IF THAT'S LEADING, I'M IN

Women Redefining Leadership

JULIA MIDDLETON

If That's Leading, I'm In
Copyright © 2023 Julia Middleton

ISBN (ebook): 978-1-7392229-0-1
ISBN (paperback): 978-1-7392229-1-8
ISBN (audiobook): 9781038654472

First edition October 2023

Women Emerging

Contents

An Invitation   7

Foreword   9

Thank You   12

The First Expedition   15

Why Explore   23

    Take a moment   43

Your Expedition   44

    Journal   51

Your Map and Compass   53

    Journal   63

Essence   64

    Motherness   64

    Nature   78

    The Body   84

    The Sacred   92

    Ancestors   97

    Trauma   104

    Education   110

    Your Essence   120

Journal	121
Elements	123
Jettison	124
Reframe	130
Journal	139
Find	141
Journal	143
Combine	144
Humble and Visible	*145*
Empathy and Distance	*150*
Collective and Individual	*154*
Quiet and Loud	*157*
Vulnerable and Strong	*166*
Dogged and Agile	*169*
Inclusive and Boundaries	*175*
Journal	188
Expression	190
Leading Performance	192
Leading Teams	196
Leading Trust	200
Leading Creativity	203
Leading Chaos	208
Leading Together	214
Leading Against the Odds	218
Leading Pace	222
Journal	225

Energy	226
Journal	243
Finale	244
Last word	248
Appendix 1: The 101 Women	250
Appendix 2: Women Emerging Podcast Episodes	255

An Invitation

I have led an Expedition of twenty-four women to explore leadership. We set out with what we thought was a simple aim: to find 'an approach to leading that resonates with women'. For months we spoke to women across the world about leading and at the end we gathered to compile everything that we had learnt.

We all undertook the Expedition because we were tired of watching women struggle to make sense of status quo leadership: a status quo mostly defined by men, and by women who think that to be successful they have to lead like men.

What we discovered was not what we had anticipated; it was something far more exciting. We don't need to define 'an' approach, because leading is individual and personal. There are common elements, but they are not common to all, and they are not done in the same ways.

What we really need is a 'map'. With a good map, everyone can set their *own* compass and do their *own* Expedition. And everyone can find an approach to leading that works *for them*.

This book is that map.

Wherever you are in the world, whatever age you are, whether your leading is done in marketplaces or temples, homes or offices, families or communities, whether you play on sports fields or in orchestras, the book invites you to go on your own Expedition and offers you a map to help you find what works for you.

We discovered something else that made us think again. The word 'leadership' suggests something that is set in stone: rigid, overwhelming and pompous. And the word 'leader' feels like a position to which you are appointed, a role that too rapidly becomes a status or a right. But the *act* of 'leading' is full of Energy, ever changing and personal. So from now on we are going to talk about leading – rather than about leadership and leaders – as much as we possibly can. And we are going to redefine what leading is.

Last of all, our Expedition confirmed one more thing for us: we are not alone in our tiredness with status quo leadership. It is turning women away from leading at a time when the world needs women leading more and more.

I hope you decide to explore and enjoy it. I did.

Julia

Foreword

Over a nearly thirty-five-year career that has afforded me great moments of joy and exhilaration, challenging times, difficult people, sad realisations of my limitations, cheerleaders and allies who have nudged me, pushed me, encouraged and supported me, I have come to realise how much leading matters. And how, when done well, it can bring happiness to people around you.

For too long, we have been shown a uni-dimensional view of leadership; male, Western, single-minded, aggressive and, most of all, recognised by one barometer alone – success as measured by wealth or power. And hence leadership has not been seen as accessible to many people and, more particularly, to women. If women's way of leading has been recognised at all, it has been as a subset of leadership.

The Expedition brought us great clarity that women bear the burden of leading without being recognised or counted for, and that women lead differently; they do not identify with the markers of leadership as they currently experience it, and indeed blame most of the ills of the world on outdated, exclusive, unsympathetic, dominating styles of leadership. This idea of leadership has led many women to say: 'If this is leading, I am not in', 'If this is how leaders behave, I don't want to be one', 'If this is what it takes to be a leader, I am not up for it'.

Over the last few decades, the need for women's leadership in the context of 'female empowerment' has acquired a new urgency. The focus has been on why women leaders are needed and what is getting in their way. Sadly, many arguments emphasise a largely economic rationale. Look how world GDP will grow if there are more women in the workforce, say most economists. Women make 50% of the world, how can they be excluded, exclaim the gender equity activists. Economically empowered women will have more voice and agency, say women's movement leaders, thumping the table. All sound arguments, no doubt.

But we wanted to do something a bit different. Not to enter the debate on why women should be leading but on how they will lead when they do.

This book brings out the voices of the thousands of women Julia has spoken to over the last few years. They were asked, perhaps for the first time, what they thought of leading and why they were unhappy with its current state. Through a process of painful 'manthan,' an approach to leadership that resonates with women was born. A 'manthan' is a beautiful Indian word: it describes a churning or bubbling up, sometimes coherently, sometimes inarticulately, sometimes with sadness, sometimes dreamily, often with joy.

I have known Julia for over twelve years now. I remember with great clarity my first impression of her: direct to the point of being mistaken as brusque, fearless, not one to brook any stupidity, but almost gentle when it mattered and, most of all, curious, always asking why, not afraid to show vulnerability and strangely maternal, immensely proud of her children. As you read this book, she will coax you into doing an Expedition of your own, or at the very least make you realise in a sublime 'aha' moment that you are already on one.

All this to say that I believe this book is important. Play with it, challenge it, embark on your own Expedition. Then, as I did, you will catch yourself not being authentic, maybe even role-playing; you will find yourself confused as to why compassion and motherhood and spirituality are seen as feminine but not good enough for leading; there will be moments when you will exclaim aloud, to the chagrin of those around you, then smile radiantly, nod vigorously or shed a quiet tear at the insights that will confront you; you will suddenly see people around you in a new light and, with a gasp, you will realise that people you least expected are actually leaders for who they are, as much as for what they do and how they do it. It is a very personal journey; after all, how you lead reveals who you are to others, but most importantly to yourself.

Enjoy your Expedition! This map will help you find what works for you. What you uncover will resonate with you because it accounts for your lived experience and your cultural context. For sure, leading is hard, with many moments of self-doubt, anger, frustration, perhaps even a desire to give up. But change cannot be affected from the outside. It will take the collective effort of millions of us to change deeply entrenched mindsets and systems that celebrate only a certain type of leading.

Vidya Shah
Executive Chairperson, EdelGive Foundation
Chair, Women Emerging

Thank You

Thousands of women have been a part of this book: women in their teens considering the prospect of leading; women who are studying and deciding whether leading is for them; women leading their families and communities; women taking a break, who will be back to leading soon; women at work determined to get leading right; women at the top of their career wondering if they have ever got it right; women juggling the many balls involved in leading; women fighting to be heard or for the very right to lead; women of all gender identities including non-binary people and transgender women; women in over 100 countries with different roots, roles and beliefs. My thanks to all.

Thank you to those who allowed me to interview you on the Women Emerging podcast, who volunteered to be a guide on our Expedition or who have been part of our Women Emerging community.

Thank you to all of you whose voices are in this book. All 101 of you are listed in Appendix 1 with your formal job titles, in the book itself I just quote you. Somehow job titles overwhelm me. Sarah Henry, a member of the First Expedition, says they never used them: "Honestly, I still do not know what half of the members do in their real lives. I know the names of their partners and their family members and the biggest mistakes they made. One day I will get to what they do in the world." (Podcast 49)

(I have put these references in throughout the book whenever I quote a woman whom I interviewed on the Women Emerging podcast. They indicate the relevant episode number so that readers can go and hear her speaking if they would like to.)

Most of all, thank you to the twenty-four members of the Expedition who have spent many long hours over the last year listening, sharing, questioning, reflecting, rethinking, refining and simply exploring. All have had competing demands on their time. All have tolerated my leading – sometimes good, sometimes poor, occasionally irritating, oftentimes fun – with great kindness. It was a long Expedition and a huge commitment. Thank you, Alia Whitney Johnson, Ana Luz Porzecanski, Andini Makosinski, Anna Kuk, Aparna Uppaluri, Ayesha Mian, Camila Pontual, Erica Su, Fatima Zibouh, Folawe Omikunle, Hinemoa Elder, Isata Kabia, Katrina Webb, Katya Guryeva, Laura Fleming, Liz Bloomfield, Melissa Kwee, Mona Sinha, Rouba Mhaissen, Sarah Henry, Selvie Jusman, Uma Chatterjee, Vidya Shah and Yvette Hopkins.

There was a wonderful richness and complexity in our group. We did have much in common but there were many differences: in our histories, cultures, beliefs, stories and experiences. Amongst us were native and settler, colonised and colonising histories. We all had different experiences of patriarchy, discrimination and privilege. So our discussions were sometimes complex, heated and challenging. We never attempted a monolithic definition of what it is to be a woman.

Some of us loved exploring without a clear plan, thriving in the white space and starting from scratch, not looking at existing models, definitions or research. And others of us found the ambiguity tough and would have preferred a clearer sense of where we were and where we were going. It was not always easy to come together.

But we did come together, magically, as an amazing group of women with open minds and deep trust. Thank you, thank you.

It is important to say that this book captures the insights from the Expedition through my eyes, though, as you will discover, I rely on the voices of members because they so often expressed or illustrated ideas far better than me.

Sometimes our voices are not as one. We all had our own discoveries, insights and revelations on our way. These differences reflect one of the big discoveries of the Expedition: that leading is a very personal thing, that there is no one way to do it, and that to pretend that there is a single way to lead is to do leading a disservice. It dooms people to struggling and inevitably failing to make one way fit all.

In one thing we are as one: in the wish to share and help women as they undertake their own Expeditions.

So we created a map. It's very simple. It has three concentric circles with an infinity symbol lying flat over the top. The middle circle is called Essence. Then one circle out is Elements, and the furthest out is Expression. The overlying infinity symbol is called Energy. From this base, the infinity symbol spirals upwards as it generates ever more Energy.

If you decide to do an Expedition, you can fill in this map so that it becomes your map. It will become thumbed and scribbled over as you unravel your Essence and how it shapes how you lead, as you pin down the Elements of your leading – which ones you will decide to jettison, reframe, find and combine (particularly tricky is combining what, on the face of it, may seem incompatible Elements) – and then as you discover ways to express your leading day after day.

It is the dynamic flow between Essence, Elements and Expression that generates the Energy of leading, which then starts to spiral upwards.

But I am getting ahead of myself. The map is simple, and it's complex too. It will take this book to know it inside out.

For now, let me tell you a bit more about the First Expedition.

The First Expedition

We were twenty-four women of different faiths, cultures and abilities. The youngest of us was twenty-four, the oldest sixty-four. We all worked in different sectors. We all spoke multiple languages. Some of us were big thinkers, others big doers. Some digested in numbers, others told stories. Some had large families, others small. Some smiled at a moment's notice, others took our time. Real women, doing real leading, right across the world.

I was the leader of the Expedition. I had started Women Emerging in early 2020 and pulled together the Expedition and the group of women in early 2022.

I became passionate about Women Emerging in the early days of Covid. Many people were talking about how the world needed to be very different post-Covid, yet there was no real indication that it would be. And change felt all the more unlikely if the same people continued to be the leaders. The most obvious and speedy way to produce change seemed to be to bring many more women into leading. Yet the women I was talking to were very clear that it was not for them for many reasons, a big one being their perception of what leading entailed. (Podcast 13)

The trigger moment came when I was preparing to do a leadership talk on a programme for women working in many sectors across the world. I saw that seven out of ten of the books recommended on their reading list were written by men. That left three written by women, mostly about how to succeed in a man's world. They were also all written by Western authors and almost all focused on how to break through the glass ceiling to reach the corporate top table.

None of the books were likely to resonate with the audience I saw in front of me. So I started Women Emerging. Not to add another book to the list, but to develop something different.

The idea of launching an Expedition came soon after. I cannot say that it was hard to persuade the twenty-four women to join it, despite the time commitment, because it wasn't. As well as the twenty-four women, we had two other women involved. Stephanie Khurana, a big backer of women social entrepreneurs, agreed to take on the role of 'enabler' to help me design the process, judge the pace and ensure that we did not lose any of the twenty-four women. Lissa Young, a woman with a long career in the US military, agreed to be the 'disruptor'. Her role was to push us to think differently; bigger, bolder, braver.

I remember asking Stephanie why she had agreed to take on the role, and she replied very simply:

"We all yearned for a new approach to leading, and there was a sense of possibility and hope that we could imagine something different and better. We saw or felt deep down that the current constructs wouldn't enable us to thrive."

What I now call the First Expedition started out in May 2022 and ended in February 2023. We worked virtually: alone, in pairs, in working groups or as a whole group. We gathered for half a day each month, online. Because of the time differences, some were in bed about to go to sleep and others were in bed having just woken up. Between these gatherings each of us explored, speaking to women leaders around the world.

The Studio

It was not always easy to persuade everyone to explore widely and resist the temptation to try to pull things together. All the way through we used the analogy of going out to gather materials which we would bring back into our virtual studio. We knew that we would eventually use the materials to draw up our approach. Every time we brought things back, we were tempted to pull up our sleeves and get going. But I would push everyone back out again to listen and search and keep exploring and gathering.

All the way, my own exploring was enriched because each week I hosted a podcast episode with amazing women, from midwives to supply chain experts and from established leaders in Botswana to young leaders in Pakistan. I brought all those insights and laid them out in the studio too.

We all adopted the studio analogy fast. Stephanie describes what she saw: "We all had our own palette and brushes, clay and pottery wheels, marble and chisels. Some painted with water, others with oil. Some started with pencils. Some shared canvases, and others had their own. We found that sometimes oil and water don't mix. Great ideas, learning and innovation emerged at the edge of difference. We found tensions among ideas. We found biased perspectives among ourselves. Our members explored their interior selves and external context. We cast wide nets looking at wherever leading could be uncovered. Nothing was excluded. We embraced messiness before order. Subgroups emerged, converged and dissolved as we worked through the complexities to surface more polished thoughts and better ideas. Ambiguity with little structure is hard to hold among a large group but it helped to foster deeper insights. Getting comfortable with the uncomfortable became a vital skill."

Though it was on Zoom, we shared our discoveries every month. Our ups and downs, the twists and doubling backs, as well as the leaps forward. There were moments full of tears and fears and then moments when we simply stood aside and watched miracles happen.

We did eventually all get together. After ten months we met in Bellagio, on Lake Como, in Northern Italy. We were hosted by the Rockefeller Foundation and it was magical. Bellagio was our real-time studio, and we started pulling everything we had learnt and seen together and making sense of everything we had brought to the studio over the previous ten months. We discovered that we had been dreaming, for sure. But that the dreaming had set us up well.

It was a bit strange finally being together. We drew on every facilitating skill within the group. We sang to each other and danced for each other. We drew pictures and created models with play doh. We found common ground and pushed each other to uncover the frictions. We went on walks together and on our own. Some swam in the freezing February lake. We wrote papers and then rewrote them. And we looked after each other as messages from the outside world came through about work and friends and family.

Without knowing it we slowly uncovered the map by doing the journey ourselves without one.

We recognised that leading is complex and layered, a quality that is specific to each person. We realised that how you lead has to be connected with who you are. That any Expedition had to be done in two parts, one internal and the other external, though they would weave together. That leading for us would forever be a verb.

We realised how often we had found ourselves reframing what are often perceived to be women's weaknesses instead as strengths. And slowly it dawned on us that the word that we were all using the most was Energy.

Perhaps, most of all, we were reminded of just how powerful women are when we work together.

I don't think we avoided either our own good or less good leading, and we didn't idealise how women lead. Nor did our diverse group start to Westernise leading in the way that we had too often seen happen. And we didn't shy away from important words such as motherhood and spirituality.

We focused right through our Expedition on talking to women. This was not to exclude men but simply to focus on women. We all knew full well that many men are in search of a fresh approach to leading themselves and would welcome the outcomes of our Expedition. We all knew men who are allies and who sometimes pay a high price for being so. But even allies can fall unconsciously into old ways. So we focused on women, while certainly never leaving our sons out.

In the very early days of Women Emerging, Vidya, Mona and I spent many hours thinking through what was to become the First Expedition. We discussed our dreamy ambitions. Mine was that women all over the world would say, "if that's leading, I'm in." But even in those early days, we sensed that we were unlikely to come up with one simple approach.

Mona, once a banker, then a philanthropist, before taking on leading Equality Now, began talking about a prism: "The prism is a powerful metaphor. Each facet can represent our individual lived experience, the experience of our communities or diverse viewpoints. Rainbows come from prisms as all the inputs feed in to create a spectrum that is a combination of seven different colour streams which stand strong individually and as a blended palette. We were determined that our journey would be like an incredibly beautiful prism: we would input our ideas, fears and hopes and the outcomes would resonate in whatever combination of thoughts, narratives and beliefs that collided to create the entire continuum of the world." (Podcast 2)

So this was what was to become known as the First Expedition. The first of many.

I invite you to do an Expedition yourself. But before I go about persuading you, let me clear one thing up.

Women Lead Differently

Those of us on the First Expedition were very clear that leading is leading. It is unchanged whoever is leading, wherever they are on the gender spectrum. But our hunch was that what was different was how women lead. We sensed that how they translate leading to action differs significantly.

So the first thing we did was agree a definition of the word 'leading'. Finding one was easier said than done, especially one that could survive even remotely intact when translated to many languages. We agreed on the following as a collation of a few we uncovered:

Catalysing people's ideas and actions
with purpose, motivation and momentum
to reach a goal and a shared vision.

With this as a starting point, we set out to test our hunch that women go about leading differently.

Nandita Das, a beautiful and brave actress in India, encouraged us: "I believe all of us have multiple identities and no *one* identity should be thrusted upon us. Having said that, I find my identity of being a woman unwittingly taking precedence over all other identities. Maybe because we are never allowed to forget that we are women. Given this, it is just natural for us to get drawn to each other with a greater sense of empathy. We have a shared sense of experience, of knowing the world the way *we* know it. This doesn't mean that every woman that we meet we are going to bond with, but there are more chances that we will. And yet the popular narrative, at least in India, is that a woman is a woman's greatest enemy. I don't even know where it came from.

"I did an Indo-Spanish film and it had an all-women crew: a woman director, producer, cinematographer, sound recordist, costume designer, everyone. Initially I thought it was just a marketing gimmick. But out of curiosity, I did it. I wanted to see what it would be like. There was one thing that was undoubtedly more present on set and that was empathy. We could be ourselves and could lean on each other more. We didn't need to hide our vulnerabilities or see them as a weakness. In fact, they became our strength."

Katya Guryeva, who works in urban policy connecting global cities, is half Nandita's age and lives on the other side of the world, but she expresses the same instinct: "There is a special kind of Energy and power that I have only felt amongst women, which is particularly strong when we come together and support each other. Something unique that we are able to draw from. We have to find the way of leading which harnesses this power that we hold.

"It might be as simple as drinking tea with multiple generations. A grandmother, a mother, a granddaughter, a great granddaughter. Women are full of juxtapositions. We are soft and strong, flexible and anchored, protectors and vulnerable, grace and chaos. So perhaps understanding these differences, the multifaceted nature of what it means to be a woman, gives us a clue."

Every woman I spoke to over the First Expedition to a greater or lesser extent shared our hunch and the wish to test it. And, in so doing, to redefine leadership.

But none underestimated how hard it would be to do so. Even if you just think of the obstacles set by language. Leading is so often seen as being the 'best': the winners in sport lead or the richest in business lead. Those at the peak of a pyramid. The 'best' rapidly drags us back to the status quo.

Anna, a glorious violinist whose ability to frame leading in musical terms never fails to intrigue, sees words as constantly getting in the way: "Leading is often associated with masculine traits. For example, when a woman is firm, she is perceived as aggressive, but when a man is firm, he is perceived as confident. Similarly, when a man is accommodating or soft spoken, he is perceived as less dominant or weak, but in a woman the same traits are perceived as caring and graceful. When a man shows empathy and is not afraid of vulnerability, he becomes phenomenal. When a woman represents the same qualities, she is just a woman. However, if her leading includes Elements of strength and firmness then she becomes a phenomenon."

So testing our hunch was going to involve unpicking a complicated labyrinth, with language playing a confusing role. But we were up for it. Well, not all of us. Aparna Uppaluri, who was leading the Ford Foundation in India when she embarked on the Expedition, saw it more as throwing down a challenge than testing a hunch.

"There is an assumption that there is a universal idea of leadership and that women's leadership is a subset of that universal idea. We are going to challenge this, and recognise that when a woman leads, she can lead very differently from how leading is assumed to be done." (Podcast 11)

It was at this point, though, that Selvie Jusman and Andini Makosinski, one a young investment banker in Singapore, the other a young entrepreneur and inventor based in Canada, rightly reminded us that status quo leadership may be largely defined by men, but many women embody it. For both, their worst bosses have been women. Andini said of hers, "she was a very old-school manager from the entertainment industry who had made her career in a 'man's world.' It slowly became very clear to me that she had found herself fashioning her aggressive and toxic personality in order to survive in the business."

Selvie described the impact of the woman who framed what leading was for her at the start of her career: "I identified leadership with something that is more results focused, very much KPI driven, very individualistic. I thought leading was about creating a punishing environment. And the effect on me of this was to feel like every day I was walking on an eggshell, feeling fearful of committing mistakes." (Podcast 7)

Laura Fleming, an ever-rising star in the energy field, based in Scotland, while recognising Selvie and Andini's descriptions, was very clear that we could change this. Laura herself refuses to become such a leader, even though the push to adopt the status quo is strong in the overwhelmingly male sector she leads in: "I have just started a new role in a new organisation. I have had to make a huge effort in order to stay myself. I know that I was hired to do the job, to bring the best of myself and bring change to the organisation. So it is vital that I do not assimilate to the company culture, but this is actually really difficult and exhausting to do. To turn up as yourself in a predominantly male environment really takes a lot of effort and a lot of Energy. Especially because it is totally counterintuitive. I think as human beings, but as women in particular, we are so good at adapting to new situations. It has been a strength for evolution and helped us survive many situations. But in order to create change, we need to avoid this assimilation and bring our true authentic self. It is absolutely worth it. I have already seen the impact that it has had on people around me." (Podcast 20)

Priyanka Handa Ram, who runs a network of schools in Botswana, was up for proving the hunch too. I had interviewed her for the podcast and though she may not have been a member of the First Expedition, she has since determinedly set off on her own Expedition. "The story of leadership has been, up to now, based on 'you need to be stronger, you need to take emotion out, it is not personal, it is business.' I think it has been a dangerous single story. It is up to us to change it. As we go on our Expeditions, I think the plot will start to twist. But let us not fall into the same trap; there is no single story for women either. I correct myself; it is up to us to change the stories." (Podcast 24)

So, with our hunch becoming rather less of a hunch and more of a conviction, let us pick up why we undertook the First Expedition and why we propose that you undertake an Expedition of your own.

Why Explore

There are so many reasons to set out on an Expedition: the status quo doesn't resonate, fitting in isn't an option, we crave something different. Leading is lonely, but it can also be wonderful. This might just be the tipping point of change, or simply that we are needed and in large numbers.

Not for Me

We read leadership books and there are many, many helpful insights, but too often they don't resonate. It's not just that they address a status quo largely defined by men, it's also one in which many feel that Western ideas dominate and emanate from a very corporate perspective. All this makes for a dissonance with many women.

Ayesha Mian, an entrepreneur and psychiatrist in Pakistan, returned frustrated from a leadership programme in the West which came with a lengthy required reading list that did not captivate her. "Lots of pedantic self-help books on what would make a successful leader out of me. I never found the 'khalish' of leading. It's an Urdu word that describes an upsetting feeling that something got missed. It's not just that their models were not designed by women, they do not work for women either. And they even compounded the ingrained perception in women that we are not leaders. Yet we know that we need to dig deeper if we are going to create a different world."

Many women agree. Ani Choying Drolma is a Buddhist Nun who leads her monastery in Nepal. She expresses the same frustration: "For many hundreds of years, women have been told what they should be doing, what they are, how a good woman, a good daughter and also a good nun should behave. How a good woman should lead. Our goodness is always validated by how we live our life according to somebody else." (Podcast 18)

Pelonomi Venson Moitoi is a civil servant in Botswana and she puts it succinctly: "We got caught in the narrative that men do it better." (Podcast 25)

Sarah Henry, from the US, adds that "women do not get to define how they want to lead and are then put into leadership roles where the way they show up to lead is not valued. We are still putting women in to survive and not thrive. We badly need to find ways for women to step into leading their way."

Meena Meenakshi Arundhati, a young student in India, hears the voices from around the world and sees the ridiculous side of all this. "It is not as if women have not always been leading. We are not allowed to think of ourselves leading and yet I, like many of us, have always taken up leadership positions. They are just not labelled leadership positions. We do the grunt work, lots of the administration and untangling of the messes. Lots of emotional and mental labour, not the glamorous or shiny part of leading. We do all the messy work and very rarely wear the shiny shoes. And, even more crazily, an outcome of this is that many of us do not even know we are leading." (Podcast 42)

So we need books that help us to be us and not someone else. Rather than be shoved into a status quo approach that doesn't fit whether you are an entrepreneur, a nun, a social entrepreneur, a civil servant or a student. Indeed, wherever you lead.

Fitting In

It is not as if the fitting in option works that well either. Many of us are told to adopt the status quo if we want to be successful, and then in the same breath, we are told to be authentic in so doing. It does not make much sense.

And the trouble is that if you do allow yourself to get shoehorned into status quo leading, you quickly start to lose sense of who you are and why you agreed to lead at all. It's a rollercoaster because what happens next is that the people around you spot that you are not being yourself and it gets much harder to lead them. Because you are no longer authentic in their eyes.

Yvette Hopkins, after a career in the US military, describes it perfectly: "I see some women stuck in a state of mimicry; she will have been given the authority, responsibility and accountability but she is shaped by the male dominated construct and will emulate its guiding hand. She basically emulates it until she can no longer see herself in it."

I spoke to Anna about how she sees this play out when women conduct orchestras. "I have the impression that they still feel the need to get into men's clothes so that they are treated seriously by the musicians. I have never seen a conductor in a dress. It seems to be more comfortable to be in trousers. This is true, but I have the impression that something more is going on. I am not sure why women need to jump into some masks that they do not need to wear just to be heard and respected. I have a picture of leaders being either men in suits or women with very serious faces, glasses, red lipstick and black jackets. I ask myself if I really must learn how to fit into this, to adapt and cut my own edges."

Hinemoa Elder, a child and adolescent psychiatrist of Māori descent in New Zealand, firmly rejects the pressure to fit in because she fell for it in the past. "Back in 2006 we were developing our Māori model of care for a new service. Management wanted to tick a box and also congratulate themselves in having a Māori service. We were excited about the opportunity to ensure a culturally safe place and a way of working for our people to be recognised and supported. One day the kaumātua (elder) and I were required to go to a management meeting and left a pākehā (white) colleague to cover us and see one of our whānau (extended family). It was not the right decision. That was a good hard lesson."

Laura, too, in her world of engineers, knows she has fallen for assimilating in the past. "Maybe now we are going too far and starting to behave a bit like men. What I have come to realise is that doing so is only going to get me so far. I need to show up as I am. Not just for the benefit of the company that I work for but also for me." I laughed as Laura said this and asked her if she would now describe herself as a radical. Her answer was a twinkling smile as she said, "who would have predicted that?" (Podcast 11)

Katrina Webb, an Australian Paralympian, says that the urge to fit in is so strong in all aspects of life that you are almost lulled into it, and then you get a rude shock. "Growing up with a hidden disability, my focus was not on leading but on being accepted. It took competing in three Paralympic Games and winning three gold, three silver and one bronze medal to start celebrating the fact that I was different and could contribute so much more because I did not fit in."

We have all done it. And not just at work. I have a strong memory of being persuaded to try to fit in by my extended family. They had come to terms with me being what they believed to be a radical when I was at work but wanted it to stop in the very traditional family. I have an enduring memory of once – only once – sitting in a room, fitting in, or attempting to, and wondering who I had become. Authentically lost.

Something Different

At first Andini looked at leading from a Gen Z perspective. "I expected myself to be more woke when it came to female leading, but the First Expedition was a wake-up call for me. I began questioning all my preconceived notions of what it meant to lead. All my life I had seen illustrations of strong patriarchal leading in fairy tales, news articles and films. I did not even know there could be a different way to do it. My only visual concept of a female leader was someone akin to Miranda Priestly in *The Devil Wears Prada*. It was not until I was fully immersed in the nine-month-long Expedition that I understood the importance of what we were trying to do."

The First Expedition was a turning point for Vidya too, one she talks about in her foreword to this book. Like Andini, she had long imbibed restricting messages about leading. "Up to then my understanding of leading was very uni-dimensional; perhaps because, at business school, and later over my career, all I encountered was a male definition and practice. In hindsight, it seems as if I had blinkers on and saw my role only as a follower. Besides, I was not impressed with some of the women leaders I met and perhaps was very judgmental of their style and found it lacking individuality and brilliance.

"As I came into my own at EdelGive and met many amazing leaders, both men and women, almost all from civil society organisations, I found myself becoming comfortable with who I am. What most resonated with me was their authenticity. Their ability to show vulnerability. Their desire to know you as a person. Their unabashed interest in your personal life. Their open admiration for you; their simplicity and genuineness. No show of power, only compassion. And I learnt that this worked for me as well!"

So Vidya and Andini both woke up to the possibility of something different in leading. Andini now has the passion of a convert. Since the First Expedition she has been driving a project to reach sixteen-year-old girls all over the world so that they can undertake their own Expeditions. "I want to tell everyone to lead their own way. Because we can all be leaders, no matter our background, location, socio-economic position or race. It is something we already possess within us; we just need to muster the courage to accept it within ourselves."

Vidya challenged us right at the start of the First Expedition: "Give me something I can believe works." Like all of us, she then began to realise that it would not be about giving her anything but more about helping her and many other women find their own way to lead.

Less Lonely

Leading is hard and often lonely. Yvette expresses it well: "You do not wake up one morning and start leading. It is a lifelong pursuit of excellence. You do not always get it right. There is no instruction manual. It is hard and that is without even layering in the complexities of being a woman; the fact that women have not been in the workplace for a very long time, that women take on additional burdens, jobs, tasks in society. And on top of this you wrap in biases about women. We look at the world through a different lens and, let us face it, the world looks at us differently." (Podcast 3)

Rouba Mhaissen, a leader of the Syrian diaspora, feels the same. "Leading definitely made me lonelier. No one ever tells you that you are doing anything right, but you get detailed feedback on what you get wrong. And on top of this, people start putting you on a pedestal. Even your close friends do it, even your family, your team, your community.

"I think it is a big moment for women when we realise that the people around us see us as leading. I did not realise it until quite late on. When I saw that they looked up to me for strength, that was scary. It is when you realise that you have some power that you are sometimes scared to recognise yourself. It is hard and lonely, but it is also rewarding, especially if you are not on your own." (Podcast 10)

Adding to this is Meena, who has not done that much leading yet in her life but has observed a great deal. She says, "most women leaders are charting the uncharted. The stakes are always so much higher for women when they lead because women cannot afford to fail. And because they know that they will take responsibility if things burn to the ground, they spend too much of their time making sure that nothing does burn and not enough on the bigger picture. Too often, I see them doing almost maintenance leading. If anything has held me back in my leading it is not having much room to fail. You have to be a trailblazer, an exceptional trailblazer. There seems to be no space for being normal." (Podcast 42)

All through the First Expedition and the many weekly podcast episodes I hosted, I got used to hearing two expressions: 'accidental' leader and 'reluctant' leader. Many women simply find themselves leading, wondering how to do it, how to transition to this new reality. This lonely new reality that Uma Chatterjee, a campaigner on human trafficking in India, describes as being put "up on a pedestal. People do not think you need any help anymore. You still need to feel loved and valued but people do not quite perceive you as human anymore, with human needs. You frequently feel hesitant or in need of space or of acceptance, but you cannot ask for them. Or you do not think you can ask for them. Leading becomes a very sultry, lonely space.

"It does not have to be this way and it cannot be. You have to search for human connectedness, relatedness and how to make leading more liberating. Leading is, after all, about connectedness, about being and becoming together even if you are leading." (Podcast 7)

And, of course, let us not underestimate the forces we are up against. Forces that are about maintaining the status quo and are disinclined to let go of any power. It does help, when you face them, if you are surrounded by other women.

I recently interviewed Anne Rugg Onwusiri. She plays rugby, and told me about 'rucking'. When a player has the ball but is down, her teammates rush across the field to 'ruck' over her. They form a sort of scaffold over her with their bodies, careful not to crush, strongly protecting her and making sure the ball isn't ripped away from her while she is down. It's a lovely analogy. Of course male players do it too, but I like to think that women players do it with love. Anne has named her own podcast 'Black Girls Ruck'. (Podcast 68)

Wonderful

There is nothing quite like getting leading right. It does not happen that often but when it does, it is good. There is a joy and a lightness, an Energy that makes the impossible seem possible, a pride in people and in work, a surprise and a delight that comes with it. A conviction that this is what it was all for. A knowledge that it is all just going to happen. It is an experience of bringing light to greyness, of being humans at our best. To me, leading is ultimately about Energy. And there is nothing quite like generating such Energy.

I remember feeling this years ago when we all sat down as a family, having realised that my son's wedding that was about to happen in two days' time needed a final push – because a few things were not ready and a few other things had fallen apart – a push that only we could make. We sat around the kitchen table and produced our plan and then we went out and spent two days flat out and we did it. We each took turns to lead at different times and on different tasks. We moved the leading between us easily. I remember it as us at our very best and will do so forever. The wedding was beautiful.

And I remember feeling it at Common Purpose – the NGO I founded and then ran for thirty years – as we pulled out of a recession that had done its best to destroy us. I was sitting after a team meeting watching the pride everyone felt at the ingenuity we had displayed, the culture we had built on, the systems that we had put into overdrive, the colleagues we had inspired to pull off not just a turnaround but even an acceleration. I remember, for once, reflecting that I had got the leading right. And I was very proud of myself and of all of us.

I have not always felt this way about leading. For most of my teens and twenties, leading was nowhere on my agenda except to try to undermine it wherever I came across it. I equated leading with abuse of power – it went hand in hand with elitism – and thought that leaders were people with unearned and undeserved titles.

I then worked at a cooperative and discovered what it was like when there was no leading. My lasting memory was of walking up and down long corridors trying to get someone to make a decision, or even to decide who would make a decision. Not for me, leaderless groups.

It was in my late twenties that I realised that if I wanted to change the world, I could not do it in the sixteen hours a day that I was awake. I needed to do it with others, and that meant I had to learn to lead. But I was going to do it my way.

That was the start of a long journey. No one can do leading for you or tell you how you should do it. It is a journey of learning, of never really knowing when you get there. Of knowing that if you ever did think you had got there, you would have already lost it. You can learn from others' journeys or Expeditions but only so that you can digest it yourself and decide which bits work for you and which bits don't.

The latest leg of my journey has been taking part in and leading the First Expedition. I have learnt a lot and unlearnt even more. This is why I suggest that all women go on an Expedition. If you are at the start of your journey and considering leading, I recommend an Expedition so that you can accelerate your journey. If you are well on your journey already, do an Expedition so that you keep on learning and unlearning as you go.

I would like Enaya Noor Mian to have the last word on this. She was by far the youngest person involved in the First Expedition. She told me very fiercely, "Leading is something you need to be proud of. I think it is an honour, an achievement. You have accomplished something if people look to you to lead them. I think that is a big thing. So do not tone it down and make it seem like it is not that big of a deal. I think leading is something I would be honoured to do." (Podcast 42)

Now the Moment

I suspect that the kind of change in leading that women yearn for is also yearned for by many men. Because as the world changes faster and faster, and the problems accelerate and spread, thinking about leading is shifting too. So there is an opportunity now to rethink leadership. The shift is uneven and certainly not happening in every company, government, village, temple, marketplace and home, but it feels like an opportunity is opening up, and that women will be crucial in redefining leadership.

I am now going to add another hunch to our first hunch: my hunch is that women's approach to leading might be the right one for our times. It might even be the best way to restore the increasingly shattered link between leaders and the people they lead around the world.

For the many people who hesitate in backing hunches, listen to Bin Wolfe; at EY she is in a perfect position to spot shifts globally: "Covid has required us to demonstrate really different leadership attributes. That is, to care for the people you work with. I think we always knew it was there, but it took Covid to surface it and bring it to the fore. The pandemic was like the human race was under attack. I think everybody felt nobody was exempt from it. Everybody needed to feel a sense of safety. And this was what they looked for from their leaders. Up to then, people intellectually knew it, but it stopped at that for most.

"One of the most basic human needs is to be acknowledged and recognised for our individual uniqueness and our individual needs. It does not matter which culture you come from, you need to be heard and seen. Leading calls for people to relate to other people and acknowledge their need to be safe, both physically and psychologically.

"I think it really highlights the need for leading to be done with empathy. This is now one of the critical attributes we look for."

I asked Bin if she thinks this shift will endure and reminded her of an Expression she once shared with me: muscle memory.

"Let me illustrate muscle memory with an example. After an intense meeting, work or family, you sometimes get into your car and start driving and before you know it, you are at your destination. You do not really think about what you are doing, about each turn you make, you just sort of know what to do. That is what I call muscle memory, when you have done something enough times it means that you could actually do it without putting a lot of thought into it. It becomes second nature. Athletes do it; they practice thousands of times so that when they compete, they do not think.

"Leading requires muscle memory too. Covid challenged us to develop a different set of muscle memory. All of a sudden you saw very senior people conducting a very important meeting, and the kids wander in or the dog starts barking. That humanised people. I think we have accepted a lot more of these human realities in the workplace.

"I am optimistic we will not lose the muscle memory, if for no other reason than that people are demanding it, both employees and customers. There is also a whole new generation demanding it and they will not relent."

Such a shift must, surely, I suggested to Bin, provide a huge opportunity for women. "Yes, women are ideal for leading in this new world. Typically, they are better communicators and listeners. They are more emotionally intelligent, are better at multi-tasking, less inclined to race from problem to solution and far less likely to let ego govern their interactions. They are a perfect fit." (Podcast 14)

It is not just in the corporate world that this shift is being observed. Claire Yorke, an expert in war studies in Denmark, observes it in conflict resolution: "There is evidence that women make a difference to the decisions made. That they are essential to peacekeeping and conflict resolution. They are often more in touch with their communities, especially in countries where you have very strong matriarchal figures who are a part of their community and know the vulnerabilities and the needs of the people within it. It seems obvious, but women are essential in designing solutions that reflect the people who are going to be at the receiving end of them." (Podcast 38)

I suspect that it is not just in strong matriarchal cultures, but that women are also at times more effective in countries where men are predominantly the leaders. Because women are able to set aside some of the challenges that arise in such environments: the egos and the need to be the person in control. In these situations, gender, rather than being the barrier, may well become the enabler.

Yvette recognises this: "It is not until you get to a very senior position in the military that this approach to leading is recognised. Where the so-called 'soft skills' finally start to emerge in greater importance. Traditionally, we do not train soldiers in such soft skills until later in their careers." (Podcast 3)

Bin is not surprised that you find such stories in every sector: "I do see that female leaders tend to be better at being more empathetic, and there is plenty of research to show this. I think this is one of those things that actually works to the advantage of female leaders. What I would love to see is all our female leaders really claiming this space.

"Once upon a time, when there were discussions about emotions, they were something to shy away from. They were seen as 'soft' in a culture where you were told to be 'tough'. I think that things have changed, and it is a change which is here to stay. And I think that will really serve well for a lot of our female leaders." (Podcast 14)

Women Needed

Over the First Expedition, I spoke to many women about what they see as the big drivers of this change. Three of them stand out and will frame the context in which we will be leading: AI, the global order and climate change. Each one badly needs women to be at the heart of addressing them. It simply cannot be done without women and in large numbers.

Artificial Intelligence

So far, AI is largely being designed by men, very seldom by women. So there is a fair chance that the old ways will be perpetuated in the data we are using and the conclusions we draw from the data.

Leila Toplic, whose life has taken her from refugee camps to becoming a leading global thinker on AI, can see this clearly: "The potential for artificial intelligence to serve humans is undeniable, and so is its ability to cause many adverse impacts on an unprecedented scale. We have this very powerful technology that is generally applicable across everything we do and care about and we have a rapidly closing window of opportunity to design and shape its direction in a safe and equitable way.

"AI is not magic. Its application will mirror our inherent human imperfections. As designers of AI systems, our biases, unfairness and injustices will inevitably surface, magnified on a massive scale. It is imperative that everyone who is leading is aware of this and proactively taking steps to mitigate risks through ethical design and implementation, as well as policy and regulation.

"Part of this will mean adopting a deliberate approach in determining who builds and deploys AI, for what purposes and based on what values. This technology, which has an impact on all of us, should be collectively designed and shaped by all of us." (Podcast 39)

Speaking to Leila reframed AI in my mind not as technology but almost as a collaborator. One that is only as effective as we brief it, debrief it, debunk it and disagree with it. If we do not set the parameters for it, do not analyse the conclusions of it, do not occasionally disagree and overrule its outcomes, then AI becomes a threat. Women are needed to play their part in this massive AI revolution, of course as coders and designers, but perhaps more importantly as the leaders who agree on the briefs, set the priorities and question the outcomes.

Lee Sue Ann, a thought leader in the ASEAN, is focused on one huge social outcome of AI. "Whether it is disinformation or misinformation, people are now really confused about what is true and what is false. And this is only going to get worse given the trajectory of AI. We think that we have got a problem now just from the social media news feeds; we are soon going to have trouble figuring out whether it is really me right now talking to you, or if it is just an animation that has somehow managed to capture my voice and my gestures and pretend I'm speaking to you. We are going to increasingly just build our networks at a local level, you know, in flesh and blood, almost go hyperlocal." (Podcast 15)

Global Order

If AI cries for women to engage, the same must surely be said of the global order. For so long, the international and national principles of sovereignty, equality and national self-determination have been relatively consistent. But things are changing. Claire sees the breakdown of international cooperation and multilateral order in very stark terms: "The differing perceptions for the future of the global order are going to be very hard to reconcile. There needs to be someone or some groups of people who are able to find common ground between them when different sides are calling out the other for their actions, their histories and their intentions. Because there is this kind of reckoning coming about what the future looks like and where we will we find security and stability.

"It is as much an issue of international order as it is a domestic issue in a number of countries around the world where people are feeling marginalised by political and economic systems that they do not feel work for them. These local foundations will need to be far stronger for people to have the capacity, desire and ability to be collaborative and cooperative actors on the international stage. Because if you have too much dominating the home front, it makes it very hard to commit resources and people or time and effort to collective solutions." (Podcast 38)

And this is in the context, says Sheila Paylan, an international human rights lawyer, of "international law turning authoritarian, because it is being misapplied and used by countries that want to launch wars and use the parlance of international law to justify their actions." (Podcast 38)

Claire has little hope of "someone, or a group of someones" finding common ground at the global level, even when we are facing such huge global problems, and when the world is full of what feels like an overwhelming number of frozen conflicts.

Whoever the someone is, there will surely need to be many women amongst them. Women like Paula Langton, who heads up a vast sustainability fund based out of London, who anticipates change emerging quite rapidly from a different place: the financial markets. She predicts that it will be global economies that will adapt the fastest. Just imagine, she challenges us, "if we took just

1% of pension funds globally and diverted that for sustainability, that is 240 billion that could go into decarbonising portfolios. And this is what investors are increasingly being pushed to do. We are really at the start of this journey, but it will move fast." (Podcast 39)

Climate Change

The scale of the challenges is daunting, and it is clear that poor, rural women in less developed countries will suffer direct, disproportionate harm caused by deforestation, water pollution, environmental toxins and the loss of ecological diversity.

Women are often more awake to this than most. Many studies have showed how women on boards and top teams are successfully pushing for change. We need women doing the same everywhere. Erum Khalid Sattar, who has devoted her life to water and sustainable water management, told me the best story to illustrate this:

"This story is situated in rural Sindh in current day Pakistan. The temperatures are very high; they can range between 40 and 50 degrees Celsius, so this is a hot part of the world. Women in these rural areas have no access to piped water. They walk long distances to wherever the well or the watering hole is to collect water and bring it back for the daily supply that the family and farm animals need. It is back-breaking work and none of us should at all try to romanticise it. Water is very heavy. When you see those pictures of women carrying big water pots on their heads, think about it, carry a few books on your head and see how you feel. It is not easy carrying heavy water pots without spilling them. It is really hard work, and it falls to women.

"So let us now skip to the World Bank. In a very broad sense, the reforms that were promoted can be described as farmer managed irrigation with the idea being to increase the role of farmers in the management of large surface-water irrigation systems. This meant organising farmers into groups and water user associations. The members of these groups were basically men and there was no representation of women. There was not even a sense that there should be a token representation of women.

"Imagine that you are the user of a resource and yet you are left out of any decision making about some of the most important ways in which water is used and the uses to which it is put.

"Switching to a personal memory from the time of my field work, I remember that there were many offices and conference rooms where I would be the only female, dressed as I may normally be dressed in bright colours and carrying a laptop in a bright Barbie pink cover. I'd find myself in a sea of sober colours worn by men, whereas when you visit women, in particular working in fields and in rural areas, you encounter a sea of bright popping colours, bright yellows and greens and pinks and reds and oranges.

"My hope is that if we are successful, we can actually enable the women most directly affected by how water is actually used in rural and agricultural areas into those – in many ways far-removed – spaces in which decisions are made that affect their lives. I want all of the lived toughness and vibrancy of women to come into that policy making space. I think the decisions we get through that dialogue and genuine understanding may begin to change many things in ways we cannot begin to imagine. We must persevere in bright hope." (Podcast 6)

Why did this story have such an impact on me? Because we talk too much about corporate boardrooms and women getting into them. In many ways, it is just as important that women get to the boardrooms in villages. The scale of the problems we face – especially those associated with climate change – requires it. And when women get there, we have to help them not to emulate and assimilate but to be different and demanding and confident and fresh. And themselves. With popping colours. And to be pulling together, especially across the generations.

Because we must remember that climate change and the consequences of climate change are bringing women to the fore and together, but they also have the potential to divide generations of women in a big way.

Twila Moon, a leading scientist in polar research, expresses this best: "For many people who are older, climate change was not something you learned in school. It was not a big part of education. So it has been a very rapid onset issue, not in the sense that scientists and many across the world actually did not understand this early on, but so much real conscious effort was put into muddying the waters around climate change that it has felt like a rapid onset issue that is moving very quickly.

"If you are young there is a particular frustration of being young and realising the full situation on climate change. You also cannot see yourself being able, in a short period of time, to step into power and undertake change yourself. So you are really dependent on older generations and people in power now to do something now." (Podcast 38)

Francesca Cavallo, whose fabulous *Rebel Girl* books are probably lining your shelves, sees this playing out across three generations: "There is young Gen Z, then there are women that are now around 50 years old and then there are the grandmothers. Grandmothers and Gen Z, on the sustainability issue, are closest, which is an interesting phenomenon.

"It may be because people who are now in their seventies and eighties remember a world that was more sustainable, whereas the generation of people who are now around fifty are sons and daughters of the economic boom, where part of their privilege was built on ignoring the environment and the challenges of the infinite growth.

"I believe that there is a lot of need to speak about these issues with an open mind and not assume bad faith from any of the people involved. This is increasingly important because, as we live in an incredibly polarized society where people want to overlap completely, with the party that they vote for or their system of beliefs, that leaves too little room to grow as a society and to understand that we do not need to agree on everything to do something together." (Podcast 38)

So we are in times of great change. Of great leaps forward. The algorithms of the world are in design mode and they have to be given the scale of the problems we face. These three in particular scream for women to be at the heart of addressing them. AI needs women designing, framing and questioning it. The global order needs women who can bring people together. And climate change needs women to work across generations as has seldom been seen before.

Ready to Go

The last compelling reason for women to undertake Expeditions and engage ever more in leading is that the trailblazers need back up.

The work being done to produce systematic change – so that the odds of women emerging and succeeding as leaders are not so heavily stacked against them – needs to be complemented with a steady supply of women choosing to lead. For this to happen we have to make leading something we gladly choose to do, and say, "If that's leading, I'm in."

Putting this right in the vast movement that is women's empowerment across the world may seem like filling in a tiny piece of a huge jigsaw, but it is crucial. Because without it in place, many women are deciding not to lead and, as a result, their talent, experience and insight is being wasted at a moment when the world really needs it.

Of course, things will not suddenly change just because women lead in a way that works for them. They will still be operating in systems that are evolving very slowly. I hear people claim that things are changing for women, and they certainly are, but very slowly. Think what a computer looked like twenty years ago versus what we have in our pockets now. Think of the speed of that change. Now think about how quickly things have changed for women. The pace has been glacial.

Catherine Ruggles, who still describes herself as a geek even after years at the top in STEM (Science, Technology, Engineering and Mathematics), observes how true this is: "I love computers, I love all the stuff about them. So when I started out over forty years ago in the technology field, I did not really have to fit in. I certainly did not have to go through what I think young women have to go through now, which I think is horrible. The twisting yourself into a doughnut to change your personality and act like a guy in order to be successful. I don't think I would have done well in the world that we have now."

Catherine as a doughnut, it made me laugh. "You mean an authentic doughnut," I said. Her response: "There you go. Don't you love that? It's a riot. And it is kind of extraordinary how good men just do not see it or get it. A few men do, but I will say very few."

I asked Catherine what she says to young women today. "That it is not them. That it is not a level playing field. It is not a meritocracy. If they do not succeed at something, it's not necessarily their fault. The concept of meritocracy has done huge damage. There is no meritocracy in lots of organisations. But there is an illusion of one. The trouble is that many people at the top genuinely believe that their organisations are meritocracies. They believe that they really did devise a system that was meritocratic and inclusive. But they are not, and this has had some really wicked consequences. It leaves women thinking that their problems are individual to them and not the result of the so-called meritocratic system. They think, 'it must be because I'm not good enough.' And it leaves a lot of young men who come in, like the young women, thinking it is a meritocracy, saying, 'if there are no women around here it must be because they cannot hack it.'

"We cannot keep on talking about inclusion and make so little progress. There are some uncomfortable conversations that need to happen. Almost certainly led by women, particularly women with privilege, because it is near impossible to take on the system if your household is dependent upon it." (Podcast 33)

While Catherine sees it from the corporate angle, Sheila Paylan sees the same but through international law eyes: "I am one of those women who wants a seat at that table, and I have one in a small way. For example, when I lived in Congo I was there as the expert on conflict-related sexual and gender-based violence. I was in a team of forensic experts. We were there to help the Congolese military authorities investigate crimes. My role was to make sure that we took rapes into account and that this form of violence was not forgotten but treated as part of the whole picture.

"I was sidelined. My team members did not understand what my role was, nor did they see it as a priority. They tried to shut me down with 'We're here to investigate murder.'

"We are just going to have to demand our seat at the table. And then demand we keep it and get heard. Talk to a survivor of conflict-related sexual violence, you will see how indomitable we are. That is the word, indomitable. That is what we have to be." (Podcast 38)

Alia Whitney Johnson has driven change on behalf of young women in Sri Lanka and California. She reflects on the indomitability of the women in Sri Lanka: "We worked with young women who have been totally cast out, who literally all of society has turned their back on due to rape. Yet they are willing to stand up in front of their whole village in public court, some as young as age eleven, with everybody there, to say, 'this is wrong, and I do not want my sisters to go through it'." (Podcast 8)

Such indomitability is a huge ask. Not every woman will be up for it, and nor should they have to be.

It is the same question everywhere, and especially in politics. Isata Kabia describes her journey as a politician in Sierra Leone: "The first hurdle is that you need money. Then to get 'permission' from partners or husbands or some family member. And once you are able to get that, you are kind of beholden. Permission can be withdrawn in a second. If the wife comes home late from a political meeting, the husband can decide that she can no longer participate, and campaign money grinds to a halt.

"A man can come home and announce to his family that he has decided to run for office without any consultation, and then he can take the baby's milk money and spend it on the campaign.

"When you get into office, you are judged not by what you do but by how much your family is suffering from what you are doing. 'Oh, your poor husband, your poor kids'. Added to this, all those who are about maintaining the status quo are going to be after you morning, noon and night. Because the moment you decide to run for office, you are challenging power.

"Then the insults start, tailored, ready-made, in waiting for a woman who raises up her hand or her head. The words, the abuse, the violence. A steady and relentless stream.

"From the beginning you have to kind of make yourself small for people so that they are on your side. It is a fight, a daily fight." (Podcast 4)

So for these extraordinary women who are fighting for systematic change, we must supply women ready to lead, and who have decided to lead their way. So that when extraordinary women make the breakthroughs and then turn round to check who is coming next, ready to go through these doors that have been prised open, there are plenty of women saying, "I'm in."

So there you have it. The reasons, the multiple and compelling reasons, to embark on your own Expedition. Whether it is because the status quo of leading doesn't resonate with you or because you yearn for something different. Or simply because leading is a lonely journey even at the best of times. Whether it's because leading is glorious and exciting and you want to get better and better at it or because you want to play your part at the moment when leading might just get redefined. Or because you have a deep sense that the world faces problems that call for all of us to lead, to scale and in popping colours. Or it may be none of the above; you just want to be ever better at leading.

Whatever the reason, explore.

Take a moment

If you are considering doing an Expedition, go through the reasons why the members of the First Expedition chose to do theirs and rate how much each reason resonates with you (5 is high and 0 is not at all). You might have more reasons that are specific to you. Add them and rate them too. The rating is simply to indicate how important each reason is to you. You could then think how you might have rated each one differently five or ten years ago.

WHY EXPLORE	NOW	PAST	Wonderful		
Not for me			Now the moment		
Fitting in			Women needed		
Something different			Ready to go		
Less lonely			My own reason		

Make a list of the people you might like to talk to about how they lead if you decide to do an Expedition.

At this very early stage, write down your hunch about what an approach to leading that resonates with you might looks like. Yes, this is a deliberately vague question. Just go for it. Don't overthink it or worry about the drafting, just write down what comes to mind. It will never be published, it does not have to be perfect, it can just be a stream of thought. Keep it short.

Your Expedition

Solo or Together

You don't have to do an Expedition at all. You can simply enjoy this book and consider a different way of leading. With so many women's voices in the book you will probably feel like you have been on an Expedition anyway by the time you have finished reading.

If you do decide to embark on an Expedition, you can either do it on your own or you can decide to gather a group of women and go on an Expedition together.

If you decide to explore solo, at your own pace, put some time aside in the coming days or weeks to speak to leaders either in your networks or in the Women Emerging community. Look out for the sections at the end of each chapter that suggest activities. Also watch out for the weekly podcast which you will probably enjoy. You can find it on whichever podcast platform you use. We also do a live online masterclass every three weeks which you are most welcome to join or listen to. For this you will need to register on the Women Emerging website, then you will get an invite.

If you decide to form an Expedition group, you want to carefully think through who might be in it. It is infinitely more interesting if it is a diverse group full of women who are likely to prompt each other to think and think again. You could choose to be local (so that you could actually meet up physically sometime) or to be a group of colleagues from one organisation or sector.

Alternatively, you may want to look wider and seek out women who are in different regions, countries or continents. If you do this, keep the practicalities of time zones in mind when setting up your calls. Whichever option you go for, keep diversity firmly in mind; it will give you much more insight. Consider women in different sectors, specialisms, geographies and generations with different backgrounds and beliefs. Try to go for people who are sufficiently open-minded, humble and curious to enjoy an Expedition.

Again, watch out for the activities and questions at the end of each chapter as well as the podcast episodes and online masterclasses.

I also try to join a few Expedition groups each month to hear their thinking and answer any questions. So please do invite me.

Your Journal

Whether you go solo or with a group, get a journal. I had a journal. It was full of pictures, quotes, diagrams, arrows, stick it notes, crossings out, scribbles, drawings. It made very little sense to anyone other than me. I found it helpful to catch ideas and questions, ones that made sense and ones that didn't. Since my Expedition I have found it interesting to look back at my discoveries and pivots, the moments of darkness, of shadows and of light as well as the ideas I was playing with at different times. When you get to the end of each chapter, consider the activities and questions and keep capturing everything in your journal as you go.

I am glad I wrote the journal because I think, if I hadn't, bits would have got lost. I have continued to learn and rethink since the Expedition, so it is helpful to look back on why I thought what I did.

Your List

You need to think about who you want to speak to while you are on your Expedition. Think widely, make sure you seek out unfamiliar voices, people with very different thinking from you. Look for women who are double or half your age. People who were born on another continent from you. Think about the men you might talk to, whose approach to leading you think might resonate with you. If you engage with the Women Emerging community either on LinkedIn or the website, seek out people to talk to. We leave it to you to connect.

Watch out for the numbers at the end of some of the quotes throughout this book. They are quotes from leaders whom I interviewed for the Women Emerging podcast. Listening to them gives you a lot more context and you will love their stories.

Good Luck

Please, as your own Expedition comes to an end, share what you have learnt on the Women Emerging website. The map will never be complete, your compass will always need readjusting. We need to share a constant flow of insights and practical advice and treasure it on the website.

I wish you luck as you read on and explore, maybe with Aparna's words in the back of your mind: "We wanted to wedge open and really take apart what it means to be a woman. To find the source of Energy inside. And let leadership emerge from that." (Podcast 11)

Before You Set Off

I asked all the members of the First Expedition to share their tips:

Start Right

Sit back not forwards, start with a smile, abandon all hope of simple answers, just take it all in and see where it takes you.

Ready to Pivot

Pivot on the big things and the small. Get the diary organised so that you use your time well and don't waste other people's time, but then be realistic; we all have competing priorities and balancing acts to perform. When plans need changing to help others, change them.

Alia: "I came into the Expedition thinking about leading others. Halfway through, I am re-discovering the importance of leading myself."

Multiple Languages

Seek out people who speak other languages from you. They will see things differently and express ideas differently. It will constantly remind you how poor words are at expressing complex or personal thoughts.

Keep That Journal

Ana Luz Porzecanski, a scientist who has led countless Expeditions, said, "you need to learn and to document what you are learning. You really have to, because otherwise it eventually evaporates. Make your journal personal, record what you are learning about yourself and about the systems you are embedded in." (Podcast 2)

Be Brave

Mona: "My fear at the beginning, which dissipated rapidly, was that because the patriarchy had already defined the parameters of leading, we would find it impossible to deviate from them. We would not be motivated to delve into places of discomfort. Let's face it, it is uncomfortable to have your alternative theory of change probed and poked at." (Podcast 2)

Not Knowing

Stephanie: "Enjoy ambiguity. Resist the instinct to overthink, even if it is hard because we all want to know where we are going, but wherever it eventually is will not be familiar. Determinedly avoid the temptation to define answers before you have uncovered all the overlooked possibilities." (Podcast 37)

Go Justajoo

Ayesha introduced me to the Urdu word 'justajoo', and when I used it with Uma it made her smile. She explained why: "It means an Expedition, but one whose source is not only to find something. It is not only the pot of gold at the end of the rainbow. It is the seeking, which is beautifully pleasurable in itself." Uma's eyes twinkled. "It is a very warm word. A word that talks about the innermost or instinctual spiritual desire for something or somebody, of the innateness of love, warmth and pure desire. It just makes me feel ... it just brings a smile to my eyes and my lips." (Podcast 7)

Then some added tips if you are exploring as a group:

Add Art
When words failed us, music did a better job. It pulled us together, opened us up, revealed things about each other. Share, discuss, perform art together including cooking. If you get together physically, cook for each other. Or chop up for the cooks. Or wash up for the cooks.

Listen to Diversity
Stephanie: "If you have taken the trouble to form a diverse group, do not try to make it all the same when you get going. Don't shy away from the diversity in the group, especially the diversity in age. We learn through our differences, not our similarities. The nuance and texture of what people share about leading from divergent perspectives is both revealing and hard to navigate."

Build in Play
Alia: "Play can help us build trust, think outside of the box, flip hierarchy and change power differential."

Meander
Vidya: "We learnt to stay away from the temptation to arrive at a consensus. Rather to go wide and even meander a bit, only narrowing down and coalescing at the very end."

Enjoy Women
Hinemoa: "I went on an Expedition to the Antarctic Peninsula at the end of 2019. If you get a chance to go anywhere close to Antarctica, seize it with both hands. One of the things that I learned was that large groups of women get on really well together. And yet we heard nothing but comments such as 'it'll be so

bitchy, there'll be so many little factions. You'll all be fighting with each other.' It just was not the case." (Podcast 1)

Worrying about this caused Laura to almost miss the First Expedition: "I really thrive in a group that is diverse, yet this was going to be all women. Women-only groups kind of remind me of school days and I really, really did not enjoy them. So up until going on this Expedition, I had veered away from all-women groups. But it has not been like that." (Podcast 11)

Expect the Unexpected

Ana Luz: "I went on a scientific Expedition to Cuba. Our vehicle broke down in the middle of nowhere, it rained for two days straight so we could not set up camp, a permit was revoked so we could not go through a certain area. You are unlikely to face these challenges, but expect your own. Zoom will collapse sometimes, 'events' will turn plans upside down. The unexpected will happen; it is a good idea to expect it to." (Podcast 2)

Anticipate Blow-ups

Blow-ups between members of the group will happen. Just live with them as part of the magic – even a necessary one. Don't suppress them. They say groups form, storm, norm and perform. Think through how to clear the air after you have disagreed or agreed to disagree.

Unconditional Friends

My friend Jude Kelly and I first knew each other when she was a theatre director. Now she is a UK activist on behalf of women, and always finds words that inspire me. As we set off, her advice to me was, "make a commitment from the outset, unconditionally, to be friends with each other. I have found it is really helpful if you just decide in advance that you will care for and love people and decide they are your friends, regardless of whether they irritate, annoy or even anger you.

"If you think about your long-standing friends, you sort of take them with all their idiosyncrasies and weirdness. It's unconditional. It is how you create long term friendship.

"When you are going into an Expedition like this, people are nervous, and they are territorial. It is much easier if you give away all of these things, as if everybody already was your long-term friend. Then, when they are irritating – and we all are sometimes – you can kind of just forget it. Get this right and you can carry on learning together for years." (Podcast 12)

And then last tip from me: don't forget; avoid job titles.

Journal

Solo

If your Expedition is solo, then who you are going to speak to becomes all the more crucial. Have a look at the list you made at the end of the last chapter. Assess it against the advice of the members from the First Expedition, and also assess it against what you know of yourself, so that you speak to people who lead in a very different way from you. You want to speak to people from many different backgrounds, but also ask yourself if your list has people who simply think, speak, act and reason differently from you. Do they counterbalance you in their instincts: if you are a doer, are there enough thinkers, if you like order, are there enough people who thrive in the opposite, if you are quite serious, are there enough playful people on your list?

Now think through how you are going to make sure that you keep exploring. There will be a constant temptation to draw together everything from this book and from the conversations you are having and land too fast on an approach to leading that resonates with you. But don't succumb.

Get it into your mind that you are painting a picture, and first you must gather insights and materials and bring them back into your studio. Only once they are all gathered will you actually start painting. Or think of it as baking a cake. You are gathering lots of ingredients and only once you have them all laid out in your kitchen will you start mixing. Every time you think you have enough ingredients, and you start to pull up your sleeves, stop, put down the new ingredients on the kitchen table and go back out there to find more. Only then will you be really exploring.

One last thought. Have you started writing and drawing in your journal? Or are you one of those people (like me) who said 'yes, yes' but privately thought you could do without one, that you would remember everything? I started my journal partway through the First Expedition and still regret the thoughts that have slipped away.

As a Group

Make sure you simply enjoy each other when you all meet together for the first time. Don't talk about families or careers, but instead about what you love doing or care about.

Talk through how you are going to keep exploring, how you as a group will avoid the temptation to start painting or baking too soon.

You may want to agree some conventions for how you will work together. Or you may not.

You might want to have your own 'enabler' and 'disrupter'. The enabler watches for divides, comfortable for them to happen as a crucial part in the creative process and yet watching out in case they flip to destructive. The disrupter watches out for group think and for moments when sleeves are being pulled up too soon in preparation for baking.

Your Map and Compass

Learning to lead has been a long journey for me, starting from rejecting the very concept, then eventually realising that my ambitions, if they were to be achieved, required me to lead. I then set out to assiduously observe people as they lead and steal from them what I thought would work for me. All the while I watched people around me to see what they required from their leaders. I was fascinated by how leaders brought about change and how they built up their own confidence so that they backed their own hunches. In my home life I was also trying to lead my increasingly large family, struggling with what people saw in me and what I saw in myself.

All the time, I was collecting insights about leading almost like collecting cards for my own eventual pack. It would be my personal collection. There would be no aces, kings or queens, no clubs or hearts, no sets or trumps, just my set of cards that together would frame how I lead. My first boss introduced me to an expression that stuck with me: "You need to have your eyes on the hills and your feet on the ground." So some of the cards were about the hills, how to keep my eyes on the big picture and tell stories about it so that everyone would see those same hills. And some of the cards were about keeping myself firmly rooted on the ground, because you can be as passionate and inspiring as you like about the hills, but you still have to run regular team meetings in such a way that colleagues would not miss one for the world.

My journey has been long, and it is unfinished. More cards have been collected over the last year on the First Expedition, ones that I wish I had had in my pack earlier. Looking back, I think it would also have been helpful to have had the map with me on my journey.

Let me talk you through the three concentric circles with the infinity sign lying across them.

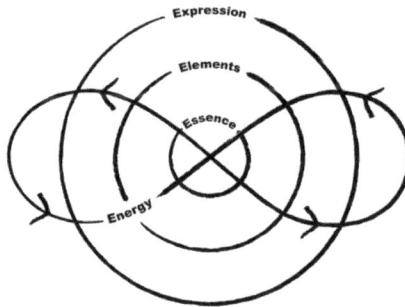

Figure 1: the Four E's

'Essence' is what makes us lead the way we do. 'Elements' are how our Essence shows up in our leading. 'Expression' is how our Essence and Elements play out in our leading. 'Energy' is what flows between the three, in both directions.

Best to start from the middle and work outwards. This makes sense because the first two circles are inward-facing, and from then on the map faces outwards.

I am convinced that when the four E's are disconnected it is harder, if not impossible, to lead effectively. Connected, the four E's provide the basis for successful leading.

Essence

If you google the word 'Essence', it comes up as: "The intrinsic nature or indispensable quality of something, especially something abstract, which determines its character." Or, more fun, "A strong liquid that is used to add a flavour or smell to something." I do like the thought that my Essence adds flavour and smell to my leading.

In the map, Essence is the central circle. It is, simply put, what makes us who we are, and specifically makes us lead the way we do. We each have different pieces in our Essence, and they influence how we lead in different ways.

On the First Expedition we found seven pieces that we felt we all had in different ways and in different proportions in our Essences, many of them deeply rooted in being women. The seven were: Motherness, Nature, the Body, the Sacred, Ancestors, Trauma and Education. We offer these by way of illustration of Essence and as an invitation to consider the pieces of your Essence. Are some the same as ours? Are some others particular to you?

I thought I was pretty clear about what made up my Essence at the start of the First Expedition and how this affected my leading, but I soon found myself out. An example was when Katrina spoke about the Body: it did not resonate at first, even remotely. I have always felt fat and I don't like my body as a result, so I have always done my best to ignore it. But as Katrina spoke, I began to shift. She spoke about how we need to listen to our bodies when we are leading. And as she continued, Sarah began to nod energetically and then burst out, "I realise that I have been leading from my neck up all my life." It was then that I got it. In the past, the Body would not have been a recognised piece of my Essence, but I can see it now.

The same thing happened with the word 'motherness' (a word we coined; I will explain later). I have always worried about using any variant of this word – motherhood or mothering – because not all women have biological children, so such words have felt excluding. I would not have named it as a piece of my Essence, even though I am deeply aware and proud of its impact on my leading. Then Aparna helped me: "We don't just mother our biological children, many of us mother other people's children and we certainly mother the Earth." So we looked for another word, and Motherness is now boldly and confidently at the centre of my Essence.

Please don't forget that these seven pieces of Essence are only illustrations. Everyone will have different pieces in their Essence. Anna, I am absolutely certain, would have music as a piece of her Essence. In almost every discussion,

Anna brings in music, sharing and illustrating complex thoughts with musical parallels. Music would definitely be in Anna's Essence, but sadly not in mine.

Elements

The next circle out from Essence is Elements. Elements are how your Essence shows up in how you lead. They are a messy and personal concoction, just as leading is a messy and personal concoction. It is silly to pretend that it isn't.

Inevitably, every piece of our Essence brings with it both light and shadows, especially in its extremes. There will be some Elements which are unhelpful. You may have to consciously jettison them. Elements like the feeling that you are never enough or that you must always be the good girl that are rooted in your Essence.

There will be other Elements which you may choose to reframe. You have probably perceived them as weaknesses for years but maybe, just maybe, they are quite the opposite and are in fact your strengths. Maybe the imposter syndrome is not a source of fear but rather a source of humility? Maybe instincts should not be dismissed as irrational but instead treated as early warning systems that kick in way before all that is rational does?

There is one Element you will need to really focus on: Purpose. It is the most significant Element that emanates from your Essence. What is your purpose in leading?

And then there are Elements that will need combining, even if they appear to be in contradiction or even in conflict. Like humility and visibility, being humble is not always about invisibility, and being visible is not always a display of absent humility. Both can and do – and must – live alongside each other when leading. You could say the same about being both loud and quiet, being vulnerable and strong, and many more.

It feels important at this stage to remind ourselves again of how flawed words are. They are such inadequate and blunt ways to express ourselves, and yet we jump so fast to judge on the basis of them. They so often mean such different things to different people. Some are toxic and you use them unawares. You can get lulled into thinking that you are speaking the same language as someone else, and then suddenly you blunder into using what is a trigger word for the other person.

I expressed a nuanced thought recently and made the mistake of using the word "oxygen" to express it. It triggered a blow-up that took us way off course. I used the word as an alternative to attention, but I used it with an audience whose main experience of attracting attention is of attracting bigotry, and oxygen is what they felt long deprived of. It triggered and I learned.

Sometimes it is not about using toxic words and it is simply an issue of translation. I remember asking all the members of the First Expedition to translate the definition of leading that we had agreed on into their mother tongue. The word 'catalytic' caused chaos. It means so many different things to scientists and artists and to different people around the world. In some languages it even has completely the opposite meaning.

The moment I will not forget as we all struggled with translations was when Selvie gave me her first literal version into Bahasa. I innocently asked her if the translation was any good, and her answer was, "it's accurate but it's awful. It's heavy and clunky and it stumbles." It sounded awful even to me. So she started again with no attempt at a literal translation, and the result rolled eloquently off her tongue. She had a sense of pride that was visible as she spoke in her favourite language, just for a change. Is it a fair translation? I simply don't know, but it looked like it might be, reading her face as she said it.

All this to say, change this map into the language that you enjoy speaking the most. Take my words only as an invitation to find your own. After all, that's what we did with Motherness.

So, the first two of the concentric circles, Essence and Elements, are both internally focused, and rightly, says Aparna: "We should not fall into the trap of thinking that all the tools to lead are to be found in the external world. That would be to do ourselves a disservice. There is a wellspring that sits inside of us." (Podcast 11)

But nor should we overdo this introspection. We must also look outwards at the world we lead in.

Expression

Expression is the third of the concentric circles. It is about how our Essence and Elements play out as we lead.

Let us go back to that team meeting for an example of Expression. Leading a meeting is one of the most important tools for leading. You must lead a meeting in such a fashion that each individual member feels visible and included, makes their contribution, comes up with great ideas, listens to everyone, finds out what is going on, feels appreciated and challenged. Crucially, you need colleagues to leave clear, focused and inspired to get on with the work in hand and knowing why they are doing it. You must lead the meeting so that as a team the whole is greater than the sum of the parts, ideas are noodled on and improved, plans are challenged and crystallised, culture is embedded and embodied, conflicts are aired and resolved, the team feels energised by being together. And do so in such a way that the work gets done, with the hurdles anticipated and overcome, the decisions made and implemented, the targets ready to be met and even exceeded.

Like all leading, it requires you to address the needs of the individuals, the team and the task so that none of the three dominates. Otherwise, the individuals may well be deeply inspired, but nothing gets done. The team is working beautifully together but on the wrong task. The task is being achieved but everyone is applying for a transfer. The team is strong and focused, but some individuals are being left out. The individuals feel motivated but are not working as a team.

Getting all this right is what Expression is about, the practical stuff of leading. The stuff of daily life when you start to lead.

Our Expedition uncovered people leading everywhere, and we went to find out what they do. Not how they are or what they believe, but what they actually do. Later in the book I have shared some extracts from my journal as examples of the conversations you need to have on your Expedition and the practical insights you are seeking. They are with people like Sylvia and Harriet Nayiga talking about midwifery, Allyson on leading in supply chain management, Erin and Elsa sharing their stories of leading when the odds were hugely stacked against them, Kelly telling me about captaining a rugby team, Monica sharing how she approaches tough performance conversations without losing all sense of her Essence, Jennifer and Vivi leading creativity in their theatres. They are all women leading in totally different contexts, holding firmly onto their Essence as they work out how best to lead in the situation they faced in the real world. As you read about them here and speak to more women as part of your own Expedition, only pick up what you think will work for you because it will connect back through your Elements to your Essence.

Just before we go on to the fourth E, let us divert for a moment. Take a step back to consider how connected and balanced the Essence, Elements and Expression circles are in you.

Your Circles

Consider the relative sizes and positions of the three circles for you. Here are three possible extremes.

Some of us have an enormous Expression circle. We are practical, hands on, on the move, making things happen. In contrast, our Essence circle at the centre is very small. We are not quite sure why we lead the way we lead. Maybe we don't have the time or inclination to bother about it.

I know successful and yet exhausted leaders who would put themselves in this category. They worry about their own sustainability. The connection between their Expression and Essence is loose and they are not quite sure about things. And sometimes it just cannot be revealed because they have to, at best, hide and, at worst, deny their Essence to succeed in the organisations or communities in which they lead.

Whatever the reason for the disconnect, they worry that their colleagues might spot it, possibly misunderstand it, and almost certainly mistrust it. As Katrina says, "you have to vocalise your Essence if people are going to trust you." (Podcast 52)

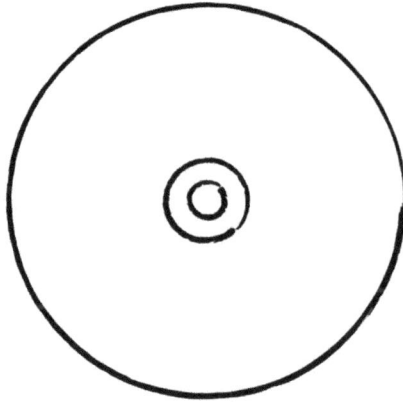

Figure 2: All Expression

Another extreme for some of us is that we have an enormous Essence circle. We have really thought through and analysed ourselves and are very self-aware. In contrast, we have a relatively limited Expression circle. We struggle to translate our Essence into Expression. We can see that nothing much is happening around us, but we cannot figure out how to breach the gap.

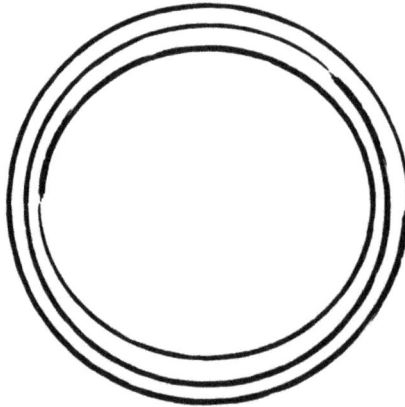

Figure 3: All Essence

The third extreme is when we have consciously or unconsciously disconnected Essence, Elements and Expression circles. We do this either because we feel that we had to do so in order to succeed, or because we have not realised that women can lead in a way that works for us. Either way, we have adopted status quo leading and it has sometimes been successful, but we are certainly not bringing our diversity and freshness to the table. Mostly we are just adding to the group think.

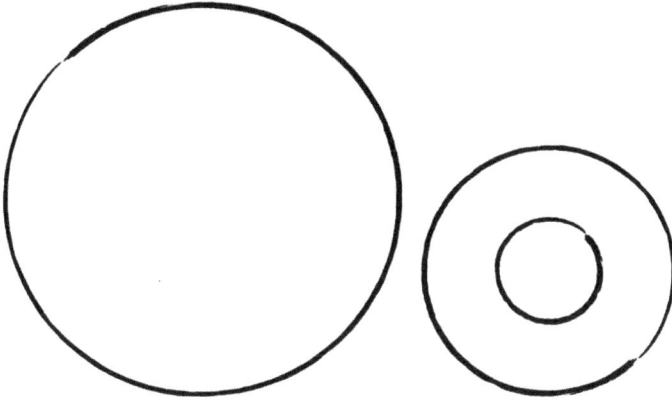

Figure 4: Disconnected E's

Uma tells me that the three E's are perfect: "I love three. In Hinduism it is the strongest number. It is a symbol of brevity and rhythm." But she says that she will have to accept the fourth E that lies across them because, "I love the infinity sign too. It is a very powerful symbol."

Energy

Energy is an infinity sign that lies across the three circles and beyond, because there is a dynamic flow between them, a flow in both directions.

The inner world of Essence flows out through Elements to Expression to frame how we do our leading. And the outside world flows back through Expression into Essence and causes us to question ourselves and evolve. The flow from in to out, and from out to in, is infinite. One anchoring everything that is built on it, the other making sure that Essence doesn't get rigid and ossify.

This flow produces Energy: the Energy of leading. This is surely what leading really is: Energy. Think of the moment when a leader enters a room and the

Energy is sparked. Or think of when they have the opposite effect and drain the Energy.

Leading at its best generates Energy, space is created, atmosphere sparkles and things start to happen, often on their own with very little leading actually called for. The Energy starts to compound and so much more begins to feel possible. Then the Energy generated starts to spiral upwards, made ever more powerful because it is deeply anchored in Essence.

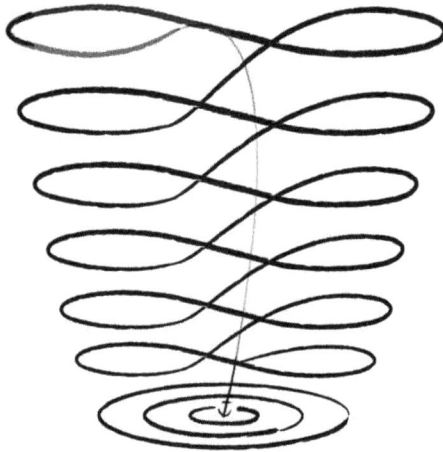

Figure 5: Energy spiral, anchored by Essence

This book walks you through this map as you embark on your Expedition. We share the pieces of Essence we uncovered on the First Expedition. Go through the Elements to jettison, reframe, find and combine. We share the advice of many women as they express how they lead. And then we lift up to the infinity symbol and show how Energy is created, all the while avoiding the dead ends when it starts to be generated big time.

But it all starts with Essence and motherness, that strange word that we coined and that I promised to explain.

Journal

Solo

Start working on your own map in your journal. Just have a go, a very rough first go. How big is each circle for you? Does one tend to dominate? Has this changed over time?

Ask people who know you well for a few words that capture how they observe you leading. What have they seen you do or not do, either well or not so well? Write down what they say. Then ask the same question to people who do not know you well, but have worked with you. Don't complicate things by asking them to distinguish between Essence, Elements and Expression. That's for you to do as you ask yourself questions like, "If I do that, where is it coming from?" And "If that's in my Essence, why is it not coming out in how I lead?"

Think of moments when your Energy has been crucial to your success in leading, and when it hasn't. Make a timeline of your journey of leading and plot out these moments.

Your journal should be filling up now.

As a group

If you are exploring as a group, do all of the above individually and decide which bits to share and discuss. If you are a diverse group there are likely to be very different and interesting insights. Listen hard to the differences and consider adjusting your own map as you do.

Once you have shared what you chose to share within your group, you could draw it all together by asking each of you to highlight something intriguing that another member of your group has written or said. Note: resist the temptation to just summarise your own thoughts.

Essence

Motherness

The word 'motherness' recognises the problems around words like 'motherhood' and 'mothering'. The first is that we do not want to exclude fathers. The answer surely is to value the beauty of 'fatherness' and recognise its undeniable overlaps with motherness.

And the second being the exclusion of women who do not or choose not to have children. Aparna disentangled this one for me: "Mothering is so much more than giving birth. I know women who have never had children, who never wanted to have children, who are extremely maternal. Maybe it gives them the ability to be even more maternal, because they do not have the angst." (Podcast 26)

But even with Aparna's clarity, I still struggle with the traditional motherhood words, and so on the First Expedition we coined the word 'motherness', which we felt was deeply rooted in all of our Essences, with a big impact on our leading.

So how does motherness shape us as leaders? We made a long, long list. A joyful and self-indulgent list. It is put together by birth mothers, adopting mothers, godmothers, women who mentor, mothers of communities and mothers of nature.

Organised

Rachel Middleton, a headhunter recently returned from maternity, has the freshness of a newcomer: "It sounds simplistic, but it is the truth. As a mother I have learnt to be organised and this has influenced how I lead. It's especially important when you have people around you who rely on you." (Podcast 46)

Kind

Rachel again: "Now I understand colleagues in a different way. I see the whole human being. Before, I might have fussed about someone being five minutes late for a meeting and drawn unkind conclusions. Now I am in this world of motherness where I am completely out of control 90% of the time. Things happen. I drop the ball, I make mistakes, I say the wrong thing and I realise nobody is exempt from ball dropping whether they are my team, my peers or my bosses. I have developed a degree of kindness as I see people as a whole person." (Podcast 46)

Samia Latif, who leads in public health and has been learning from teenagers for some time, declares, "Yes, kind, and also I do not blame or shame anymore. Because if you have teenage kids, you discover that it is the worst thing you can do. And this translates to work. When you debrief a difficult situation, you ask two questions: What went well and what could have gone better? Mothers get this right because they know how a culture of blame or shame is hugely detrimental." (Podcast 47)

It took a while to persuade Melissa Kwee, a businesswoman and campaigner in Singapore, to talk about her motherness. She kept on telling me that she did not have children of her own, but then she spoke about being a CEO during COVID: "Once a week we held a meeting where people could just drop in and check in. They did not need to turn on their camera, just drop in. I became known as the 'hugging chief executive' during COVID. That is what motherness is, isn't it?" (Podcast 54)

Boundaries

Myrna Atalla, who leads Alfanar, which invests in women social entrepreneurs in the Arab world, reflects back on the baby phase: "I finally learned that it is OK to have boundaries. I knew I needed them in theory; I had been on all the leadership programmes that told me to draw them, but it had not sunk in. Now I finally got it. In the first year I was actually turning off the notifications on my email because I found I would get home after a long day, during which I had been missing my child, and an email notification would come up. Even if I did not respond to the email, it sullied my time with my child. I realised that it is OK; I can pick up those emails later if I need to when I am in the right head-space. Before, I would have responded to the emails instantly, feeling frantic and frustrated, and I would inevitably have responded incorrectly because I was in a rush." (Podcast 46)

Bigger

Uthara Narayanan works with women in villages in the south of India. She talked about being a perfectionist, or rather about how motherness had cured her of perfectionism. She held high the adoption certificate for her son, signed by the Chief Registrar in Karnatake, as she told me the story: "We were in an orphanage for something else and somehow it happened. He is severely differently abled. I started down a road that changed me as a person and as a leader. I am a perfectionist; I like things a certain way, I like things to be just right and I strive towards that. Suddenly, here is a child who does not have a so-called 'normal' body structure, and he is not able to do things that others can do, but he is so happy. Just being around him every day changes how I lead. Nobody is perfect. We just use our own abilities to the best that we can, and it is in your hands to find happiness." (Podcast 64)

Innovative

Back to Rachel, who has a glorious illustration of innovation in motherness: "I remember once with my son, he was crying and crying and crying. I just could not work out why he was crying. So I got in the shower with him. I didn't turn the shower on. I just stood underneath it. Then we got out. We flushed the loo and he suddenly stopped crying. In moments like this, you are really, really tired. You have tried everything. You have gone through the list: he isn't tired, or hungry, or ill, he doesn't need burping or a clean nappy. You just think, right, I have got to be creative. I have got to think of something new, something different. So you stand under the shower and flush the loo. And that is what was needed.

"It is ridiculous, but actually it is that sort of innovation we need, particularly when the world seems to be crumbling down around us. We just have to be calm, to rethink and reset, then come up with something new. I think that is probably the greatest thing I will take into my leading from motherness. If something is not working, don't panic. Find a place of mental peace despite the screaming, calm yourself and just think of a new idea and try it. If it doesn't work, start again. Some ideas do not work, but you have to try them, and if they didn't work today, they might work tomorrow or they might work in two minutes' time. There is nothing wrong with failing, even when you know the stakes are high. I mean mothering is the thing that you really do not want to fail at, but you fail at it all the time. Just pick yourself up and try it again, even if it is exactly the same thing. I guess that is what resilience is for leaders. That is what innovation is too: try new things and if they don't work, try again tomorrow." (Podcast 46)

When Melissa Kwee heard this story, she laughed and quoted her mother, saying: "You know children never come with an instruction manual. Motherness is figuring out what to do without one." (Podcast 54)

It made me laugh too, because leading is the same, though I now think that a map does help.

Samia smiled too. She suspects that when Rachel has her second child, she will find that if she goes into the shower, it might not work. Samia says that is the other thing that motherness teaches you, that the people you lead are all very different: "You have to get savvy enough to be able to say, 'okay this is what works for this person, but it is a no-no for someone else.'" (Podcast 47)

Agile

For me, motherness made me better at spotting when to act and understanding the hazards of delaying or avoiding and the impact of compounding. Once my baby got into a state, I started to get into a state myself. Then the state started to accumulate and compound and things rapidly got out of control, and then everybody around me got into a state too. If I didn't take the time out to spot what was going on early on, if I avoided and hoped and prevaricated, things got more out of control at an extraordinary speed. Most often it is because I was too tired to see what was happening or too distant to sense it. And by the time I acted, it needed a disproportionate effort to put it right.

There is a direct link here to leading, having the instinct or judgement to hold back or get in there at the right time. If you let the wrong things run wild, they compound, and by the time it gets your attention it is massive. It's also why, if you are leading, you have to be careful not to get too tired if you can possibly avoid it.

Consistent

Another big pull through from motherness to leading, for me, is consistency. Talk to anyone who fosters children, their top secret of success is: boring, incredibly boring, consistency. I learnt fast that my kids valued consistency, even when they were not crazy about what I was being consistent about. I learnt this with my first child and even more as I had more children. Of course, they are all very different, but I knew that I had to be consistent about the boundaries I set.

Ok, I can sense my kids reading this. Tom (the youngest) got away with far more, says Emma (the second eldest). True. But if anyone came to the house and any of you ignored them, you were sent straight to your room, weren't you?

Consistency is at the root of safety and of trust in both motherness and leading. Try working for someone who changes the boundaries constantly, who moves the goalposts regularly, who responds to problems in completely unpredictable ways, who has random favourites at random times, who switches from hot to cold almost in an instant, and quite inexplicably. You will not thrive and, crucially, you are unlikely to trust them.

Uncontrolling

Samia adds something more nuanced to our list: "Mothering teenage children forces you to rethink power and authority. Sometimes we feel we need to be in control, so as to stop disasters that we see unfolding from happening. But what I have realised is that we need to let them make their own mistakes. Leave them to walk on the path that they have chosen. We can guide them, help them to navigate, but we cannot steer the way for them. They have got to do that them-selves. Because then the lessons they learn are more meaningful. I try to take this lesson into my leading. To give my team the autonomy to make decisions when I know full well that there is a risk, but then again there is risk in every-thing. Things may not work out, but the learning does.

"You learn fast that if you do intervene, it must be with lengthy explana-tion and detailed background logic. I try to avoid it sometimes, to fob them off when I am really fed up, but it does not work. They need to know the reasons and the logic behind your intervention." (Podcast 47)

Upskilling

Samia is on a roll now, this time on communication: "With children you realise how important regular check-ins are. Nothing fancy, just 'are you ok? How was today?'. Then they begin to feel safe. Don't expect too much by way of reply in return; they will talk when they feel like talking.

"Kids also force you to upskill. For example, they use all of these emojis and slang and gifs. I ask my daughter what they mean. I'm constantly upskilling my communication because they use a totally different language that is very alien to me. But I know that I need to understand them to lead teams and read a room whether I am at work or at home." (Podcast 47)

Modern

Samia pauses and smiles gently at this point. "I remember reading something very poignant by one of the companions of our prophet in Islam. His name is Ali; he went on to become one of the leaders of the Muslim Community after the prophet died. The saying goes, 'Do not raise your children the way [your] parents raised you; they were born for a different time.'

"It has always stayed with me. The pressures that our children are facing are different, it is true of every generation. The environment we live in has changed rapidly. Our children see things through a very different lens. I think our lens gets very jaded; we see things the way they were when we grew up. We get cataracts in our lenses. I think that is metaphorically true as our perspective on life becomes jaded. So how we lead needs that fresh influx and perspective. We have to evolve. We have to constantly check and recheck ourselves." (Podcast 47)

Vulnerable

This word had to be in this list. An ease with vulnerability comes hand in hand with motherness. It makes Saba Al Mubaslat, based in Egypt where she leads the Ford Foundation, laugh: "I remember how adamant I was on me being there to teach my kids. In fact, I rapidly realised that I was learning from them way more than I was teaching them: to be humble, to say I don't know, just to be vulnerable. They see the human side of me, that I am not a machine, that I get tired and do not want to talk and that sometimes it is me who wants space for myself. I did speeches for years about this stuff, but it was my kids who forced me to do it as a mother and now I do it when I am leading." (Podcast 47)

Tough

Saba wants to counterbalance some of the gentler words associated with motherness with the tough ones too. "My son came home and said, 'Mom, the exam did not go well today.' I said, 'okay, fine, we cannot change the result. Were the questions you messed up on covered in the textbook?' He nodded. 'Why were you not able to answer them?' His answer was, 'we were not given enough time.' It was clear that he thought it was all someone else's responsibility. So I kept on probing until he owned his mistakes and learnt from them. I do not see any difference here from daily leading."

Saba gave me another example: "Sometimes you have to put your heart aside. You have to discipline. I invented a variation of the 'naughty chair' of my childhood: I called it the 'thinking corner.' I would ask my boys to go and sit in it and think about their action, why it was not pleasant and what could be done to fix it. It used to break my heart seeing them sitting there with tears coming down. They were pleading, 'I have not done anything wrong' and I just kept to, 'take your time, think about it.' I told myself that at least it was a paradigm shift from the 'naughty chair.' I cannot remember the number of times I just wanted to run to them and hug them. But they needed to know that they were perfectly loved and that the imperfect action could be fixed. It is the same when you are leading. You have to be clear and consistent about what is not acceptable, what must be done better, what can be done better with reflection. To go away and re-think a proposal or whatever you are working on and then discuss it tomorrow. I try to nudge colleagues not to allow themselves to do a mediocre job, if for no other reason than that I know they can do better." (Podcast 47)

We talked about all the words associated with mothers. Tough is seldom on the list. But it should be.

Nurturing

Saba then went in another direction: "I think the only way to lead with love and care is to behave as if you are stuck with your team forever, like your kids. You may reach a point where it is not working, and you must let go, but even then, the mentoring and support you have provided will stay with them forever. You have to take responsibility for being part of their journey. Whatever good or bad you leave them with might affect them for the rest of their journey. I take it very personally when I fail to help one of my team members to flourish."

I asked Saba if she ever takes too much of those mothering skills into work. Her answer was yes, but she drew a distinction: "With my boys I try to be loving, fair and firm. With my colleagues I try to be fair and firm with love. The order of the words matters a lot because I am leading professional adults who are responsible for their own behaviour. You can care, but over caring can hinder their ability to grow." (Podcast 47)

Visibility

Anna explained this concept of visibility to me with a story told her by a friend who played in an orchestra with Maestro Bernard Haitink as the conductor: "There is a small cello solo in the Alpine symphony. The principal cellist played it. Bernard stopped and said, 'it was very beautiful, but maybe a touch less vibrato?' She played again and he stopped again, looked at his score, then put his hand on his heart with a sad expression on his face and said, 'I am so sorry; I do not have the words to describe what it is I am asking from you. Can we do it again?' And the third time was just sublime. It was completely transformed.

"By thanking her and not coming down on her and by appealing to her musicality, the maestro had lifted her. She was visible and liberated to have her own idea about the music. So she tried again and found something else which was exactly what he wanted. He transformed her way of playing just by giving her visibility and the permission to try something herself."

Anna believes passionately that great leading makes everyone feel visible. Even if they are one in a vast orchestra and only have a tiny note to play. Even, in Anna's case, if you are the second violin in a sea of violins.

It is important to say that Anna carefully distinguishes visibility from exposure. "Leading well makes people feel visible without feeling exposed and without making them feel that they need to expose themselves to be visible."

Anna believes that motherness inspires us to give this gift of visibility. To see others and not just ourselves. And that the best leading does this too.

Enabling

Melissa is convinced that, "Motherness somehow creates an enabling environment. One that is sometimes supportive and sometimes quite challenging, but even in the challenge there is a foundation to build on. This environment enables people to thrive. I feel like that is a huge part of leading, creating the conditions in which people find it within themselves to take action."

When I asked Melissa to give me an example, she was still pushing back on the basis that she never had biological children. I replied to her, "You expressed your motherness to us all, all the way through the First Expedition." And so she began to talk about the community where she lives in Queenstown, Singapore: "It is a mixed income neighbourhood where people do not necessarily connect, where there is not a great care for the public spaces or a strong connection to place or to each other. When I moved there, I started opening my house, listening to my neighbours about what they loved about the neighbourhood, finding ways in which their interests and talents could be shared. We have slowly built the community."

Now it is not just Melissa running activities and programmes in her home, it is also the many neighbours who until then had lived there for decades not knowing one another and never saying a word to each other. Melissa explained: "Now, if my neighbour loves to cook and he is only able to have a job two days a week, people are ordering from him, and we have got a little catering business going. It is birthing possibilities through just creating the space where people's gifts and talents are discovered and shared. There is a lot of sitting, eating and laughing around a table. It is about creating the conditions for others to find their voice."

I asked Melissa how important food is to motherness. She said it was essential. She described her kitchen as a "War Ready Pantry" (Podcast 54) and I can visualise it because she created a mini one when we met together at the end of the First Expedition. We kept asking "where is Melissa?" The answer was always that she was at the local supermarket buying more food for us "just in case we got hungry." Her bottles and packets filled the shelves in the tiny kitchen. When we left it was a joy handing them on to the women who came to prepare for the next guests.

Less ego

Melissa also put her finger on a final light that emanates out of motherness, one that she has already illustrated: much less ego. I asked her what would happen if she left Queenstown.

"I do not plan to leave but I do not believe that community can or should ever be built around a single person. So the most important thing is raising up a core with common values and a common sense of what we want to see in our neighbourhood and ensuring that we are constantly bringing in new and different people. I don't actually show up every Saturday now. It never should be about a single person. It is motherness, isn't it: built-in redundancy? Or built in evolution, letting the chicks fly." (Podcast 54)

That completes the list we put together. I am sure there are many more from Rachel, Samia, Myrna, Uthara, Melissa, Anna, Princess and Saba. Motherness is undoubtedly in our Essence and has had a significant impact on our leading.

Melissa Kwee describes it as: "a set of life-giving attributes which focus intently on the well-being and thriving of another." But she recognises that, as with every piece of our Essence, there comes both light and shadows, and motherness is no exception to this.

Shadows

I asked Melissa about the shadows of motherness and how they translate to leading. Here are three from her:

The first is 'smother-hood': "It is being overly present, overly concerned, overly cautious, overly interventionist. It is when the unbridled gifts of empathy and care overwhelm others with their singularly focused emotion and action. It is a dead end for motherness and also for leading."

Everyone needs fresh air and space to breathe, rather than a tornado of concern and remedies. Smotherness can repel and disempower people. Melissa is clear: "The leader who draws smotherness into their leading prevents themselves from raising others to discover their own agency and become their highest selves."

Princess Ashilokun, a young poet and rapper whom I admire, reflected on this and put it into her context: "Mothers want to protect their daughters and inadvertently pass on a sort of cage mentality, so that even before we experience the things which caged our mothers, their mentality shapes us to fit into those cages. It becomes a repeating cycle.

"Your mother is telling you that there are certain ways in which a woman can – or rather a wife must – exist. If you do not conform to these things, then there is going to be 'wahala' – the Nigerian term for trouble. What she does not realise is that she is taking away your childhood and autonomy, your ability to figure out for yourself who you are. She is trying to shape your existence to conform to the idea of a husband who does not even exist yet but whose existence already shapes your being. She is trying to save you rather than allowing you to save yourself."

Back to Melissa's shadow. It is 'mini-me': mothers with unmet needs, unfulfilled dreams and an inability to let go end up trying to create mini-me's. Melissa observes that, "Motherness can unconsciously slip into this trap when emotional closeness is exchanged for mirrored action. And it translates to leading in a way that does not create space for the beauty and strength of each individual to be seen, felt and nurtured."

The third shadow is 'respect your mother': Princess jumped when I uttered these words of Melissa's. She began to talk about the hierarchies in families and took over describing this third shadow in motherness: "It is a motherness that demands respect even when it is wrong. Blind respect. Blind obedient respect. It comes from when the lines are blurred between respect and deference."

The result is that for the people you mother or the colleagues you lead, being respectful becomes prided above autonomy and sense of self. Princess kept going: "I am having flashbacks to those moments that prevent girls from speaking up because they are thinking about being respectful. It is the saddest of things because it shows you that your mother's beliefs are already entrenched. She has accepted the cage and is passing it on. She is now, inadvertently or not, shaping you to fit into it. As we try to change society and patriarchal structures, we have to remember not to become too much like our mothers."

We have all watched leaders obsessed with hierarchy, who demand respect and in the same breath demand that colleagues speak up. Talking to Princess, I was reminded of Andini's words about *The Devil Wears Prada* and grasped the full damage that film did to ideas of women leading. Sadly, the Devil still seems to wear Prada.

Smotherness, mini-me, respect your mother; I am sure there are more. They all translate from motherness into leading, and we see them everywhere.

As I write these, I see little glimpses of me, and it hurts. I recognise how some of the shadowy sides of my Essence have translated into how I am as a mother and my leading, and that hurts too.

Hiding motherness

I know that many women choose to keep clear dividing lines in their lives and would rather separate motherness and leading, but I hope it is their decision to do so and not the result of pressure to do so.

Going back to Rachel: "Motherness is a rollercoaster." At this point she was muttering, "motherness, or whatever you want to call it, Mum." She was irritated by the cumbersome word and felt entitled to say so. Yes, I must admit it, Rachel is indeed my daughter, and the screaming baby in the shower is my grandson.

"I feel that this experience has changed me more than any experience that I have had in my whole life, and I think that needs to be a bit more celebrated.

"It is so important that you can bring the learning with you when you return to work, because it will have changed you dramatically and wholeheartedly as a human and as a leader. If captured and acknowledged in the right way in the workplace, I think it can be completely transformative. But if it has to be concealed, or if you have to be ashamed of it, then I think it can do quite the opposite to your leading. It can lead to you losing confidence or empathy. You might end up putting loads of effort into trying to conceal a part of you that is quite dramatically different to what you were before you left." (Podcast 46)

Celebrated would be great, even acknowledged would be a move in the right direction. It is not always easy to do so because we risk being written off as weak or wrong, or patronised for our newly acquired 'soft skills'.

Rachel ends with a plea: "I don't think there are many women who, when asked, 'has motherhood transformed you as a leader?' would reply that it had. I have not heard of many apart from you." (Podcast 46)

Rachel has seen me do this in every speech I have made since I had my first child. I promised myself then that I would always tell some motherness stories when I spoke about leading. But Rachel has also seen how half the audience delighted in them, while the rest wrote me off as unprofessional.

Aparna pulls this together: "I feel like to be a maternal leader is so incredibly powerful in whatever context it is performed. Why would we not allow that side of ourselves to emerge in a world where there is so much conflict?

"I have this huge dream that one day we're going to have women leading everywhere. And especially in interfaith dialogue, because we have so much religious conflict in this world, and I cannot imagine not needing an element of motherness in it." (Podcast 26)

Two last thoughts from me:

I think that getting good at leading helps you to get good at motherness, too. It works both ways. It certainly has for me.

It works both ways with nature too. If we use our motherness in caring for nature, I think nature will care for us too.

So we move on to nature as the second piece of the Essence discovered by the members of the First Expedition.

Nature

Nature is surely another piece in our Essence, though I am not sure that we are all conscious of it and its impact on how we lead. It cannot be a coincidence that we express ourselves through nature so often.

The Baobab

Priyanka sees nature through a Botswanan lens where, for her, nature is the start and end of everything: "Nature is everywhere you look and when you start to look at it you have to see things differently. We have this deep rootedness to our soil, the soil of Botswana. We have got the most stunning Baobab trees, they are called the tree of life because so much comes out of them that is nurturing; from food to medicine.

"I think the more time I spend in nature, the more I start to look at myself differently and at how I lead. I learn about flexibility, resilience, about the permanence and unpredictability of change. About what actually grows when you give it the right environment. And most of what I see goes against what I have been taught.

"One of my favourite things is the Botswana sky. When I look up to the sky, I think of an expression used by the poet, Rumi: 'Even after all this time, the sun never says to the Earth, "look at me, you owe me".' I think that is what we must do, light people up. It is what I have learnt to do by spending time in nature in Botswana." (Podcast 24)

The vā

Sina Wendt, originally from Samoa in the South Pacific before becoming a business leader in New Zealand, speaks of the Vā – or rather of its absence: "We talk about the Vā which, translated to English, literally just means 'the space'. Most Polynesian societies see space as a relational space, not a physical space. It is a sacred space that connects us, not just to other humans but to the environment and to the ecology of the world. In Samoa we believe it to be our duty to be in a collective, to be in relationship with each other and to nourish and nurture and cherish the Vā.

"During COVID we realised how bad the Vā had become. It felt like the planet had said 'enough is enough. Look at the way humans have treated our planet, look at the way humans have treated each other.' It is not that the Vā was that good before, but the isolation of COVID magnified how empty it had become.

"I suppose to create a different Vā we have to have a better idea of what it is we want to create together, and that is the biggest challenge. That is where I get completely frustrated and sad and angry. I look at the way people who lead in different parts of the world come at it with what I consider to be a really Western mindset. It is kind of a 'last person standing' mindset. If we continue to see things through this lens we will get nowhere."

The Vā is a beautiful expression that I must introduce to Fatima Zibouh in Bruxelles. She spends her life bringing women together in the city, and describes it as, "building bridges to connect up islands in an archipelago, but in a culture where you only get recognised if you are leading an island."

Nature seems to very naturally sit in our Essence and play out in how we lead in beautiful ways.

Not all light

We often use beautiful words to capture nature's impact on us, such as serenity and wisdom, yet, as Ana Luz says, "it too has its shadowy sides which curiously might prepare us well for the tough realities of leading.

"I have always felt a deep connection to nature, but it is not what I would call a spiritual one, an interconnectivity, a Oneness with nature and an understanding of its complexity.

"I like to say that I have travelled the journey as a scientist from trying to *understand* nature when I was doing pure research, to looking to *conserve* nature. And now, two decades later, to really focusing on our relationship with nature: *sustaining* it and ourselves.

"I think that women have a special way of connecting to nature. We are more cyclical beings and many of us feel deeply connected to nature in a way that is restorative. But I worry when people become over-emotional and start to romanticise nature and assume that it is inherently good, because we risk forgetting how very powerful and very destructive nature can be. You may romanticise the lion cub but if you go on a safari and you watch the lions hunt, it is a brutal business. We must approach nature with a certain reverence, recognise there are mysterious ways of functioning that we might not ever fully understand, and take on board its nuances and complexities."

For Ana Luz, nature being central to her Essence has had a profound impact on how she leads, both from the light and the shadowy sides.

"You start to understand that there are different ways of leading at different times because there are cycles, and there are cycles within cycles, as in nature. It has an acceptance of cycles, of death and destruction. There are also seasons; it is not always about grow, move forward, produce progress, generate more incessantly. There is this sense of enoughness in nature. And nature makes you pay more attention because you do not know exactly what is coming next. It can be unpredictable, deeply uncaring and unfair. So we cannot assume a stable world. Change is the norm today and it will be the norm for the rest of our lives.

"If you hold on to nature in your Essence, you avoid the trap of the dreamy quality in leading. You recognise and anticipate that the world is not always benevolent however much, as women, you have a desire to see more benevolence. It means that you are not surprised when the hard realities of leading actually hit you, nor are you unprepared when the system is unfair. When I was younger, it hurt me when I found colleagues in positions of power who were unkind and unpredictable. It was a shock, but I have learnt to navigate around these and to adapt. Much like nature does.

"And yet I think the greatest impact that it has on my leading is this sense of harmony that we see in nature; this deep sense of gratitude for sustenance and all of those things that sunlight brings." (Podcast 53)

I asked Ana Luz if another impact was linked to the expression 'the infinite game,' which she once explained to me.

"The idea is that we are here playing an infinite game. It is not a finite game. We are not here to win or lose. When we play an infinite game, the goal is to keep playing, not to end the game.

"If victory is to keep playing, it means we have to do things differently. We have to collaborate. We have to figure out what the next step is together because if we just eliminate the other player, the game is over. We have to be inclusive because everyone is part of the ecosystem that needs balancing. In real life we are mainly surrounded by finite games; sports that have rigid, unchanging rules, tight timings, most of them are competitive, most of them have winners or losers. The infinite game gives you a different way of looking at how we are doing as a society, as human beings, as Earthlings." (Podcast 53)

As Ana Luz spoke, I remembered a podcast episode with Sarah and Paula. Sarah the social entrepreneur was reflecting with Paula Vaccaro, a film producer, on *The Hunger Games* series (Podcast 17). It is an example of the ultimate finite game, designed quite cynically to pit people against each other. Ana Luz laughed. "That happens in nature too. I mean, resources are finite. Nature teaches us that. Sometimes we go into a meeting and see it is a finite game. Whether we like it or not, only one of us will emerge winning. It is a reality, but it is important to remember that ultimately it is an infinite game." I asked Ana Luz for an example. "It means that sometimes you pass on an opportunity because you don't think you are the best person to deliver it. By doing this you are nurturing the ecosystem." I asked her if she has even been written off as a weak female leader when she did this. Her answer: "I think there is a risk of that, yes. A risk you just live with." (Podcast 53)

Generational

Our commitment to nature makes us deeply focused on the issues of climate change. In many parts of the world, these issues are dividing women into generations. Without any doubt it is a dominant piece in young women's Essence – as is the trauma it generates.

Hila Davies, a young student from the Philippines and passionate volunteer for Take Action Global, says, "I feel like the climate crisis has been dumped on our generation. As young women we feel that it has taken over our entire lives and is causing serious climate anxiety. Young people do not have agency. People like Greta Thunberg have been given a platform, but there is no point getting to the table if it is to fill a quota or to allow the inviters to claim, 'look, we're listening to young women' if it is just for show on social media. Young women specifically are the butt of jokes. Every single thing that a teenage girl gets caricatured and nit-picked by the media, by the existing leaders and also by older women. There was one campaign called the 'VSCO girl'; she was being ridiculed, amongst other things, for using plastic straws. It became a joke, everyone imitated VSCO girls. It is so sad to see important issues dismissed. They only seem to become important when they come out of the right mouth, because a young woman's voice is heard as her being angry or bossy, or a social justice warrior. Whatever you do, you always feel powerless.

"Think of the 'seat at the table' idea. It is almost like someone has pulled up a chair for you, you have sat down and now you witness what is going on. It is happening in front of your eyes, all the dominoes are toppling, there are flashing lights focused on the things that you cannot control, but no one has asked you to speak. You are just sitting there, silently, like you have a piece of tape over your mouth. It is morbid, you see everything, but you can do nothing. Not because you do not want to, but because no one has given you the platform or, if they have, it is like you are speaking into a mask. You are speaking into nothing, everyone's nodding and agreeing but they are not going to do anything.

"Ever since I was little it was my goal to be a mother. I was like the kid who was always playing with baby dolls. But in the last couple years, I question whether I should.

"I want to ask for help. As young women we feel we are facing this on our own, in the middle of the tornado. We need older women to help to stand behind us. To use their voices to help amplify ours. We have got that seat at the table, but we need generations of women behind us holding that seat down and making sure that we stay in place. Then we will rip the tape off young women's mouths and speak."

I hope that the many generations who have nature firmly in their Essence either because they choose to care for or to fight on behalf of nature will come together and not let this divide us.

To me, it is on us older women to breach this divide, to stand aside when needed and hand some of our power on to the next generation and then watch their backs as they use it. On this issue of nature and climate change there is an overwhelming urgency to do this. I don't mean abdicating all responsibility and declaring, "it's over to the next generation now," that is not leading. I mean working together; that is leading. After all, nature is almost certainly in all of our Essences to a greater or lesser extent.

The Body

Alison Coburn, with whom I worked for over thirty-five years at Common Purpose, loves yoga. I have always had a theory that our longevity as friends is rooted in her yoga. When I drove her mad, yoga helped her. She has always balanced body and mind with an elegance I could only dream of, one that yoga seemed to be at the heart of. "You imagine yourself riding two horses, body and mind; you are trying to get them to work in harmony. When you are leading it is the same, though we sometimes feel we are riding more than two horses, maybe four or five." (Podcast 19)

Right through the First Expedition, women talked about the body: of reaching the right relationship with it, of challenging notions of 'mind over body', of getting to a place of connection rather than control, of the cycles of nature that weave into the cycles of women's bodies, and of how all of this frames our leading.

Placing body into my Essence did not come naturally to me, and I have slowly realised that it's not just refusing to love my body because it is not perfect. It is also being the mother of my middle daughter Kate who has an autoimmune disease called lupus. It's her lupus and not mine, but fifteen years of trying to get my motherness right, of avoiding what Melissa would call 'smotherness' so that I can help her, has had a deep impact on me. It's the nature of autoimmune conditions that has deepened my distance with my body. I will let Kate explain: "Seven percent of the population have autoimmune diseases. They are invisible, they strike in the mid-twenties and are mostly incurable. There are eighty of them; some, like MS, diabetes and Crohn's, are more well-known than others. Something triggers your body and your immune system starts attacking itself. So your body becomes your worst enemy." It's the attacking that has got to me. Kate started a gloriously successful charity called The Wren Project to address head on the psychological problems caused by this happening. My response has been less admirable; I have trusted 'the body' even less.

But Aparna, Katrina, Martyna and Anna have managed to place body into my Essence, taking in the light and not just its shadows, and Alison will be delighted to hear that I have finally got there.

Aparna went first: "For years, I have struggled with the unwritten and conditioned response, where we turn to the intellect to solve and resolve problems. I am asked to overcome what I 'feel' in my body, to accept the pressure to be objective and to value rationality above all else. Meanwhile, I inhabit the body of a woman, a body that is continually expressing intelligence in ways that appear to be far beyond my control, a body that responds to its natural environment and generates its own rhythm, its own clarity on when to rise up and when to sink down. To listen to its wisdom I do not need language, I do not need to think, I have to allow myself to simply be. Because our bodies and minds are inextricably linked.

"By centring the body, I am also pushing myself towards a 'non-Western' view of leadership – one that values instinct, mystery and nature over reason, knowledge and technology. I am experimenting by leading with the wisdom of the body rather than simply the information in my mind."

Katrina picked up from here as she spoke of her relationship with her body and her journey as a Paralympian: "Now I look at my own body as having the gift of Cerebral Palsy. My left side is my able side, so I understand what it feels like to be able. What a gift. My right side has my cerebral palsy. It is where things do not work. I have this understanding of when people cannot do things or do things in a different way. Another gift. I have grown into this understanding. I wrote a letter to myself twenty years ago. I had tears in my eyes, and I wrote the words 'what a gift'. I have been born in a body that understands both lives. I physically cannot curl my toes on my right, and I never will. But I can do it so easily on my left. It is almost too easy. And that fascinates me; in this one body how easy something can be and how hard something else can be." (Podcast 52)

A barometer

Katrina is convinced that the body is the Essence of all Essences, the primary Essence. She talks about it as her 'barometer.'

"As an athlete, the mental, emotional and spiritual parts are crucial, but the physical body for me has been something I have learned to really master and listen to. I don't just rely on the intellectual component.

"I listen to my body as it sends me messages all the time. I have to listen hard to hear them. The message may be about re-energising, telling me to go for a run or to lay on the floor to be still. Or the message might be about being triggered, that I am now feeling emotional and need to go for a walk quietly on my own.

"It happened when we were together at the end of our First Expedition. One of our discussions triggered something in me, so I went for a walk in the dark. I didn't care about walking away; I just knew I had to dissipate that Energy from a physical point of view so I could come back and have more wonderful conversations.

"A big part of leading and understanding yourself is having a strong sense of what your body needs. Only then will you have that ability to understand others' needs. To judge when to step in and when to be quiet. I love the infinity sign that we have lain across our three E's. It's about fluidity, knowing when to come in and when to come out. The infinity symbol opens a flow of Energy that goes from you to me, then back to you, and then back again to me. But remember it is physical as well as emotional.

"Think about what happens when you are in a room. What is the Energy exchange? And what happens when you leave it? What are you leaving behind? And what about other people? As we lead, we do so often forget to watch the physical in other people. We are intellectual and spend a lot of time in our heads and maybe have not found that connection to the physical yet." (Podcast 52)

I asked Katrina about the balancing act. What happens when you go in the opposite direction and let the physical dominate? "I certainly realised coming from sport that you could not pile everything on just the physical. At the Sydney Paralympics, I got out there and I lost. I only won one silver and one bronze in Sydney. And I did not even run a personal best.

"After those games, I sat down with my psychologist coach because I felt like I had failed. We unpacked how my life was then. I was saying yes to every opportunity that came my way. We looked at everything that I had on my plate leading into the Sydney Paralympic Games and we said, 'there is no way I could have won a gold medal, there is no way I could have done a personal best because

I had too many competing agendas in my head, so I was performing at a silver or worse level in every aspect of my life.' So I made some significant changes and got a gold in 2004 in Athens. It was extraordinary. From then on, I knew that I needed checks and balances in place. Because I can easily go back to that default of having too much on my plate and ignoring my body's messages and thinking I can do everything and be Superwoman. And I just cannot." (Podcast 11)

A prop
Martyna Pastuszka, the conductor of a Polish orchestra, talks about the role of the body in leading not as a barometer but almost as a prop. She gave the most eloquent of examples, beautifully illustrating that it was so much more powerful as a conductor to invite an orchestra to play and do so with the body. No tapping on a lectern or a loud clearing of the throat for Martyna, instead a gesture.

"I know the power of a gesture. You can say so many things just by the way you look or by the position of the chin. You can be proud and unbeatable because your chin is slightly higher. And then you can be modest because you put it lower. You can inspire someone else by this beautiful suggestion while not taking away any freedom of interpretation. You only suggest with your body, so players can then give what they want. I think that we should use much more our body."

Martyna talked to me about a wedding she attended when she saw that, "dancers can dance together without speaking. If you dance with an old aunt or uncle, you actually synchronise much faster than some of the players in the orchestra can. We should learn from wedding dances to adjust quickly using our bodies; as the tempo of the dance changes, our steps to each other adjust. We take care because we suddenly remember that this is the elderly aunt who has a problem with her right hand, so we should not press it too much. All these things, the sensitivity and the intuition, they play a huge role because you cannot talk. The dance music is far too loud for talking.

"When you are leading you use your body to have influence, only with a suggestion so that you do not take away the freedom of the people you are leading. Freedom is something musicians and artists value a lot. Most people do. They do not want to lose their individuality. And that's why it is best to suggest but not to instruct or to force. And do not forget to smile. The troubles are never so big that you cannot smile. And move your hands so that they are embracing. I think about how to lead without verbalising." (Podcast 45)

It was Anna who introduced me to Martyna; she had never played for Martyna, but she had seen how physical Martyna's conducting was. Observing it was a breakthrough for Anna.

Sarah made the same breakthrough when she heard Anna play when we met at the end of the First Expedition: "I had thought that my head controlled my body until I heard her music. I realised my body actually deeply controlled my thinking. I saw ways to express myself without saying a single word, I discovered gestures that are more powerful than all of the words that I will ever string together". (Podcast 49).

Anna discovered gestures from Martyna, and another breakthrough came from another conductor she once played for. "He said to me, 'allow your body to smile.' I was in the first year of my studies and I was very serious and ambitious. It transformed my playing and there was a big change in the room." (Podcast 45)

Smiling is such a big message from the body, a glorious generator of Energy and hope. When I first met Ani, not a conductor but a nun, not in Poland but in Nepal, smiling was all she did. "Smiling is one of the healthiest things to do, and singing and dancing as well. Some people think that serious people should not do this. Or they think they are going to be powerful so they have to be strong and boring. Boring and unemotional. I do not consider a person who is boring to be leading well. Not so inspiring."

I told Ani that my father described people he did not trust as "smiling with everything except their eyes." Ani laughed. "You can also have sparkling eyes without actually stretching your lips. I see it often. You need to let your face tell the story. I like to be comfortable, I like to be happy. I like to be joyful and if it is too rigid and too constrained, I feel suffocated. And if you have a very suffocated face and attitude, you cannot inspire or lead anyone."

Ani had just returned from a shopping trip to buy "silly, pretty shoes" for one of her young colleagues. "She is a young lady and I know her desire to look pretty and attractive. So I fulfilled her wish. And then I can sense how happy she was, and I got that happiness transmitted to me. See how smart I am?

"I make sure that I do not feel stingy about giving a smile. It can be very infectious. Somebody will definitely smile at you. But only when they see a true smile, not a plastic smile, a robotic smile." She added, "The stock of joy in your heart through your smile will increase more and more. The more you give, the more it will increase." (Podcast 18)

Three insights

I cannot finish talking about the body without sharing three entirely random insights.

First from Martyna, she gave me a tip about stretching. She shared it because I asked her about how she copes when she stands up on stage knowing that thousands of eyes are focused on her. Her advice: "Stretch your legs and just stand like the guard. Think of guards on borders. They stand in a special way, this stretched position of the shoulders and of the hips. It actually makes you produce more testosterone than cortisol. That is what men do as they go on the stage. I see girls trying to be so small, almost trying to shrink, shoulders so close and the legs crossed, making themselves so tiny. My advice is stand like a guard. It will help with your breathing too." (Podcast 45)

The second from Liz Bloomfield, whose career has spanned the army, the corporate world and now film making. Hers came as a warning, one that made me think hard: "We must find effective ways to project our strength without relying on physical or verbal dominance." Physical made total sense. I think of the huge men who have peered down at me, consciously intimidating, so that I end up on my tiptoes, poking my finger at them. But verbal made me step back. It brought to mind the people who talk without drawing breath and repeat louder when people do not get a point on first hearing. Their voices eloquent and dominant, their speech firing out, using words some of us need to google. They often do this even when they are wrong and know that they are. Back to Liz: "Because the result of leading based on physical and verbal dominance is people getting more and more passive and less engaged, as they drop their creativity in order to follow instructions."

The third of the random insights on the body before we move on is very beautiful, and came in the form of a powerful challenge from Katrina: "We see someone and then judge in an instant if this person is a threat or a danger. Sometimes we meet people who have the gift of expressing a warmth and empathy from the start which helps people trust them or value their competency. I think a lot of this is physical. I know that I can make people feel warm and at the same time give them a sense that I am strong. It is a lovely combination.

"An important component of this is that I have a disability that is hidden. It means that I understand that there is a lot more going on for people than what can be seen. I understand that we are all different physically. I think it is why my empathy comes across in the first instant.

"I think that we need to vocalise our Essence when we lead. I try to tell my story. I start with, 'I am different physically and that is what makes me who I am,' and by doing that I enable others to share their own Essence. Then you connect and you get the infinity symbol flowing, the Energy exchange.

"When I led my team to the Commonwealth Games, I made sure there was a moment for us to share our Essences. It is really curiosity; I try to lead with curiosity instead of seeking out difference. For me I look at people now and instead of looking at the deficit model and searching for the weakness and negatives, I have the curiosity to search out their strengths. Because we are all so different, I wonder what skills they have got because of their difference. It is hard to do this because our brain wants to do the opposite. Think about the medical models of disability. They focus on the medical deficits. The doctors ask, 'what does not work?' It implies that you have 'less of' something. I think we should flip it and say, "what have I got more of, because of, rather than in spite of?" (Podcast 52)

It is up to you to decide if 'body' is in your Essence, but I urge you to consider it. Especially if you are like me: you have only really noticed your body when it has got in your way, prevented you from doing something and not delivered in its scaffolding role.

How can someone who has been healthy most of her life, had five children and made it to sixty-five be so very blind? Body is firmly in my Essence now. I want to be a conductor who invites people to follow her lead without saying a single word. And I want in my very physicality to convince people that I am that wonderful combination of empathetic and strong.

Aparna sets us a challenge: "If we can start with our body and the truths that our bodies hold, I think there is a different source of Energy that we begin to generate. My experience as a brown woman will not be the same as the experience of my sister as a Black woman and will be different from your experience as a white woman. But we are all connected to our womanly bodies." (Podcast 11)

The Sacred

We move now from the body to the sacred.

We spent a long time trying to find the right word for this piece of Essence. Just as with motherness, Aparna offered us a solution. But first we must allow Katya to express why this piece of Essence is so hard.

"We are almost afraid to put the sacred into our Essence and leading. To bring things that are not solid or that are perceived not to be solid, into something that many of us are told should be strong and fixed. And of course, we want to understand things and our assumption is that to understand something we have to be able to see it clearly, to feel it tangibly and define it in clear and fixed terms. And yet I think that spirituality prompts us to broaden our understanding of leading. To think about why we do what we do, as we lead, what the path is that we are pursuing, and why we are pursuing it. How we best use the Energy, power and privilege of leading."

Katya spoke to me about how, in her eyes, spirituality makes us more empathetic, more aware of the bigger picture and more willing to share for a greater good. At the heart of spirituality for Katya "is the belief in something much bigger than us."

When Katya uses the word 'spirituality' rather than words like 'religion' or 'faith,' it is to respect and recognise that everyone has a different understanding of spirituality. But it was then that Aparna proposed not using the word 'spirituality' but rather 'the sacred.'

"I think we have conflated faith, religion, belief, divinity and the sacred in a very secularised way into 'spirituality'. Maybe we do this as a conscious choice because it avoids the more problematic things that are associated with faith traditions and religions which undeniably have had deeply misogynist histories. But I think the important thing to recognise is that all these things have always been a deeply powerful resource for women. I think for us to centre sacredness would be a very beautiful thing to do."

This inspired us, so sacred is what this piece of Essence became.

Greatest resource

For Aparna, it is a central piece of Essence for women: "Women have had to rely deeply on the sacred. There has been very little else for them to rely upon. It has always played an enormously powerful role and acted as a resource for all women and especially women at the bottom of the social, economic and family ladders. When you are the last person who gets to eat in a family, how do you cope? I do not mean to reduce the sacred to a coping mechanism, but I do want to lift it up as something that has been and is today an important resource, and should never be underestimated.

"Women have always had to fight to seek out and then hold power from the margins. So we have to draw strength from unknown sources, which are not always obvious to us. A lot of times those sources are from our innermost recesses, from our deep lived experiences, from our intergenerational memory. And from our own understanding of the miracles of nature that happen within our own bodies, whether it is the cycles of the Moon or experience of pregnancy or ability to bear pain or to offer care. Where does this all come from? We really do not know. But it does.

"I believe that women all over the world and through time have been holders of the secrets of what is sacred. We have an ability to reach deep down inside and access our inner resources of power. For many women the sacred is their central Essence, and not just a label that we give to the religious tradition that we might be born to or the faith we might choose to adopt. To me it is the mechanism through which we all access our inner power."

Every day

Aparna says that as a leader she is constantly trying to reconnect with the sacred in life because it is her compass for being a good person. She takes the time each day or each night, no matter how tired she is, to sit with herself, to acknowledge the presence of the sacred in her life.

"I find that in times when I am rushed and do not do this, I am more flustered, perhaps angrier. This happened to me between September and December of last year when I just did not make the time or the space to honour the sacred in my life. This period took its toll on me. I have a horrible habit of being angry with myself before I am angry with others, which really hurts my sacredness. I draw ethical power, my moral Energy and also my physical presence from being in a sacred place or state."

Many ways

We were with Anna when Aparna and I spoke. Anna was visibly holding back, but then burst out, "but you are a scientist, Aparna. How do sacred and science work alongside each other?"

Aparna replied, "I believe that there are many things that science teaches us that are gifts in terms of how we see and navigate the world. Equally I believe that science is just one of the many ways through which one can understand the world; in fact, one of the dominant ways that has garnered enormous amounts of power. But you also see that there are many places where it has been ineffective, and where rationality has not always won. We know, too, that rationality should not always win because it can lead to unethical actions.

"I think that the fundamental quest of science is to answer questions about the unknown. And I think that the sacred is about respecting and holding the unknown. So I see no conflict."

I must tell you about Aparna and Anna. One a foundation director, a scientist – and also a dancer, though few of us knew this. The other a young violinist. One from India, the other from Poland. About twenty years apart in age.

I walked into a room to collect something on the first day of our meeting at the end of the First Expedition. As soon as I opened the door, I knew I was an interloper. I could not see either Aparna or Anna, but I knew it. It was in the air; it was not that I heard anything. Then Aparna and Anna walked past me out of the room, Anna cradling her violin. Still nothing was said. That evening, Aparna danced and Anna accompanied her on the violin. We all watched, transfixed. At the end I asked them what had happened in that room. Their connection must surely, I thought, have started in that room, and yet I knew they had not been in it for long. They did not really answer me that evening, but sitting there speaking about the sacred, they decided to tell me more: "We can give away the secret of what happened. We tried to speak to each other without words. Anna through her music and me through my movement. We were both a little bit nervous and uncertain because we came from very different places. We did not share the same cultural idioms and we did not share the same structure when it came to our art form. But once we began being our best selves for each other – and I think that is the only way I can describe it – it was magical and profoundly sacred."

With this I finally understood more about what I had interrupted. What I had blundered into and sensed but could not explain.

Later I asked Aparna if she had always been so ready to talk about and reveal what was sacred to her: "I get more comfortable as I get older. I have had decades to figure it out. At twenty-eight I would have been very uncomfortable. It makes me think that this is something we should talk more about in inter-generational spaces. We do not normally have enough time and, even if we did, I suspect we would still not discuss it. And even less how it affects us when we lead." (Podcast 51)

I cannot add much to this other than perhaps to repeat that the sacred and connecting with the sacred is so very different for all of us. Uncoupling sacred and theology, as expressed by Aparna, had a lasting impact on me. The truth is that I have never known properly why I do what I do and have no confidence that I ever will. Katya tells me that she runs in the mountains: "For me it is a 'sacred' experience. A way of doing inner work."

Aparna's voice has dominated this piece of Essence, maybe you now see why. To her go the final words.

First, to urge us to "come face to face with the rules of the theologies and to challenge them. Because theology and the way that theologies have been constructed and written have too often created power structures and gender binaries. It will be incredibly hard to do this, because it feels somehow heretical, but I do not see how else we will take a really deep next step, even if we only do this on behalf of the body. Sadly, religions have done a wonderful job of making us be ashamed of our bodies. I think that we must honour our body as a very sacred thing to do."

And second, to take the sacred into how we lead: "I think that to draw upon all this as we lead is what gives us powerful ways to be empathetic. To see connections that others cannot see. To be instinctive about making connections when connections are not obvious. There are things that happen beyond the intellect or beneath the intellect. So for me, that is why the sacred becomes a very deep well that I draw upon. And a way for me to really connect with the larger universe. By 'the universe,' I mean my fellow beings." (Podcast 51)

Ancestors

This must be the right moment to move on to Ancestors.

I want to start this with Chulu. You will rapidly discover why.

"My name is Chulu Lucy Tendai Chansa. Chansa means 'an ant hill'. An ant hill in Zambia can be as high as seven meters. They are big and majestic and made by something as small as an ant. My name speaks to the limitless potential that we as a community can have when we come together. The names Chulu and Lucy were the names of my paternal grandmother and were gifted to me at birth. Tendai means 'give thanks to God.' It was given to me by my maternal grandmother when she was a political refugee in Zimbabwe; it is Shona for 'we are Zambians.' Chansa is my family name' it means 'wealth and prosperity.'

"I hope you can see that my names are a symbol of my heritage. They are the legacy that I inherited, and they are a reminder of the history of my family's struggles and triumphs. My names are the means by which I can trace my family lineage, and they are a source of my pride and strength. My names are also a prophecy; their words call forth certain attributes to my life going forward.

"I have been fortunate enough to have travelled to a number of countries and met all sorts of people. The repeated inability or unwillingness to learn my name the way it is supposed to be said and pronounced deeply saddens me. My name only has five letters and yet I have been called everything from 'Chula,' 'Chuli,' 'Chalu.' I mean, the list goes on. Where I come from, 'Chula' means 'to suffer,' and that completely changes the destiny that was intended by my ancestors when they gave me the name Chulu. The names were given with intention, they were given to be a blessing to me for the rest of my life. When you do not bother to learn my name, what does that mean? I know a lot of African women who accommodate the environments they are in and change their names to sound more English, but it is like rejecting yourself, your identity, part of yourself.

"So please call me by my name. It is ant hill, a monumental feat that was driven by community. I am a living Expression of giving thanks to God, and I am the daughter of wealth and prosperity." (Podcast 6)

Recognising

For Chulu, ancestors are firmly in her name, her Essence and her leading. For many of us, recognising ancestors in Essence has been a journey. A journey Selvie is mid-way through:"Recognising, taking ownership and honouring my cultural roots has not been an easy task. It almost felt unnatural in moments. Looking back, I have not been courageous enough to own and be proud of my cultural identities. The English language may unite our multicultural society, but globalisation has made it difficult to define where I belong.

"I ask myself who I am and what does it mean to be Chinese/Indonesian/ Singaporean? As much as I have tried to diminish my cultural identity, it has shaped my likes and dislikes from a very young age and influenced my perspectives and my preference for a certain approach to leading. Now I want to integrate my culture into all my work, to create a safe space for other women to share how their cultural identity has shaped them and take on board that there are diverse and nuanced approaches to leading that I need to embrace."

It was Hinemoa who shifted Selvie's thinking when they were together on the First Expedition. Hinemoa had spoken of the female leaders in her Māori culture and how they influenced her: "I look to our whakapapa, to our genealogy of women. Papatūānuku, our earth mother, is the ultimate female leader. Her ways of leading help us navigate; her fundamentals make sense for me. Strong, nurturing, predictable, integral, honest, fierce. She provides a safe collective space from which to stand and flourish. A place of life cycles and of growth.

"The ocean we can see, Hinemoana, is one of Papatūānuku's children and gives her own insights into female leadership: of tides, persistence, energy, drive, abundance, depth. Hina is our Māori moon. She has a different name for each face she shows us across the month. It is a female Energy that leads time. I have been exploring her influence over many years.

"I am descended from Muriwhenua, daughter of Pōhurihanga, navigator of the Kurahaupō waka. The land was named for her and she for the land. That is our ūkaipō, the land that nurtures like mother's milk in the night. When females lead, they have this nourishing aspect. I wonder about key moments where we have experienced a sense of mana wāhine, female strength, standing in our own Energy."

Long journey

Hinemoa has a very personalised cultural sense of leading. It gives her an enviable certainty. For Fatima Zibouh, it has been a long and difficult journey balancing the Moroccan part of her identity and the Belgian part, a journey finally reconciled: "I can eat a Belgian chocolate with a Moroccan tea, and it is very delicious. The principles of Islam, I can find in Buddhism, Catholicism, even in atheism, because it is all about serenity, peace, justice, solidarity and love. When I understood that it is possible to combine all of my identities, I felt a kind of peace in my heart. It is very hard, for sure. But when you do feel it, despite everything around you, you can be proud. It is happiness.

"I cannot pretend that it has been easy. I would love for someone to give me some keys to understand the contradictions and paradoxes. Eventually you get there and accept the contradictions of chocolate and tea and you say, 'it is okay'. For me, this has been letting go but not a passive letting go. It has been a choice of being who I am, with the priorities I have, and not being too worried about what other people think or about people who ask me to simplify my identity. I have, after all, multiple ancestors like everyone else." (Podcast 9)

It has clearly been and continues to be a hard journey for Fatima: "When people want me to be just one identity, I say to myself, 'I am who I am, and I am brilliant. I am beautiful. I am powerful.' And I go ahead with people who want to go ahead with me and for me and I give priority to the many voices which are inside me, my many ancestors. Of course, I face the intense social pressure from the majority, but it also comes from my own community. I have just come to accept that I am different and multipolar.

"For too many years I thought that the key to peace and stability would be found through study; with study I would gain legitimacy. I tried to always smile and to be perfect. To be simple. But now I say no. I am forty years old now. I will stop. I am who I am." (Podcast 9)

Ayesha in Pakistan also recognises a contrasting balancing act emanating from her ancestry: "I know I have an internalised colonialism and an internalised patriarchy within myself. I grew up in a culture and household where patriarchy was the norm. I could never have escaped it. I was raised by a mother for whom the world was created for men and women were there to serve men's interests. And yet I was also raised by a father who continuously, without realising it, countered all this and gave me wings. I must own this tug, this push and pull, as part of my own journey."

Connecting

Like Selvie, I know that Hinemoa has prompted me to think about my ancestry more and how it has influenced how I lead. Because ancestors have so fundamentally framed and defined how Hinemoa leads, they are ever present for her as she says, "they create a source, a wellspring, a puna, of female Energy that I can draw on at any time.

"My mother died a long time ago and I remember feeling and sensing so profoundly that I had to move up into another generation. I was pregnant with my son; it was all very intense, but I also felt welcomed. Soon after, as a medical student, I was on a field trip. I was asked to do the karanga, the traditional call of women. I remember vividly feeling my mother next to me.

"I love bringing forward the story of my great-grandmother who passed away in the great flu of 1919. I grew up with her picture in our home and I never thought about her death in the same way until COVID happened. Then for me it was like she was reaching forward to share all the ramifications of that era. It helped me to navigate the complexities of COVID.

"I feel this connectivity across generations. I want to connect with our young women and our girls and at the same time I do not want to leave our older women behind. A lot of them have come through different kinds of colonisation, and they carry their own pain. I have a sense of this role, of the cultural baton being carried forward and passed on. It gives me Energy. We talked about leading as a source of Energy. I think about this Energy coming from our female ancestors." (Podcast 55)

Hinemoa told me about the role that music and language play in this: "I uphold our tradition of opening discussion with waiata (song). Introduction is with pepeha, which is our time-honoured tradition of how we introduce ourselves, how we respect those around us and how we locate ourselves in space and time. Singing is so important for us as leaders. It releases different energies. It is honouring a different experience of being human. And it is simply joyful, even if the waiata is sad. I have not learned a new song for a while, but I know that I want to and there are new songs and parts of songs that I will become more confident with. There is a unique Energy singing together.

"I seek out experiences of using our Māori language. I think when you have had to learn your own language, because it has been suppressed for so long, then that is very emotional. Because your language has become a separate and crucial part of your Essence. It does not matter if you cannot understand the words, you sense the vibration, and the vibration is healing. Using our language is a transformative aspect and it connects us back to our old people." (Podcast 55)

Tebogo Matenge, a businesswoman in Botswana, told me how determined she is to do the same, however old fashioned it may sound: "The danger is that because everybody is doing it the Western way, we feel that we should fall into line and do it the 'sophisticated' way. But if we do, we risk forgetting our own ancestors. In Africa I think we are increasingly realising that we must not. As we see other cultures, it sometimes makes us see our own more clearly. For example, if you look at our history, we have always shared, we simply do not want to have a full belly when our neighbours are feeling hungry. So people who do not have this instinct to share do not achieve much when they lead in Botswana. For a while when we were colonised, we sort of lost all this a bit, but I think we are slowly coming back to being who we were.

"I also see in some societies women think that in order to lead they need to be more like men. More outspoken, harsher. In Africa there is a growing trend of women realising we can take our caregiving status and nurturing nature into our leading. Westerners seem to be going on courses to do this; on this side of the world it is natural." (Podcast 24).

Pragmatic

Rouba is pragmatic after years of leading in the Arab world. She agrees, but also says that sometimes you have to step back, too: "I identify myself as a progressive, liberal, modern woman. But at the same time, I identify myself as a woman with deep indigenous roots in my culture. I draw on them – not just for my Essence; they are also a source of my power.

"I think you have to be able to make the link with your ancestors, but at the same time I think you must be able to uncouple from it too at times. The link is deep, and it empowers you. But sometimes a break from your ancestors empowers you too.

"I was invited to the UK parliament to speak about Syria. I had never done public speaking before. I had never done anything at all like that before. I was so scared as a twenty-two-year-old to talk about politics and human rights and refugees. It was a leap of faith that I had to make because I thought of the men and women in my Syria who were dying. The least I could do was to step up and talk about what they were facing. It was not even a choice; it was a responsibility that I had to take on, because so many people were making far bigger sacrifices than I.

"What helped me was being outside my context. I was disconnected from my place, my ancestors, my mothers and grandmothers, nowhere near the place or culture that I grew up in. A place where women are expected to act and be a certain way. Because I was outside of that context, I was operating outside of the norms, the paradigms, the structures that were designed for a woman in my home context. I could be whoever I wanted to be. I could reinvent myself and think about my identity differently. I could reinvent who Rouba was as a person, as a human, as a leader, as a speaker, as someone who is trying to do something bigger than herself." (Podcast 10).

The Seeds

Uma thinks about her ancestors in a way that is helpful. She names three kinds of seeds: the dream seeds, gift seeds and incomplete seeds.

"Dream seeds are the seeds we were born with and have somehow forgotten as we grow up. Gift seeds are the seeds full of promise and potential bestowed by our ancestors. And incomplete seeds are the seeds that our ancestors felt that they could not use to complete their dreams, so they pass them on to us.

"Ask yourself, what are the dream and gift seeds that you carry from your ancestors? How will you pass them on? What are seeds that you need to let go of or even destroy? And which seeds must you cherish and hand on?"

Uma is focused on the incomplete seeds. She is determined "to name the incomplete seeds I carry and, in so doing, recognise the hurt and pain they have caused and still cause. And, with this, recognise the power that I now have to transform the incompleteness to wholeness. I also want to recognise that if I don't, the angst, the negative Energy and the pain will pass on. I might do it unintentionally, but it would be forceful if I did.

"This is why I have worked hard on myself to heal and transform that incomplete seed and hand it on as a gift seed. I know the incredible Energy of the gift seed. It radiates through us. We absolutely must pass on wisdom so that those who come after us can remember their dream seeds, access their gift seeds and heal their incomplete seeds. Only then will we generate the Energy of leadership."

Looking backwards and forwards is fascinating. Ancestors matter, and so do the ancestors we will be for future generations. It makes me think of driving a car; you need a windscreen to look forwards and a mirror to look backwards. There are drivers whose eyes are constantly peering into their rear-view mirrors, and there are also drivers whose eyes are fixed on the windscreen. It requires a balance of both, otherwise you will cause terrible accidents.

Uma's idea of seeds makes sense to me. It has made me think of my mother and grandmothers in different ways. And certainly now, also, my daughters and granddaughters, and which seeds they will inherit from me.

Trauma

How we lead must be influenced by the trauma we have experienced and inherited. This feels self-evident, but as with some other pieces of our Essence, maybe we put the trauma piece aside in the eagerness to fit in with status quo leading.

Experience

It feels right to start thinking about trauma with words from two women who have faced it head on: Harriet Adong, who experienced war in Northern Uganda and its aftermath, and Asifa Hassan, a young Yazidi refugee from Syria now in Germany. They share their thinking on how their leading has been and will always be shaped by trauma.

First, Harriet: "Nobody understands the depth of what it means to be a survivor of war. You do not even understand yourself how it takes your mind, your body, your spirit from you. Now they call us the builders of community, but to do that you need somebody who is whole, who can recollect herself. It is because of this that rape is used as a weapon of war. It puts us in a space where we cannot recollect ourselves.

"When the guns are silent, the only thing everyone wants to rebuild is infrastructure. They forget about helping women to pick up the pieces of what happened to them. And yet women will not rebuild a place that is not safe for them. They revert to the only place where they feel comfortable, and that is a closed space that nobody understands. People expect you to come out of this closed space in a snap. They say to you, 'now it is time to get into the development processes,' as if you should or could just close that door.

"I am very passionate about helping the girls and women rebuild themselves and our community. Because nobody is going to help us, we have to do it ourselves. We have to find what we felt was lost and tell our stories like we used to when we sat under the tree. It is our role to share the story of peace and change the negative stories that are being told.

"And yet violence continues to happen. We have men who were abused, abducted, returned home with anger, who have now become violent again. We have parents who have forgotten their role and do not even know how to handle their children born of war. This violence is like a time bomb; we do not know what will happen to this generation if we do not bring it back to life.

"So as we lead, we have to tell stories and make them about peace. Yes, we went through dark times, when children were separated, where a parent was forced to kill their own child, when Northern Uganda was covered with the darkness of rape, of killings, of slaughter. But that is the narrative that my community and I can change, to ensure that we know ourselves as people of peace. War should not determine who we are."

Asifa Hassan is part of the generation Harriet Adong fears for, born in another part of the world, in another part of the broken world.

"When I was in Iraq, the Yazidi genocide happened and I luckily survived it with my family. Many of my friends and two of my cousins were kidnapped by ISIS. They were in captivity for five years.

"I have seen so many things. I try to always claim to myself that I am exaggerating them. That compared to the others, I have seen nothing. I tell myself that I am so lucky that I did not lose my father, my two sisters, my brothers. I tell myself that I am the luckiest person on Earth. I have been holding myself together by comparing myself to others and always thinking that when I get to Germany, I will be free. I will be so mentally and physically free and happy and safe. But it is not like that. At this point, I realise that I also have been through so many things. I have never been a child." (Podcast 16).

Speaking to Harriet and Asifa, and to many women like them, I am reminded of what Jude said to me: "Women have something in common, which is an acknowledgement of pain. They have been through obstacles, vicious knocks, difficulties and self-searching. And they make that available. They have compassion, the ability to self-reflect on the scars – the scar tissues. It is an empathy without sentimentality." (Podcast 12)

Impact

Ayesha sees such trauma daily in her work as a psychiatrist. She spoke to me about its impact on how we lead and on how she herself leads because, along with inherited and experienced trauma, there is secondary trauma.

"Trauma generally affects your emotional regulation, your cognition, your processes, your behaviours and your body. All of these are crucial to leading and show up in many ways. For example, trauma affects your decision making. So you are not able to make sharp, timely and confident decisions.

"It affects your relationships. And given that leading is all about relationships, this will have a huge impact. It affects your self-belief. It is not easy to illicit confidence in your team if you are not confident yourself. It affects your body. Katrina used that expression, 'the body keeps a score,' and she is right. The score being things like irritable bowel syndrome, eczema, chronic fatigue, depression, anxiety, stress; they all show up in all sorts of different ways in your body as a result of trauma. This automatically affects your leading.

"When we think about trauma, we often think of war and displacement. But trauma comes in many shapes and forms. The most common kind of abuse in children and adolescents is not sexual or physical abuse, it is neglect. Neglect produces avoidance attachment problems that continue down the generations. And this inevitably shows up in leading too. Another example is that if you are a minority and you live in a space of fear, it might mean that you live with caution. You are often unable to say that you belong, and do not want to attract attention to yourself. Again, this will play out in your leading.

"Then there is secondary trauma, where somebody living in, say, Pakistan may not actually see first-hand the trauma of race that resulted in the Black Lives Matter movement. But if you read, watch the news, watch movies, have exposure to social media and the rest of the world, then you are actually imbibing trauma from your surroundings. Because if you are remotely empathic to what is happening around you, which most humans are, you will feel the pain of others.

"This secondary trauma can be intergenerational. It is passed on by narratives in the family, by stories that are told from one generation to another. So you are able to feel the pain of others, just as if you are there and actually feeling it first-hand."

Personal

I asked Ayesha about her own experience. We started to talk about Islamophobia.

"I saw it on the rise around me as I was moving up in the space of leading. I saw it mostly second-hand, sometimes first-hand, but mostly through hearing stories. You hear of the trauma that people have suffered who look like you, have been raised like you and share the same faith as you. You start thinking, 'if it can happen to them or their children or their spouses or their families, then it could happen to me.' So it shifts automatically. Little things make you question where you would not have questioned before. You have an oversensitive smoke alarm inside you. Even a tiny statement or reference somewhere automatically ignites something in your brain. You stiffen up and you start thinking, 'is this happening because I am a Muslim?'

"What this does to me, as for most of us when dealing with trauma or the presence of trauma, I go to denial or minimisation. I have tried both of these. I have tried to keep 'Muslimness' in the back corner, not to talk about it because it feels unsafe.

"I will give you a very concrete example. A colleague and I have started talking about the idea of incorporating cognitive behaviour therapy and religion into our work, looking at how growing up in a specific religion might manifest itself when doing cognitive behaviour therapy and how the ideas of religion affect people's thought processes. Then we would look at how a therapist would bring them to light and try to work with them. We have still not gone ahead with making this happen because it feels vulnerable to me. Even though in any other space, I would have jumped at a new idea right away." (Podcast 56)

Global

This conversation made me think about trauma at a global level and about colonialism. It was an issue that came up regularly amongst the First Expedition group. I asked Ayesha if she thought colonialism had and continues to induce trauma for a large part of the world.

"Yes, it is an interesting trauma. Because colonialism is all about a 'greater' power coming in and proclaiming, 'you're not good enough, we need to come in and shape you and your society.' Slowly, the colonisers' views become part and parcel of how your systems function. It puts you in the back corner. Eventually you start to believe that you are not good enough and that whatever is coming out from the 'greater' civilisation is better. Your sense of self becomes affected, your cognition becomes affected. You are unlikely to take decisions the way you would otherwise. You are unlikely to adapt to different environments. You do not trust your own instincts or your own sense of self.

"This one is intergenerational. Even today, in Pakistan, that gained physical independence over eighty years ago, there still exists the idea that anything that comes from the West will be superior to whatever we are building indigenously. Even in the simplest of things. When I was growing up, I would go shopping with my mother and aunts in the cities of Quetta and Peshawer. The Baara, or markets, where you got imported material, especially cloth, like silk, chiffon or georgette, etc, were exciting for my aunts because these were not indigenous goods, they were 'imported' and therefore considered to be superior.

"Even in our attitudes to women leaders, we think it is best to think like Western women. And yet, the whole South Asian region has a long history of matriarchy and of very strong and well-respected female leaders. And mother-hood used to be considered such a noble thing. We talk of pregnant women needing to be safe, healthy, happy and content as 'bearers of the future gener-ations.' But the Western influence has shifted things. Our women leaders got written out of our history and the idea of motherhood is more of a burden, or an obstruction to a career pathway, like the West." (Podcast 56)

Healing

Ayesha: "I think when we lead, we have to make the idea of healing trauma possible and safe, and we can only do that by modelling it ourselves. The dis-cussion around trauma scares people away. We need open conversations around it. I don't mean just going to the therapist; healing trauma comes from music, cycling, being close to nature. It comes from narrating our own story or from using humour.

"I am not saying this is easy. Where I am, making yourself so vulnerable can have challenging repercussions. But we must listen to ourselves when we feel burnt out, want a pause or need silence. Because once we have stopped for a moment, then we might be ready to go again. If we go at full throttle all the time it will be hard to muster the Energy that leading requires." (Podcast 56)

As I listened to Ayesha, I was thinking about myself. I wanted to add to her list of what helps to heal trauma: the word 'friendships.' I will tell you why. My childhood had too much experience of women who drank too much. Now, fifty years on, if I go to an event and there is a very drunk woman there, my children circle around me, watching me carefully. Because they know that 'Mum's judgement will go all askew,' not necessarily because the woman is behaving badly but because the presence of drunk women triggers something in me. For sure we need to spot the trauma in ourselves, but it helps if we have friends to circle around us, who spot when our trauma is going to manifest itself.

I think Stellah Bosire, a woman born in the streets of Nairobi who is now one of the most powerful voices in health in Kenya should end this section on trauma. She declares, "I have been a patient of severe depression despite many of my colleagues saying, 'how can you be depressed when you are one of the overachievers?' I tell them, yes, but it doesn't mean that I can't get depression. I am human, I have pain, I love and I cry. And that doesn't take anything away from my leading.

"I refuse to be branded 'a strong black woman'. I am a 'vulnerable black woman'. I am a girl who loves soft life, I am a pearl and I love soft feathery pillows. I don't live to other people's scripts; I write my own script and it has trauma in it." (Podcast 66)

We all hold trauma. It is real for all of us, and it plays out in how we lead, for all of us, but I am still in awe of Harriet Adong and Asifa's determination to name and deal with their trauma. Thank you.

Education

On to education, the final piece of Essence that we uncovered on the First Expedition.

Education must have a huge impact on how we lead, especially if we take the word in its broadest sense – informal and formal, early years to lifelong, the education your family and community give you and the education that formal institutions provide. The biases our education instils, the instincts it nourishes, the confidence it bakes in, the opportunities it opens up – this is a big one.

Informal education

Saba gives us an illustration from the Arab world of the education that family or community gives us. It has parallels the world over. She captures the sayings that she grew up listening to and reflects on their impact on how she leads.

"'Ham elbanat lal mamat.' This is said to you on the day you are born. Translated, it is 'You are a burden from birth to death.' Why would a new life of a beautiful, innocent girl be a burden? Because everything about you is heavy, starting with your body. If it is beautiful, men will pursue you. If it is not beautiful, no one will fancy you enough to want to marry you. As you grow up, anything that goes wrong is your fault. If you are harassed, it must be about what you were wearing, how you walk, whether you smile. You force men to misbehave.

"'Kol e'lak wa e'lbes lel nas.' Basically, 'you do not have a say in how to live.' Your opinions and decisions will be your father's until you are handed over to another man. Your secrets should never be shared, even if they burn from within you. Keep quiet, stay silent, it matters that your light shines on the outside, make it look as if you are living a perfect life. If you work, that is a plus because you generate income, but it does not necessarily mean that you have a say in using the income.

"'Shouroohum wa khalfoohum.' Men are taught from a very early age to consult with their women and then do exactly the opposite. So with time, you will learn to give the opposite opinion so that men do exactly what you want.

And so, the dance starts, you learn how to live around men. But you never get the full life because as an individual, you do not exist. You are someone's daughter, wife, mother.

"'Haki tentain bekhreb betain,' or, 'if two women get together and start talking, the result will be two ruined houses.' You are told never to trust women. You just do not talk to them." (Podcast 6)

Sayings such as these exist in most languages, accompanied by words like 'Huss.' Saba utters it with her finger across her mouth. It says 'keep quiet' in Arabic. In Nigeria, Folawe tells us that the equivalent word is 'farabale,' pronounced with flair. She almost sings it as if it were the first word of a song. In Hindi, it's 'chup' said crisply. The 'p' has finality in it, clearly pronounced with the intention of shutting down. There seems to be an equivalent word in most languages used to pin girls' lips closed.

No one bothered to say it to Katja Weisheit, though, as she grew up in Germany. They didn't need to, instead they had programmed her to 'act the boy.' She showed me a picture to prove it.

"What you can see are two children dressed in sportswear, at a sports event, having a short break before their next big challenge. At first sight they might be two boys. Elbows on knees, sitting forward, cropped hair. But I can give you second sight. One of them is a girl and this girl is me. She is acting like a boy. She knows that the camera is pointing at her, and this is why she tries even harder to look and act like a boy. She wants to present herself as a strong and tough boy. She wants the people to think, 'wow, what a tough boy he is. I think he is the winner.' In the following years, this girl will do everything to hide that she is a girl."

Katja was heavily pregnant when we spoke, awaiting the birth of her son. "My mindset for the last twenty-nine years has been that if you want to reach something in your life, you need to be strong, fast, calculating, competitive, rational, analytical and bold. You must not think or talk too much, and you must never let emotions get in your way. 'Stop whining, do not feel pain.' Up to now, all these successful behaviours have been connected in my mind with boys, so my logical conclusion as a girl was that I need to act like a boy. Do not wear too much makeup, do not talk with a high voice, do not talk with a baby voice and, in general, do not be interested in girl stuff.

"Feminism always gave me a distant feeling that I never felt connected to women. I never asked myself why I had no vision of success via a female approach. But then suddenly I gained access to the world of women and since then I cannot not stop uncovering myself as a woman. Now I am thinking about my future son, imagining him being the one in the photo, not me. I do not want him to act like a strong superhero. I want him to feel absolutely fine with just being himself." (Podcast 6)

Impact

I sat with Andini and told her about Saba and Katja. She smiled. As an inventor she has often seen the consequences of this.

"I see a lot of inventors who sign contracts with the people that they sell their rights to without reading the contracts because they think 'all the legalese' will be beyond their understanding. I say to them, 'these are your rights, the rights to what you have created. They are a portion of your soul. How can you assign them without reading the contract?' I made this mistake in the past, and I learned the hard way. The real question is: how do people manage to convince us that, as women, we are not capable of understanding certain things?"

The answer is probably education. I do not think I have to make the case for the impact of it on how we lead. It feels self-evident. But just before we move on to formal education, it is worth taking a step back and speaking to women who moved countries or cultures and assumed that it would mostly be the same for women wherever they went. Though Huss, farabale and chup equivalents are everywhere, there are unexpected differences too, and sometimes there are surprises.

Surprises

Tebogo talked to me about Botswana: "We are a very small country, where the men went off to a different country to work in the mines. So a lot of women were left at home, running the household, making sure kids were fed, making sure jobs were done. It is in our DNA; we have always led because our men went away."

She laughs about how confused Westerners are when they land in Botswana. "They ask questions like, 'can I speak to the owner of the business?' and I say, 'it is me.'" (Podcast 24)

Sometimes it takes moving away to look back and see home in a new light. I talked to Anila Dehart, a successful woman in financial services who grew up in Albania and then moved to the US. "One of my surprises relates to educated women putting their career on hold, in some cases indefinitely, when they become mothers. I'm not referring to women who prefer a different lifestyle or can't afford childcare, I'm referring to women who feel they have no choice due to societal norms and expectations, particularly in cases where their male partners are high earners. I had assumed the opposite would be true in societies which are further ahead on the journey for women's equality and equity. In contrast, my experience in my home country, Albania, is that while there is still a lot of change needed to elevate women's place in society, education and careers are seen as non-negotiable." (Podcast 35)

Anna Afeyan Gunnarson, a scientist and philanthropist, had a comparable experience. When she moved from Sweden to the US, Anna did not think that she was going to a more developed country but rather an equally developed one, and yet, "In the US, the men I worked with wanted to take care of me. Now, in the beginning it can be nice that people want to take care of you when you are new in a country. On the other hand, it also implies that you cannot take care of yourself. I knew who I was, and I knew I could take care of myself and make choices for myself. I did not need to ask any of my male co-workers or friends how to do things. I had never sensed this in Sweden." (Podcast 35)

I suppose we all see things through our own eyes, sometimes thinking that our experience is the experience of all, and we make assumptions about others' worlds, assumptions that seldom survive travel, and the surprises come both ways.

Formal Education

Let this start with just how crucial formal education is and how deeply it frames how we lead. Isata sees this every single day: "I work with mostly women in a rural area of Sierra Leone who are lowly educated or sometimes not at all. Never underestimate the limits this puts on somebody's life.

"When I moved back to my community as an adult, I ran for elected office. If I had never been to school, I would never have dared do that. I would not have seen myself as worthy to represent people because I would know that I did not know everything that I should know.

"Only once you have been in a classroom and learned something do you realise there is always more to learn. Only then do you realise that you do not know everything, and that you don't need to know everything. Education opens up your world so that you are able to seek new knowledge and find out about things. You can learn things on your own afterwards once you have already got that basic foundation. But if you have never been able to be in a class-room, you place limits on your life because you realise that you do not know as much as other people. And for women in particular in these rural settings, it does not just limit their economic activity. It limits their mothering, their revenue and what they measure within themselves. It is education that makes you able to question your current situation and to change it." (Podcast 57)

Breadth

It is not just knowledge you gain. When I first met Folawe Omikunle, who runs Teach for Nigeria, we talked about the school she went to as a refugee when she left Nigeria because of the military regime and how it formed a piece of her Essence as a leader. She talked of the headmistress:

"Part of my primary education took place in Benin, where Mrs Edna Tounou was the owner of the school and, at the time, it attracted students from across the African continent. I have vivid memories of the songs Mrs Edna had us sing together every morning. One particular song that has stayed with me begins with the words, 'No man is an island.' When I reflect on who I have become today and some of the values that shape my life, I can trace them back to that school. Mrs Edna recognised potential in every child, even the most disruptive ones, and she saw some form of talent in each of us. Every teacher, parent and individual played a role in uplifting one another. Looking back, our lives were uprooted, and we entered a community that was overflowing with love and support. I can still recall every word of the song she taught us: 'No man is an island. No man stands alone. Each man's joy is joy to me. Each man's grief is my own. We need one another. So I must defend each man as my brother, each man as my friend.'" (Podcast 10)

Folawe had formed a fist as she sang and thumped the air with it, though I don't think she realised it herself. Watching Mrs Edna Tounou lead must have had a profound effect on Folawe and instilled in her that women could be fabulous at leading.

This dawning awareness of women leading must be so important: seeing them lead and also making sure that girls get an experience of leading when they are at school. Lulu Raghavan is one of the foremost leaders in advertising in India. Looking back, she tells me that it was school that instilled leading into her DNA.

"I was appointed School Prefect when I was in grade twelve. We had a beautiful uniform and I had all of these badges to say I was School Prefect, House Vice-Captain, Badminton Captain and Basketball Captain. And we had this sash with the colours of all the houses. It was a visible signal of leadership. That was the first time I realised that I was a role model that my juniors were looking up to. I had to be conscious of how I spoke and how I behaved. When I think back, it made me feel I was a leader, it instilled in me the desire to lead and to inspire others, it sowed the seeds of my ambition and what I wanted to be." (Podcast 67)

For Katya, education instilled knowledge and leading – and also something more, as she found herself surrounded in her school by people from everywhere.

"I studied in a school where the premise was to have young people together from different countries and socio-economic backgrounds; countries that had historically been in conflict with each other. The hope was that by living, eating and studying together, we would build friendships that were beyond the typical interactions between people of different countries. The experience shaped everything in my life since then.

"Every time I hear about something that is happening in the world, I associate it with a person that I know from that country. It humanises things. It is why I am very careful now about seeing things in a binary sense. I understand that there are so many truths behind every conflict and version of history. And I think that this acknowledgement of nuance is something that I continue to carry with me as I lead." (Podcast 5)

The power of education to open things up is clear. Opportunities, possibilities, ambitions, self-confidence, insight. But of course, as with all pieces of Essence, there are shadowy sides too.

Baked in

Ayesha is determined to bake out the competitiveness that was baked into her by her education: "It is sometimes a monster that keeps growing. This idea that somehow you will be left behind. I have to push it back and say to myself, 'the world is about coming together.' I grew up in a very competitive school, college and higher education system. But it doesn't sit well. I want to be different. Ambition is fine. It is great to want to have a dream and work hard towards it. But competitiveness, I think, works against achievement.

"People talk about 'leaning in.' I just do not want to do that constantly. It is just not right for me, and my sense is also that you really can only lean in when you have a certain privilege. I am not white; I am a woman. I have not grown up with privilege. I do not come from a very high socio-economic status. It is okay to lean in and people will allow you to lean in if you have privilege, a certain accent, certain skin colour or certain degrees all stacked up, then it works fine. But if someone like me leans in, it is not taken well at all. You are told that you are too pushy, you're making people angry, or frankly upsetting people." (Podcast 4)

For Jude, it has taken a conscious effort to make sure her education does not frame how she leads. She sees things that were baked into her that she has since consciously strived to remove.

"I think we were given terribly damaging ideas of superiority. We were told that we were better. It had a hugely damaging effect. We go into dialogue with a sense that we need to just persuade somebody else and that eventually they will come around to what we think. Because we're right. To counter this, we have to start again, with humility. And it is not easy." (Podcast 12)

Isata reflects: "I often see such a sense of superiority play out with leaders who confuse intelligence and education, and yet they are not the same thing. Somebody may not have a formal education, but they have something to offer in terms of solutions regardless of how long they have been in the classroom. We must recognise the impact of learning even outside of the classroom. This sense of superiority is often then compounded when they measure somebody's education or intelligence based on how well people speak English. Speaking English is absolutely not a benchmark for intelligence." (Podcast 57)

Permission

Isata also talked about how some leaders don't recognise that education is delivered differently in different places: "In Sierra Leone we have a more instructive way of learning where you repeat everything you have been told, first by your mother, then your teacher and eventually your boss. You do not disagree with adults. In the UK, you are encouraged to challenge what you've been told and find solutions for yourself. If you have been educated in the UK and find yourself leading in Sierra Leone, you need to take the difference into account. Understanding it takes a while because initially you assume everybody is educated in the same way. You have to know that there are differences and make allowances for them."

I asked Isata how she had seen this play out as people lead. "It takes a while for people who have not been in an environment where the permission to push back has been granted to do so. I think they are suspicious. I remember when I was Minister of Social Welfare; in the first couple of meetings, the civil servants at the ministry thought, 'who is she and which sky did she fall out of?' Ministers are supposed to be in charge and tell people what to do. And my take was, I am here, I am new. The civil servants have been here for years; they know better than me, even if it is just institutional memory. So if I do not seek their advice, I am not going to learn anything. But they were suspicious. Only after a while did they realise that I was genuine. Then they started to bloom. You have to really listen and keep on listening, because education does not prepare everyone for this. You have to create the space for people to have their voices heard, feel safe enough to make mistakes and suggest solutions, contribute ideas and overall feel valued. You have to listen with your heart. Only then will they give you theirs."

But there is a caveat here, says Isata: "It goes both ways. Once questioning is allowed, then you have to accept that somebody is going to question you. Many leaders do not like this. I do."

Then Isata sees another angle: "Sometimes I can question others too aggressively. Some people may not be ready to have the – as they perceive it – rug pulled out from under them. So I have to go more gently and find ways of moving together until we hit common ground.

"Basically, you have to evolve as a person who knows that there is always more to learn."

We return full circle to Isata's first thoughts: "You have to be sure enough about the learning that you have already received to do this. Only once you have learned to do so will you become teachable." (Podcast 57)

Rebels

As Isata and I talked about education, we realised that there was another aspect of our schooling that we had in common. It had instilled in both of us a rebelliousness – or at least it had failed to erase it from us, because I suspect the rebelliousness was a dream seed handed on by our ancestors for both of us. I told Isata about how, aged twelve, I took my class out on strike because our head teacher had said that we could only have a Christmas tree in the main entrance of the school and not in every classroom. Oh, what privilege I have had that this was all we had to strike about. Anyway, we all went on strike and refused to be educated.

Isata started giggling at this point. "I want to go back to a twelve-year-old me as well. I was the class rep in a campaign to change the school uniform. We were able to change what we wore every day to school. After that, nothing is impossible. Will I ever wield that kind of power again? It is really hard not to believe that anything is possible after that."

It has been a few years since either of us were twelve. We have both worked with many 'highly educated' leaders since then. I asked Isata what she finds the most irritating when she does. "It is arrogance that you know everything. The idea that one person can know everything. The very idea shows a lack of education, and it makes for bad leading because everybody who has been in a classroom knows that there is always more to learn and that you can learn from people that you are intending to teach. If you are sitting on a high horse from a position of 'I know more than you,' it will limit you." (Podcast 57)

So education is well established in our Essence. Informal education which, with good fortune, instils deep confidence, and formal education, the gift never to be undervalued or understated, especially at its best. Both have a huge impact on how we lead. But not quickly, says Ayesha:

"My mother's voice keeps resonating in my head, that 'nothing is going to come out of it, this struggle toward gender parity. This is just a completely lost cause. And I do not know why you keep fighting it and losing so much sleep over this.' Being a realist, I don't think it is going to change in my lifetime. My hope is that it will change for the generations to come. To me, that is enough of a reason to work on change right now." (Podcast 4)

Your Essence

These have been seven possible pieces of Essence: motherness, nature, ancestors, the body, the sacred, trauma and education. Yours will differ from mine, but they will all, to a greater or lesser extent, deeply influence how you lead.

I make no attempt at a summary. Leading is personal and messy; I leave the summarising to you. Take the pieces of Essence that make sense to you, add the ones that need adding for you, put aside the ones that do not resonate. I say put aside rather than discard because you may want to reconsider them some time in the future, just in case you change your mind. Indeed, I hope that you do change it and evolve– that is a crucial part of leading and of the infinity symbol.

So before we move on from Essence, please don't forget to add your own pieces of Essence. There will be eighth and ninth pieces that are right for you. Anna will have added 'music,' I am sure. I would add 'outsider' into mine. Why? Because I have always felt like an outsider from the age of three when my parents delivered me to a playground where everyone spoke French and nothing but French. I spoke nothing but English. I stood at the back of the line to which I was allocated with hand gestures. I stood there wondering how I was going to talk to anyone. I have never experienced huge bias as so many have, I have not survived war or been a refugee, but I have always felt like an outsider. I suppose that I have become one as a result. I know that I feel very uncomfortable if I am ever invited to go 'inside'. No, I must be honest, I behave badly if ever I go inside. I love the outside; I am privileged enough to be able to choose to remain on the outside. I know this has affected how I lead. For a long time, I thought behaving as an outsider was one of my weaknesses, now finally I recognise it as a strength. But when I offered up 'outsider' to the Expedition members, it did not resonate with anyone. So, like many, I will be adding a personal piece to my Essence, quietly.

Journal

Solo

Do any of the pieces of Essence described by the members of the First Expedition resonate with you? Which do? Which don't? What might you add? Once you have named the pieces of your Essence, write a paragraph on each one. Why is it in your Essence? Has it always been? Describe it a little to yourself. How has it affected how you lead? Now put the pieces into the central Essence circle in your map. Make the size of each one reflect its relative importance to you in how you lead. Remember this is not about how important each piece of Essence is to who you are, but rather to how you lead.

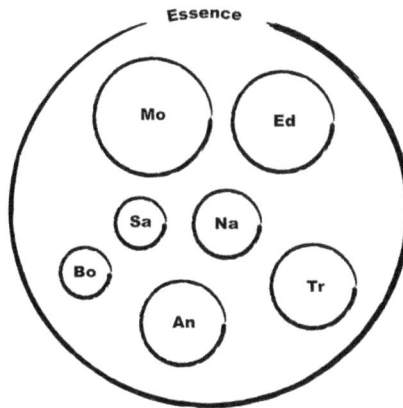

Figure 6: My Essence

Maybe, quietly, go for a walk and think of the dream, gift and incomplete seeds you have inherited and intend to hand on.

Capture everything in your journal. Some will be points that you may not fully understand at this stage. Just put them in as questions to come back to.

As a group

Share your maps as they evolve. If you have a sufficiently diverse group and you have invested in enjoying each other, you will start to discover very different thinking as you discuss them. And this might trigger changes in how you lead people who are very different from you.

Elements

With Essence pinned down, we look at how it shows up as Elements in how we lead. As these Elements become clear, some will definitely need to be jettisoned, some reframed and one very clearly identified. Then many others will need elegant combining even though they may appear to be on opposite ends of a spectrum; even in conflict, they are best combined. Because leading requires us to operate along a continuum between them, constantly reassessing and repositioning what becomes a sliding scale between two Elements. Combined, they make the whole greater than the sum of the two Elements. This is something that women are very adept at doing. Indeed, it is often the tension and creativity sparked when they combine that generates the Energy of leading.

But more on this later. For now, what do we consciously and deliberately jettison, abandon and dump?

Jettison

I am going to leave it to some great women to list them. Let's not spend too much time on them, they don't deserve it – just dump them.

Good girl

Mai Chen, a famous lawyer in New Zealand, says, "I was brought up in the Chinese and Kiwi cultures. I was told to keep my head down, swallow my views and opinions, never complain, do not fight, do not be angry, walk away, please people, be agreeable, be silent, never aggressive, toe the line, be a good girl. And this was from the people who loved me. They did not want to see me hurt. Confucius had good advice for tall trees in strong winds; he said that if you wanted to avoid them, be a stump." Mai does not hold back: "To change the world you need just sometimes to be disagreeable when there is a good reason for being so."

Camilla Sievers, who has survived the endless ups and downs of successful entrepreneurialism, adds, "Why in my professional life have I always needed approval from older, mostly white, more experienced and more 'superior' men? I never really feel that I have done a good job until they tell me that I have." Camilla promises me, "this stops now."

Room at the Table

Sarah: "I have decided that there is plenty of room at the table for us all. And that there is sure to be even more room if enough of us get to the table and put down the ladder for others to climb up. And that if there is not room at that table, there are plenty more tables." (Podcast 49)

The ladders need putting down – and more. When someone climbs one, they must then turn around when they get to the top and look back down it to then stretch out their hand and help others as they climb. The look in their eyes as they stretch out their hand must be beautiful to see. It has been done for me a few times over the years, and I will never forget the sight of the outstretched hand and the belief in the eyes. We must jettison the 'not enough room at the table' attitude.

Mona believes this passionately and adds, "Don't forget the option of creating your own table, a table that you love being at, with the people you choose around it". Then no ladders are needed.

Dividing by Age

The diversity in ages was one of the most important features of the First Expedition. Aparna and then Anna described its impact on them: "The positive restlessness amongst the younger women on our Expedition was something I was grateful to witness," says Aparna. "As they tiptoed around their sense of power and established their own space in the room, in them I saw a mirror that reflected my own transformation. A transformation that has been brewing within me for years, but I only discovered it as I looked deep into the eyes of these young women. I realised just how much I needed them to know myself."

And Anna: "There is a moment in life when you want to be a sister, not a daughter. I'm thirty-one. I was craving for women's wisdom. I was trying as a child to feel accepted by the women in my life. But this unique group of powerful women on the Expedition made me feel my own power. I no longer feel like a child. Being seen as a woman by a man is ordinary. But being seen as a woman by a woman is another thing."

Divya Kapoor interviewed both Aparna and Anna when she joined the Women Emerging team. "You got the impression that on the First Expedition everyone had left their hierarchies – especially the hierarchies of age – out of the room like you would leave your shoes out of the temple."

I balk every time I hear the expression 'harness the talents of young people.' Just think about what a harness is. A large, thick piece of leather that we strap around an animal's neck to force it to do something it doesn't want to do or to prevent it from doing something it does want to do. The last thing we must do is harness people, and most especially young people.

Ignoring Self

Leila: "I learned this the hard way. There were times when I saw taking care of myself as optional, as secondary to other priorities. It did not end well. Caring for yourself has to be prioritised intentionally, not seasonally or occasionally, not on my birthday but every day.

"Twelve months or three hundred and sixty-five days is a long time, so we cannot be at the same level every minute. Nowadays I think of the seasons, expanding and contracting Energy to nurture myself so that I can give what I want to give to the fights I'm fighting. If I don't, I am not useful to the people I lead." (Podcast 36)

Latanya Mapp Frett, who runs the Global Fund for Women, has seen this too many times: "The biggest mistake is to just keep going. Thinking you are not doing it for yourself but for other people. That you will keep going until you cannot function anymore. You think it is just you doing the sacrificing, but in truth everybody around you has to sacrifice themselves in order to get things done. You feel it is all on your shoulders. You know that success means you have to work like a dog, be everywhere at once. This is when decline starts, not just for you but for the work." (Podcast 29)

Minimising Me

Antonia Belcher is always looking for talent to work in the businesses she runs: "If I look at a male CV and a female CV for a job, I will find the guys have upped the ante on all their things that are marginal, and the girls have taken them down. And when I interview the girls, I ask, 'You put here that you have done a bit of this; how much have you done?' I then rapidly realise just how much they had 'done.' Whereas if I challenge the boys, I might illicit one small example which is made to sound like it was a full-time sprint for six months. We have to get the balance right, to stop minimising while resisting the pressure to swing to the other extreme." (Podcast 27)

Alex Moore, now so successful in the med tech field, looks back at opportunities she almost missed: "I minimised myself. I was doing quite well; I had two children and a husband with a busy job, and I was really enjoying my job. But I had this self-imposed limiting view that I could not go any further because of my children and the industry that I was in. Without speaking to anybody. I resigned myself to it. I was dissatisfied but just getting on with my lot. I convinced myself that this was as far as I could go. That other women might choose to work long hours and be in the office every day, but that I couldn't.

"Then a promotion offer came up. I politely refused it. This lit a light bulb for my boss. She said, 'you do not have to do it my way. I work the way that suits me. I am interested in what you can bring to the business, not in making you a carbon copy of me,' and that lit a light bulb this time for me. I applied, got it, found my way that works for me, my family and for the business.

"When I look back, I am embarrassed by what I imposed on myself."

Falling for Flattery

Erica Su looks back at her successful career in financial services in China, at the moments when she has said 'no': "Flattery can get you into a mess. Into accepting roles that you are not right for or not right for now. All the time you should say to yourself, 'it is my story, not yours.' You should ignore the flattery and ask basic questions of yourself:

"Can I do it? You should not be tempted by the tendency to overstate competence. You have to have your own realistic assessment about your capability and also the job requirements. You will not be a 100% match, but it should be reasonably reconciled.

"Do I want the responsibility? Sometimes you feel you are better off to step back a little bit. Do something more comfortable or not stretch so much. You must have the courage to step out of your comfort zone, but how much you want to stretch yourself is a personal judgement not only for yourself but also your family, as they are going through the journey with you.

"Am I OK with the sacrifices? You analyse them and do not pretend that there are not sacrifices. Ask yourself: if it is something of a sacrifice now, will you get it back later or will you never get it back?

"What will I miss? If you are really excited about the new things in a job, even if there is a lot of uncertainty, then go for it. But if you feel passionately about the things that you are doing right now, then think carefully.

"Is it really worth it? There are sure to be politics and lots of managing people and conflict and also you will be scrutinised more as a woman. Would you feel more comfortable and happier with more sense of achievement by staying where you are?

"Do I have the power base to support me in this new role? You will need a power base to carry out a new initiative or to show a result. This one is very critical.

"Will I accept the trade-offs on my health? Health-wise, if you get to your limit and have to stretch too much, then you will have mental stress, and your physical body will react to that pressure.

"These questions are not self-limiting, they are self-defining. I suppose the outside world may see them as self-limiting and people around you will almost goad you into doing what you should not do. Of course you do not want to appear to be self-limiting, but don't let this lead you to say yes if you really know it should be no. It takes more courage to do self-defining and to say no when everyone around is flattering you because they want you to say yes." (Podcast 10)

Enough

Katrina: "Am I smart enough? Am I attractive enough? Am I kind enough? Am I thoughtful enough? Am I helping enough? Am I grateful enough? Am I professional enough? Am I fit enough? Am I relevant, positive, slim, loving, good, old, wealthy, valuable, quiet, important, objective, loyal, sexy, clear, authentic, flexible, confident, spiritual enough? Am I interesting, ambitious, honest, caring, passionate, happy, successful, healthy enough? Am I calm, mindful and funny enough? Am I strong enough? And humble enough? Am I gentle enough? Am I open enough? Am I curious enough? There are so many enoughs for all of us as women, and then it goes one step further for me. Am I disabled enough?

"It was that last one that was enough for me. Enough is enough. I am absolutely tired of seeking that sweet spot of trying to find just the right amount. It takes an incredible amount of Energy, time, attention, and it's simply exhausting. I decided to take the risk of abandoning the enoughs and to believe deep down that I am enough."

I just could not resist the temptation to tease Katrina with a memory, so I asked, "do you remember you once wore a Wonder Woman outfit?"

"Yes, I did. A friend was putting together a series around gender issues. She asked if I could be her subject. Erica is right about flattery. I was flattered into wearing a Wonder Woman outfit. We took photos of me at work, shopping in the supermarket, holding my baby, hanging out the washing and then coming home and being that sexual goddess to my husband. I talked about doing everything, with a beautiful smile on my face. Isn't that interesting? Some twenty years ago, I did that. I am a different woman now, though I am not so sure that the world is all that different." (Podcast 11)

So seven things to jettison. Some you won't need to jettison because you have never suffered from them. I have never felt the pressure to be a 'good girl,' though I have seen the effect it has on others. And you will no doubt add some that are specific to you, strange things that emerge from your Essence which you may not see at first but definitely need to be dumped.

Reframe

This might take a bit longer. For whatever reason, some of our greatest strengths as women have become framed as weaknesses. We will be reframing and regaining them here.

When people ask me about whether I 'suffer' from imposter syndrome, my answer is "yes, thankfully." I add 'thankfully' because the syndrome keeps me humble. Think for a moment: what would it be like if the alternative to having imposter syndrome was to think that you know everything or that you have a right to be where you are? I prefer imposter syndrome any day, even if it is sometimes a struggle.

When people push back on my passion or anger with the words, "let's not get too emotional, shall we?" my answer is, "I am so sorry, can't you do emotion? Is there some way I can help?"

When people, steeped in analytics and data, dismiss my instinct as 'irrational,' my answer is, "let us combine forces. We need both."

When I struggle with privilege, now I frame it as responsibility. When noisy people tell me to speak up, now I ignore them. When everyone on the First Expedition decided to dump the words 'leader' and 'leadership,' now I simply reset to the verb 'leading.'

There is a lot of reframing to do. I will leave it to more beautiful voices than mine to elaborate.

Imposter Syndrome

Jude: "Most of us have a version of imposter syndrome. Or most of us have a level of appropriate humility where we would not claim to be leading. I am told that I am leading by others. If this is the impact I have, then I am grateful and will carry on working towards being better at it.

"I think it is a good thing that you never fully own a sense of being a leader, even if other people urge you to believe that you are one, because the essential quality of self-reflection and self-doubt balanced with confidence is a good thing.

"We must own the imposter syndrome as an asset and not let it shy us away from leading, because we need each other to lead." (Podcast 12)

Rouba: "I did not know I was leading until quite late on when people started telling me that I was. People were coming to me for advice, and I was always thinking, 'who am I to give them this advice?' I remember one of the big moments during my journey to leading was when one of the first people in my team left. We had an open-hearted chat and she said, 'Rouba, I expected much more guidance and mentorship from you.' I had only ever thought of her as a very strong woman to whom I had nothing to teach. At that point I realised that the way I look at myself is not the same as how other people look at me. Maybe we are scared to recognise ourselves and hold ourselves to our true value. Maybe it is a form of the imposter syndrome. Maybe it is about time that I step up into the shoes of how people see me." (Podcast 10)

Zenna Hopson Atkins has just said yes to joining the advisory board of the Shetland Space Centre, which will launch the first vertical rocket in the UK: "I said yes because who would not? It's space. It's rockets. It's vertical launches. It's really exciting.

"We need to just say yes to doing things that we do not normally do. We get put in boxes, we slide into our swim lanes and then we want to stay there. It is vital just to get out there and say yes to stuff that we at first think we cannot do.

"I said yes years ago to chairing OFSTED, which is the organisation that inspects and regulates everything to do with education and children services in the UK. I said yes because I got expelled from school. I did not pass my exams. I had to start from scratch, get a career and work my way up the ladder. I remember when the OFSTED board were talking about 'those parents' whose kids were currently getting into trouble at school. I had just received a call to say that my son had been given a fixed term exclusion because he had been naughty.

"I said yes to being on the board of the Royal Navy because I could see that I could get some real change in thinking and attitudes towards the climate through. I turned out to be the longest serving non-executive in the Royal Navy.

"I have learnt that all-male teams don't do themselves any favours; they get stuck in group think. So we have to overcome a sense of being an imposter and say yes. Get in there and challenge the group think."

Catherine, who has heard the expression 'imposter syndrome' right through her career in STEM, says, "I don't think women actually have imposter syndrome any more than men do. I think the difference is that women are self-aware enough to know they have imposter syndrome. I think that men tend to feel like that is not an OK thing, so they cover it up even to themselves." (Podcast 33)

Emotional

Hinemoa: "I have had covert and overt messages to not be so emotional. They say, 'if you are going to lead, to be out front and in a position of responsibility, you need to stop showing emotion.' I think that is absolutely wrong. One of the things that we need to do more of as women leaders is to show feelings, both the vulnerability and the anger." (Podcast 1)

Jacqui Gavin has worked in government and the corporate world in the UK. "I am proud to be able to cry. Now that I have transitioned from being a man to being a woman, I am not ashamed of crying any more. I never cried as a man. I had to show strength. I don't think I could have cried, but if I had it would have been behind a closed door. Now I see crying as a wonderful strength. I don't mean uncontrollably; I don't sob uncontrollably. I cry simply because it is a good thing to do." (Podcast 27)

Ani is all over this one, looking at it from her monastic community in Nepal: "I find men suffer more than women because they need to control their emotions. If you cry as a man in front of the society, they will say, 'Oh, such a weak man.' How men are brought up in our society is very unfortunate. In the name of being brave and tough, men can become unkind and inflexible. In the name of strength, they become very weak and fragile.

"Women are comfortable to shed tears. It helps us to release our stress and our suffocating emotions. I cry very frequently. At times, I feel bad about it. I ask myself why I so easily have tears in my eyes. I think maybe I am going through pre-menopausal symptoms. But then on the other hand, I feel like it is good, it is healthy.

"I see the great monks gradually becoming more and more soft and sensitive. The tone of the voice starts to change, it becomes more motherly." (Podcast 23)

Catherine wishes that, as with the imposter syndrome, men would catch up: "I think they are just as emotional as women; they just cannot show it. Women are used to showing their emotions and it makes them lead better. Men do not have that awareness. They only really allow themselves to show one emotion and it is a negative one: anger, because it is the only acceptable one for them. They don't allow themselves to feel hurt or sad, and certainly not in the workplace. They must exhibit the stereotype, that very confident and lack of emotion kind of thing.

"The problem is that emotional men who are hiding it do often raise the emotions in meetings by displaying the only emotion they allow themselves: anger. Then meetings become too full of anger too quickly." (Podcast 33)

Ayesha is sick of the remarks about emotions. These are the ones she dislikes the most: 'Why are you so angry?' 'Why are you so angry all the time?' and 'Why do you take it so personally?' She suggests banishing them: "There are things that happen that make me angry, and I am right to express them as such, even if it is not what people are used to. And if it is personal, then I am going to take it personally and respond in whatever way I should. Too often the question is followed by 'let it go' even when it's something that is overtly unfair, wrong, unethical or unprofessional. I am really clear. If it feels right to express emotion and anger, don't let people stop you." (Podcast 4)

Instincts

Mona: "Somehow, we must reframe instincts as something that we ourselves trust. Only then can we persuade others to trust our instincts.

"A hunch, an intuition or instinct is a powerful tool for leading and often overlooked because it is not a quantifiable hard skill, yet that is exactly why it is so powerful. Intuition is the ability of our brain and sensory nodes to store the information that feels right and warn us about situations that are potentially dangerous. These highly developed nodes are pathways in our brains forged from our unique life journeys. They allow us to sift through the myriad of our lived experiences without too much conscious effort."

Liz illustrated this with a story: "I was with my family in France. I was about ten years old. I was a confident swimmer and I wanted to cross a river to buy an ice cream. I started off swimming towards the ice cream shop. Then I got caught in a current and I started to panic. It was pulling me in a different direction. There were people on the bank yelling where I should go to on the bank. I panicked a bit more and I decided to swim harder. My body tensed up. It was truly exhausting.

"When I got to the other side of the river, I sat on the bank. I realised that, actually, if I had trusted my own instincts and just relaxed into the current, I would have landed on the bank a little further down than I had intended. Fighting against the current had not been necessary. I should have had confidence in my ability as a swimmer and trusted myself and my instincts."

Listening

Not long ago, I was sitting with a group of professors at a college in the US. Good people, they had been trying to sort out a problem: that male students dominated their classes with questions, and women were often silent. Silent, I thought, or listening? Anyway, the professors told me that they had set up workshops for women to help them 'speak up.' The trouble was that the workshops were having no effect. I suggested that they might run workshops for men on coping with silence, listening and resisting the need to jump in. I had very little impact; I don't think they were listening. Somehow, we have to reframe listening as active, engaged and committed, and stick to it when it feels right.

Liz explains: "It seems obvious, but it is surprising how often listening does not happen, quite often because ego permeates the situation. The best people who lead make the space to listen, not just to hear what they want to hear or to pick up on the bits that they were waiting for, eager to catch confirmation bias. They listen in a genuine way, with their ears and their eyes. They seek both the verbal and nonverbal cues and pick up how people are behaving with each other. They sense the dynamic of the room, in the Zoom call, at the community meeting or within the team. And they reflect on it, ask questions, get people's perspectives. Never in a tick-box way. I think such a degree of curiosity is only possible when ego is set aside by people who know they do not have all the answers.

"And when the listening is done, the final step is to say, 'Okay, I have listened, I hear, I see. And now this is what we are going to do. Do you want to come with me?' They create a space where people cannot do anything but say yes, because where they are going looks interesting, fun and exciting."

I asked Liz if this is always possible. Surely from her years in the army there had been times when there was no time for listening.

"I have seen this in so many contexts and in some really challenging situations. It may seem that this listening approach is best in a nice comfy conference room, but I would say it is even more crucial in a more hostile situation. It is then that you really need to double down on listening and pay attention, because that is when it really matters. People who lead well do that in abundance, and when they are under pressure, they do it even more.

"I have a simple answer to people who say, 'there was no time to listen.' There is always time to listen. The false economy of not listening is what people often overlook in their urgency to act – to act or to be seen to be acting. It does not require bringing people together for a long discussion or retreat. Sometimes it is about listening for one minute. It is about pausing and saying, 'can you give me your thoughts on the situation? What is your perspective?' It can be transformative even if it is a few minutes.

"Teams can really get themselves into an upward spiral when listening is done well. If as a leader you get into good habits with your team, they know they will have an opportunity to share and be listened to, then they get really good at expressing what they want to say – and quickly. It takes a while, and at the start it can be quite frustrating, and some may take quite a long time to say their piece, but as you get better as a team, it very quickly becomes a really effective and efficient process of sharing. Because you have built that trust. They know they will be heard so they are willing to step up and give their perspective." (Podcast 59)

Melissa Berman, another huge investor in women, says that listening is not just extremely active, it's also extremely exhausting "as you try to understand what both the text and the subtext are. To sense the context, to spot what people want you to hear. It takes a lot of emotional labour, to the extent that it needs to be stepped back from at times so that you do not get burned out." (Podcast 30)

So listening is a crucial part of leading. It needs reframing as an active and not a passive activity.

Privilege

Folawe put a great deal of thought into the issue of privilege during the First Expedition: "I have always acknowledged the privilege I had. My father, a successful businessman with connections to government officials and elites, possessed native intelligence and strong business acumen. He made a lot of money early and that gave him access to some privileges. I was well aware of the privilege that came with it.

"Over time, I have witnessed privilege from various perspectives. I have seen marginalised and discriminated people who are continuously blocked and unlikely to taste privilege. I have seen women who have been oppressed while pursuing power and are now using it to oppress others. I have seen some women who use their privilege as a weapon, others who exploit it for personal gain and women who trample on those with less power.

"On the other hand, I have also witnessed wonderful women with privilege who use their power to uplift others, to open doors and sponsor other women. They recognise that privilege comes with responsibility. So I have stopped viewing my privilege with embarrassment and discomfort. Now I see privilege as a responsibility. It is my duty to use my privilege in practical ways for the benefit of others."

Leading Itself

Right from the start we decided to reframe to the verb. It is a verb because leading is adapting, evolving, reforming, caring, listening. It is not static, rigid, sculpted or established. Liz and Alia want to go further and reframe leading in our minds as water.

Liz: "Leading, like water, takes many different forms. Water can be ice – strong, hard and resilient – and sometimes that is what it needs to be. Water can be liquid – flexible, evolving and adaptable, moving into the spaces where it is called for. Water is steam – reaching everywhere, almost invisible; it cannot be caught, and it must be about this sometimes. Water can change shape to fill a tall bottle, a round vase, a long pipe or a deep tank, and that is what it is about in this ever-changing world."

Alia: "Seas hold things that are bigger than themselves, whether you look under the ocean surface or at what life is being birthed in marshes. When I think about my own journey of leading, it has been most powerful when it is bringing people together to build something that is greater than the sum of the parts. In the ocean, we find coral, fish, and all working together under the surface. The water is holding it all.

"And water comes with Energy. It can be angry and destructive or calm and supportive. When we lead, we have to be aware of the Energy we're creating and the spaces and ecosystems we are birthing.

"I think there is something deeply powerful about seeing leading as providing a container for connecting things that are greater than ourselves."

Liz sees more parallels between water and leading: "I often think about what is happening above the surface and what is happening below it. About what am I projecting to the world above the surface, and about how much I want to share of myself below the surface. How much of my Essence should I carry and reveal in the rooms that I walk into? Because Essence is with us all the time, spoken or unspoken, useful or not useful. There is something really beautiful about this as a metaphor of the above and below, what we can see and what we cannot see. Both are important.

"Then there is the ripple effect of water. Sometimes the challenges that we face in the world can feel pretty overwhelming. You think, 'how I can possibly as one person address these enormous barriers?' I think water offers the analogy that as one droplet or one pebble we can make our own ripple. And a multitude of us each making our own ripples make change feel more achievable."

So there is a lot to reframe as well as to jettison. Again, not all of these six reframes will resonate with you and you will undoubtedly add more that are specific to you.

I admit, the reframing won't happen just like that. But it might be faster than you think. Once you adopt the imposter syndrome; once you see emotions and instincts as the assets that they really are, as soon as you decide that whatever privilege you are fortunate enough to have is a responsibility; and once you have dived deep into the waters of leading, then you might surprise yourself how rapidly you reframe.

The next question must then surely be: for what purpose?

Journal

Solo

Think through what you intend to jettison and reframe. Some of the things the members of the First Expedition chose to jettison and reframe might resonate with you, others won't. You may also have things to add.

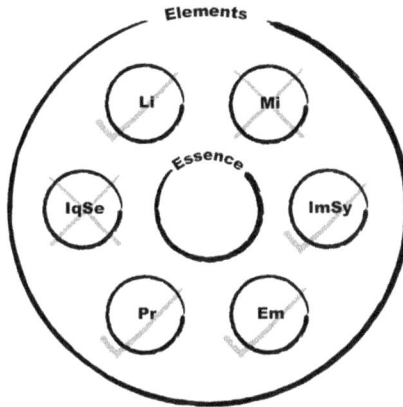

Figure 7: My Elements

The priority for me is to jettison IqSe (ignoring self) and Mi (minimising) and I need to reframe Li (listening), ImSy (imposter syndrome), Em (emotional) and Pr (privilege).

Give yourself practical examples of what you need to stop thinking or doing for each one and write down in what circumstances you think this will be most difficult for you to do. Set yourself a few targets. Make them as specific as possible, like 'at the next team meeting on .... I will ....'

Speak to some of the leaders on your list and ask them about reframing. How have they managed to do it? Ask them under what circumstances they forget to reframe and instead revert.

Think of someone you trust with whom to share your thinking. Preferably someone who will be good at reminding you if you forget to jettison or reframe in the future.

Keep capturing the insights as you go in your journal. Your map should now be getting more detailed.

As a group

Talk through what you all agree should be jettisoned and reframed. Figure out why so many of you have some in common. Push each other hard on practical ways to sustain the jettisoning and reframing.

Write down what each of you is determined to jettison and reframe. Then save them somewhere so that you can send them out to each other in six months' time.

Find

From our Essence we must draw a crucial element: purpose, an Element never to be jettisoned and only to be reframed with great care. Whether it is a clear choice or accidental or even reluctantly, why are we leading? Motherness, nature, the body, the sacred, ancestors, trauma or education and all the pieces of Essence that you will have added; how do they frame your purpose?

I believe that leaders who are not clear on why they lead will struggle to lead people and they will struggle to lead themselves. To build the resilience to keep going. My father said, 'don't lead if it is a round of applause you seek' and he was right. They are rare; you need something else to sustain you.

It might be for Harriet Adong the vision to rebuild the war-torn communities of northern Uganda. Or for Erum, the determination to get water to villages in Pakistan. Or for Laura, the commitment to greener energy in Scotland. Or for Camila, the dream of a Brasil that protects the Amazon. Or it may be Fatima bringing the women of Bruxelles together. Or Erica building the economy of Shanghai. Or me trying to inspire women to lead. Or Paula Langton focused on climate change:

"We have been setting our science-based target as a firm. We have decided to go for raising fifty billion dollars towards climate funds. We started off with a thirty billion target. We have raised eighteen billion so far and I have just convinced everyone to go for fifty. We kept pushing it up bigger and bigger. Breaking the target down made it feel OK, and even I began to think, 'I can actually do this,' and now everyone feels it and it has become everyone's shared vision. It is what I can do from where I am, and it will have a huge impact."

Or for Leila, it's about hope: "My first job was as a teacher in a refugee camp. It was during that time that I came to understand the significance of hope in the face of adversity. I realised that despair, which is the absence of hope, is a luxury that individuals grappling with displacement, loss, poverty or natural disasters cannot afford. And neither should we. I discovered that the starting point is to believe, even if the outcome is uncertain, in the potential for a positive result. Simply having faith that we will navigate the path as we go along."

Leila adds, "Purpose is the key to generating and sustaining the Energy required for effective leadership. It allows us to remain optimistic about the future and to choose which problems are truly worth fighting for. Once we have identified those issues, we can determine the specific Energy we need to bring to the fight. For me, that Energy is synonymous with hope. While it is natural to feel anger towards inequality and devastation, I believe in channelling those emotions into unwavering determination and optimism. Intentionally choosing not to succumb to despair, and instead fostering hope and trusting in the possibility of change is to me synonymous with leading a fight worth fighting." (Podcast 36)

How do you find purpose? Go back to Essence; part of it has to be there. And go out into parts of the world you don't know, maybe across your street, maybe further afield, part of it has to be there. Alison would then advise finding a way to reflect: "One of the things I have learned most from yoga is that it gives you the space and time to really consider what is most important. Certain thoughts float to the surface, others float away. As women we often have many, many priorities. We are wrestling with too many challenges and all at the same time. Having a way of reflecting and giving yourself the time to figure out what is really important and what is your most important goal is hugely valuable."

Your purpose then becomes your compass. You will need it to accompany your map as you explore. It will also make leading easier because the people you lead will sense it in you and choose to let you lead them.

Journal

Solo

Go in a dark room or walk up a mountain and ask yourself what your purpose is in leading. Capture it however you want, but keep it. It won't be perfect, it will evolve; that is the way of things. Remember, it's not your purpose in life, it's your purpose in leading. They may or may not be the same.

I was mystified when I was given this advice, but then a friend told me to quietly and privately write down the few things that I will be proud of as a leader when I am on my deathbed. It was a bit morbid, but I have them and they have provided me with a good compass over the years, especially when big decisions have had to be made.

You don't have to share your purpose, but people will sense that you know it. Now you have added your compass to your own map which is evolving fast.

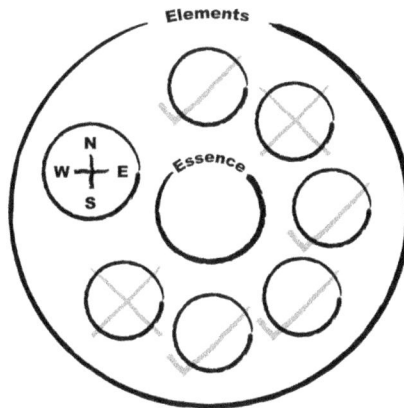

Figure 8: The purpose Element

As a group

Help each other to find the questions to ask themselves which will help them find purpose. Deathbeds don't work for everyone. Then leave each other to find their own answers, with no requirement to share them or not to share them.

Combine

Before we go any further on Elements, Uma is going to insert a health warning: "Self-awareness and delving into our Essence and Elements is a double-edged sword. It brings a lot of pleasure and confidence, but it also brings its share of pain. The more self-aware you become, the more you need to co-hold the pleasure and the pain of things that are both within your control and those that are way beyond your control. This is one of the reasons why I think leading is so hard to do." (Podcast 7)

I said earlier that one of the reasons to do an Expedition is that leading is wonderful, and I meant it. But it is also at times very tough, excruciatingly lonely and it makes you frighteningly vulnerable. They say you are there to make key decisions, but in my experience you are there to make fine calls often between two perfectly viable options. They say you have to forgive people easily for their mistakes, but in my experience it's the forgiving of our own mistakes that is the hardest. They say that you should not seek praise or credit, but I must admit that if you never get any credit at all, you can feel that everything you do is pointless. This list could go on for pages and pages. But the hardest piece is the one Uma highlights: you get to know yourself far too well, the good and the bad.

Like everything to do with leading, it's undoubtedly both wonderful and tough. Keep your purpose firmly in mind and hold on to the reality that you are unlikely to achieve it alone. Remember that if you lead well, you will occasionally make something good happen and you will get to watch the people around you achieve more than they ever thought they could.

So with Uma's health warning in mind, we proceed on from jettisoning, reframing and finding purpose to combining. Katrina was up for this from the start: "I love that opposing Elements combine. We can be incredibly warm and loving and at the same time direct and strong. It is all about knowing when to step into one or the other and knowing that you can have a mix." (Podcast 52)

The word is 'combine,' not balance, because balance is too much about trade-offs. I am confused when people talk about 'work-life balance' as if one exists without the other. They are not parallel universes, never to be bridged or revealed to one another. There is no balancing here, only combining: they are both me, each one enriching the other. And combining is something women do excel at, even those things that seem diametrically opposed.

Here are some examples of Elements to combine. You will have many more, but here are some by way of illustration. They are combinations of Elements emerging from your Essence which may appear to be almost diametrically opposed and even in conflict, but it's in the combining of them that sparks fly and Energy is generated.

I think of them as on a sliding scale along which you move to different positions at different times. Never get stuck at one end or the other, keep assessing, calibrating, adjusting all the time.

Humble and Visible

Visibility is a prerequisite for leading. Whether you are leading from the front, the middle, the side or the back, you are always visible and must always be visible. Not all the time and in every place, but overall visible. This is important for many reasons: to gain trust, inspire others, generate Energy, be accountable… the list is long.

This visibility does not indicate a lack of humility. The two combine unexpectedly well. It was Mona who first linked the two words: "Visibility and humility are two sides of the same coin. They are not mutually exclusive. You can be humble about the work you do but, to really amplify your impact, you must be visible. Visibility does not mean that you are bragging or that you're showcasing yourself; you are highlighting an issue so people can identify the path to change. Many of us struggle with this, but it is a false narrative that if you are visible, you are not humble. As a child growing up in Calcutta, I worked with Mother Teresa. I remember someone observing that Mother Teresa was both humble and visible. And, of course, she was. I realised then that you can and must be both." (Podcast 20)

Anna thinks humility and visibility are often seen as irreconcilable in leading because 'ego' is such a misunderstood word: "You can also have ego and humility. Ego is simply an awareness of yourself. You cannot be a conductor of an orchestra – you cannot lead a group of musicians and stand in front of an audience – unless you have a certain level of ego. Quite a low level, but it has to be there. It is like chilli in a recipe that just boosts the taste. It is all balanced. We need all the ingredients; they just have to be combined well."

Humble

Liz reflects that sometimes we complicate leading too much, that it is a humble activity: "The women all around the world who get leading right are the ones who are simply paying attention. There is nothing magic, loud or theatrical about it, they just pay attention and do so with humility. They have the simplicity in just looking at what is around them, observing, listening – really, actively listening – and then acting. When they come up against challenges, somehow they are able to set aside their egos, really focus on what they have been told and what they have observed. They reflect on this and then do something about it. I think that is great leading in its rawest sense. I have seen women do this in some of the most challenging of circumstances, be it war, natural disaster or in just day-to-day living. They bring a level of simplicity and clarity that inspires confidence and calmness in those around them. It is humble, and humbling to see." (Podcast 7)

I asked Liz how she displays humility. "By uttering the words, 'hey, I just do not know.' They inspire confidence in others so that they share, bring their own answers to the table, know they will not be laughed at or ridiculed for coming up with unexpected suggestions." (Podcast 7)

And I asked the same of Terri Hord Owens, who describes herself simply as a pastor (a successful pastor at that); her answer was by "not claiming the credit". She added that her ultimate inspiration for this was Mary in the Bible: "Her story is painful and difficult. She became pregnant at what scholars think was probably about fourteen years of age. She lived through immense shame and then the angel came down. From then, she raised this amazing human.

"We can look at Jesus and say the success of that mission had a whole lot to do with who Mary was. But I do not imagine that she was the kind of person who was walking around saying 'See what I did.'

"I think real leading is not about credit. If you fight for it all the time, the chances are that it is not justifiably yours. If the credit belongs to you, you will get it.

"I worked for someone who needed to have vocal credit for everything that happened. I said to her once, 'do you not realise that the success of this place reflects well on you? People will ascribe it to you whether you claim it or not.' If you are constantly looking for credit, then people begin to raise questions about what your real motives are." (Podcast 22)

Latanya, who backs so many women leaders, says that one way to lose humility is to "surround yourself by a bunch of yes people who are just so enamoured with who you are that they never tell you the truth about where things are headed. Instead, you need to surround yourself with people who will tell you what is right and also wrong. People who will call you on your bullshit, because otherwise all of us get very big heads." (Podcast 29)

Alison believes that yoga provides a source of humility: "When you start out doing yoga, you think 'I am going to be able to turn myself into human pretzel' when you may not have the bodily aptitude to do it. You must know what you are good at.

"Leading is just the same. It may turn out that you are not a financial genius, but you need to be financially literate, and you will have to push yourself to develop basic financial knowledge. But to do the finance really effectively, you are going to need to find an accountant to support you.

"Of course, in leading as in yoga, if you do not challenge yourself, you will never know what you can do. But you do sometimes have to allow the other person to become the human pretzel."

Julia Neuberger, too, describes herself simply as a rabbi (she is a very successful rabbi). She believes the elegant combining of humility and visibility lies in "getting on with it." Deborah from the holy texts is her inspiration in this: "She is a judge; she has been given this title and named a prophet. This is something that normally only a man would do. But Deborah just gets on with it. She judges without any complications or any excuses. The practice at the time was that judges sat where the people could find them. Deborah does this and she sits under her own tree. What I really love about Deborah's story is that she makes no excuses for who she is.

"I think one of the most important aspects of leading is to be comfortable in your own skin, not to be afraid of who you are, humble but not too humble, not making excuses for why you are there or for how you do what you do. I think a lot of times we feel that there's some accommodation that we have to make about either our femininity or our approach. We think we have to step into a system and assimilate into it, as opposed to bringing who we are and how we do things and sit there visible under a tree." (Podcast 23)

Fiona Campbell is a partner at McKinsey who advises many leaders. She loves this, and adds that once you get this level of humility and ego right, "the same level of ego maturity translates to that of the organisation you lead in. And that if you don't get it right, whatever purpose you may want to put in place for the organisation is going to be lost at the door."

So we are after a level of humility that does not shy away from visibility, it just does not crave it.

Visible

Why do we then shy away from visibility? I certainly did, for two reasons, both connected with my Essence. The motherness piece caused me to confuse visibility with lack of privacy: my kids were young, I was exhausted most of the time and also I didn't want them to get dragged into my work. An ancestry piece in my Essence also played a part. My family came from the northwest of England, where 'showing off' or 'getting too big for your own boots' was almost the greatest sin. Visibility could never have combined with humility in their eyes.

So for years, as Common Purpose got bigger and bigger, my profile as the founder and CEO remained low, maybe even decreased. It stayed that way for a long time until I discovered that if you don't talk about yourself then others will talk about you on your behalf – especially online. Some pretty unpleasant people locked onto me and talked about me obsessively, unpleasantly and completely inaccurately, and I spent years on the back foot. It passed but it was not pleasant. I discovered that if you lead, you must be visible even if you don't want to be – and it has nothing to do with a lack of humility.

It is not as if I didn't know that already. I was very visible with my colleagues, customers and stakeholders. I knew from the very early years of leading – and I was lucky, I started young – that if you lead, you must explain who you are to the people you lead so that they understand where you are coming from. They don't always have to agree with you, but they do need to know a bit about your Essence. With luck and consistency, they start to trust you, even sometimes feel affectionate enough about you to forgive you for your mistakes.

You have to explain yourself, to reveal yourself and your thinking, and you also need to be physically seen. I recall years ago giving this advice to a fellow chief executive who was painfully shy. Her colleagues assumed that because she was invisible, she must not care. Far from it, shyness is very hard to deal with. I suggested to her that each day when she got to the office, she walked around the building to see and to be seen. A week later we met for lunch and as I went up the stairs to her office a young man stopped me to complain about the lack of electricity and lift. He asked if I knew how to contact the new electrician. "New electrician," I replied. "Is there a new electrician?" He said, "She started last week. She has been going through the office every morning looking at the overhead lights." When my friend and I sat down to lunch, I suggested that she continue to walk around, but stopped looking up at the ceiling as she did. I promised her that if she prioritised being visible then people would start to talk to her.

My colleagues, customers and stakeholders were never the problem for me. It was the wider world – especially the online version of it – that was. I learnt to apply my commitment to visibility beyond my normal circle, however much I hated it.

One last thought on visibility: make sure you learn to make a speech. It is a crucial skill for leading and it is only acquired through endless, painful practice. It makes you deeply visible and it means you can share your dreams and ideas in a way that is humble and humbling and generates vast Energy.

Empathy and Distance

Leading is about relationships. Building relationships requires empathy. Empathy can get in the way of distance. Leading requires some distance. Empathy and distance form an elegant duo and combining is difficult: it requires regular attention, a sensitive radar and acute judgement.

Empathy

If for no other reason than that today's world is full of trauma, primary and secondary, empathy feels ever more essential to leading.

Both Claire, looking at global security, and Twila at global warming, echo this point. Claire: "Given the scale of conflict and uncertainty across the world, you're going to have to deal with trauma. You're going to have to deal with the legacies for generations of people who do not have a place they can call home, where they can feel at ease and feel they can settle." (Podcast 38)

Twila: "I sometimes hear people talk about a new normal and that is simply not a concept. Change is now and accelerating. No one will know precisely what the full range of change is to come. But they will know that we have to work our darnedest right now to minimise the change. And for many, they will never see the upside of the actions they take now. This means that there are a wide range of emotions that leaders have to be aware of, because they will need to give space for negative, fearful, difficult, angry and sad emotions in many of the people they lead, as well as for the sense of loss of things that were familiar and memories of youth.

"Leading will mean helping people to change those difficult emotions. To inspire, bring people together and move forward." (Podcast 38)

Bin, who, from her position at EY, has second to none access to data and research globally, agrees: "Empathy is a critical component of leading today. It's now the level one stuff; having the self-awareness to relate to other people. In the end, leading is about inspiring, motivating and relating to your fellow team members, colleagues and to everyone." (Podcast 14)

Folawe reflects on who she 'caught' empathy from and how much she cherishes it. "When I speak of leading with love and empathy, I am reminded again of my former headteacher, Mrs Tounou. She operated with love and empathy towards everyone, from the cleaners and security personnel to the teachers and students. If a child was disruptive, she would inquire, 'Have you had breakfast?' or 'How did you wake up today?' She always paid attention to what was happening around her and to whom. This approach has shaped the way I engage with people. Before passing judgment, it is important to understand why someone may be behaving in a certain way and to consider the deeper issues they may be dealing with, which we may be unaware of. It is simply about being kinder in our interactions and relationships with others. Everyone is facing their own battles, and everyone is striving to be better and to give their best. Engaging with people fully requires having that kindness within you." (Podcast 10)

For every woman involved in the First Expedition, empathy was a priority. Leading requires it, but it has to be real empathy, says Victoria Cordoba, a woman who has had a tough life made all the tougher by intolerance. She is sick of what she sees as the casual and vapid use of the word empathy. She has heard it used a lot, but not often been in the presence of the actual emotion.

"People today claim they are empathetic because it is a good word to call themselves. But in reality, they are not, because empathy is shown by actions, not by words. Being empathetic requires a great internal work, to take yourself out of your comfort zone and into the life of a completely different person. It is not easy. It is a very brave act to be empathetic to someone who is completely different from you. To be curious about other people's religion or lifestyle.

"I have grown up in Argentina. I felt feminine since I was four years old. I dressed up with my mother's clothes. All my world was always feminine. People in school isolated me, and I isolated myself to protect myself. No one wanted to play with me, everyone was calling me names. When I started secondary school, for two years, I never went to the bathroom. I was petrified to go there and be harassed by the boys. I listened to music, watched films and read books to survive. At seventeen, I had my first boyfriend. Then I found out what nightlife was. It was heaven to me. I became a drag queen. I was so famous. It was my revenge for all of the years that people bullied me.

"I concentrated on being the best artist that I could be. It took me all over the world. It was a triumph to me. I was showing the world who I was without any mask. I was a drag queen for eighteen years, and then I decided to change my gender. Growing up in Argentina at the time, it was very difficult to become a trans person straight away, so when I reached forty it was the right time.

"It has been hard. To get through every closed door, you have to pay double the price. But you keep going, and going no matter what and when you fail, your sister will lift you up.

"I will tell my story to anyone just to see if I can plant that seed of empathy. Real empathy, not fake empathy."

We come back again and again to words and their ineffectiveness. Victoria says that the word 'empathy' is used carelessly, as a badge, with little depth.

Ayesha and Harriet Nayiga add that empathy is not even the right word. They distinguish it first with compassion and then with sympathy.

Ayesha: "Empathy is the quality of feeling the pain of another person. It is wonderful, important and rooted in kindness. But when empathy does not lead to an action, it can be an emotion that keeps you layering and adding on without being able to do anything about it. This very quickly leads to frustration and empathy fatigue. It is too strong a word, but you feel useless: I am feeling the pain of the human existence around me, but I cannot do anything about it. Compassion may be a better ambition; it is when you shift the emotion of empathy to an actual act of kindness."

Harriet Nayiga is a midwife in Uganda. "Sometimes you see that a mother is in need. Sometimes it is urgent and sometimes she imagines that it is urgent, but she definitely thinks she needs something. And sometimes, according to you as a midwife, it is not what she needs at that moment.

"Then you have to boldly tell her that this is not right. She may be going through a painful experience and your heart and mind may be taken up so that you want to cry with her. But if you do, you will fail to provide the necessary care. So during her painful experience, you stand with her to show her love and care, but you remain strong and standing on the truth as you see it. That is being empathetic, not sympathetic. If you are sympathetic, you may become so weak that you cannot help this mother appropriately."

So we proceed to distance, as Harriet Nayiga says, "because empathy slides to sympathy too easily if there is not enough distance." (Podcast 28)

Distance

Back to Folawe: "I found myself in a position of leading almost unintentionally. It was something I stumbled into and had to navigate. I was an introvert who preferred solitude. Overcoming my introversion was the first challenge I had to face. The second challenge was that my intention was always to ensure that everyone was fine and happy. But at the same time, I am results-driven, and I struggled when people did not meet expectations. I distinctly remember someone telling me, 'If you want to be liked, you can sell ice creams, but do not lead.' In that moment, I realised that leading does not guarantee universal approval or happiness with your decisions. I learned that I needed some distance to make sound decisions and to cope with a certain level of unpopularity. Sometimes you have to make decisions based on what is best for the cause you're fighting for, rather than seeking approval or empathising solely with people's problems. You must be prepared for others to become angry or upset with you. This realisation was one of the most game-changing discoveries of my life." (Podcast 10)

Vidya expresses the combining of empathy and distance beautifully: "Sometimes what I see in myself is too much empathy. As a leader, there is a danger that you put yourself too much in the other's shoes. You do so to the extent that you find yourself always finding excuses for somebody else's underperformance or lack of understanding of your vision or the way you expect things to get delivered. As a result, you are always giving a lot more room than is required.

"Nurturing has to be done to the extent that it enables people to become the finest versions of themselves, but not so much that you keep compensating for what they do not do or that they do not understand.

"This has been my personal journey. I have taken refuge in not being aggressive because I felt it was not me. It is not only masculine, but also something that I cannot be. The result has been that I was often fighting a not very articulate battle for what I felt should be.

"I have found myself to be on the journey to be assertive, so that I stop giving too much rope, and this requires me to keep some distance. This is my new self. I wondered at first if people would not like it. But they do. A lot of people have told me that they see a very different me, and they like it." (Podcast 20)

Maybe we need to untangle empathy and kindness a bit. I don't think empathy is only love and kindness, sometimes it is about being loving and firm, very firm, almost bordering on unkindness but always falling just short. 'Firm' can help someone achieve something they had never in a million years thought they could achieve, and to do this you need empathy but also distance.

The last word on empathy and distance goes to Enaya Noor. Enaya Noor was the youngest person I spoke to over the year-long Expedition. She is of a generation that deeply associates with the word 'empathy': "I'm not very good at telling people what to do. That has always been very difficult for me, because I am always the one who is being told what to do.

"It is tough when people have not done their work correctly. It was extremely difficult for me to tell them because I did not want to discourage anyone. I did not want to let anyone down. I wanted to be an empathetic boss. But then at the same time, the work was not being done correctly. I found it extremely hard to communicate to them because I had this need to be kind to them. "(Podcast 42)

I urged Enaya to keep going. We have all been there and struggle still with this difficult combining. Combining the next two Elements, too. Getting buried in one or the other means neither will thrive and the task will never get done.

Collective and Individual

I believe so deeply that building partnerships, connecting people, inspiring collaboration is one of women's greatest strengths: the instinct and ability to convene, to bring people together. Even people who may never have done so before because they have history, or because they are blind to the possibility of combining their efforts. Women know how to resist the pressures of competition and seek out common ground, to frame and phrase the task in a way so that people see the opportunity and moment to come together. And we do so with good grace and Energy even when we ourselves do not quite believe it is possible.

It is an Element that is in short supply in the divided world in which we operate. Almost every problem we face is complex and messy and crosses boundaries between sectors and specialisms, geographies and generations. To address them, we must cross these boundaries too. Pulling people together to work collectively, whether this is about drawing in colleagues from across many different disciplines or identifying and engaging with a wide range of partners and stakeholders. I have watched so many women triumph in this way. But like all great strengths, it can dominate and then the individual gets subsumed and eventually lost unless we take great care.

Collective

Latanya: "Leaders who do this are wonderful to watch. They have instincts for who to bring round the table. Who are the right people and from where? They get them together to say, 'How can we engage? How can we partner? I think we can align and do things together. I think our partnership can be more than just a conversation.' This Element must form part of women's genes because you see so many women who have it. They have the right instincts about who to bring into the circle and the right relationships to persuade them to join together." (Podcast 29)

There is something else in those genes, says Paula Marra, a founder of companies and cooperatives in Latin America: "Women do it pragmatically. When we get together we don't start talking about values. I see many, many collaborative processes start by trying to agree upon values, and yet people have different values. What they mostly share is a vision of what is better for their community and for humanity. It is better to focus more on that vision than on values. Because some people are in favour of abortion, some are not. Some people like organics, some do not. Some people want to be given orders, some do not. Setting out from the start to agree on all the values makes the process impossible. Society is complex and has different approaches to things. It is far easier to agree on what we want for the future. Just keep going and, in the end, values will start to emerge as you work together. At the start, remember only the vision and what you are achieving together.

"In my case it is simply about planting chow. We do not all have to agree on abortion rights to plant chow. We are not evangelists; there are many times we have very interesting and spiritual conversations, but this does not distract us, and it does not mean my values are compromised, and nor are theirs. We plant chow. That's what we do together." (Podcast 14)

Individual

We use this collective strength in abundance, but we keep the individual front and centre at the same time because every individual must feel visible within the collective and not invisible. They must know they are heard, recognised for their contribution, and that whoever is leading will adapt where possible for them.

Think of Anna in her orchestra. Even as the second violin, in the second row, tiny (because Anna is the same height as me), Anna is visible. Or think of Martyna the conductor. I asked her how she makes sure everyone feels visible in the large collective that makes up an orchestra.

"First you need to really place people with the right character to the right role, because if you settle them wrongly, they will have a constant feeling of being not appreciated. I think it will be fantastic never to make a mistake on where to put them and with whom to pair them. You never can be sure that this time will be successful, but try to be.

"Second, you work really hard on telling them where they are and why they are there so that they are settled.

"Third, you make them feel appreciated, listened to, if they have a new idea. You may have someone who always comes up with the ideas that might not work. Find a less prestigious concert, a less prestigious moment when you can afford for them to trial the idea and fulfil their needs without losing prestige.

"Fourth, know the dreams of people. I mean, someone just might need to play solo for a few bars, just to appear for a certain moment. It might not be very well played, but that moment may be what gets them up in the morning,

"Leading is to appreciate people and to place them in the right role in the orchestra, never to be buried in the collective." (Podcast 45)

Uthara reached back to nature and ancestors in her Essence to illustrate the fierce attention she feels is needed to nurture each individual as her organisation grows: "I had always been one of those people who killed a lot of pot plants. Then, two years back, I just told myself, 'I got to learn this.' I heard that my grandmother had a green thumb. She would just stick something in the earth and it would grow. So I thought genetics would show me the way.

"Discipline played its part in my eventual success, but what it really taught me was patience. You cannot command a plant to grow. If you give it too much fertiliser or water, it will die. Plants are like people. You need to be around them and constantly nurture them and, in nurturing, you will sense when they need water, what impact the season is having on them, and you will adjust and change your leading just as a gardener does." (Podcast 64)

How beautiful is that? We need to collectively address the vast, messy problem, and this is our strength, but we must never lose sight of the individuals in the collective. They are beautiful plants that need fertiliser, water and air.

Quiet and Loud

Combining these two is a little different. You need to flip from one to the other at the right moment; judging when to flip, then flip back, then flip again, and then revert with another flip. You get the point. 'Quiet' is probably the right word, 'loud' is probably overdoing it, but for people who prefer quiet, it does sound quite loud when you flip out of quiet.

One thing to remember is that silence and saying nothing is often quite 'loud' when leading. When you stay silent as a leader, people speculate on what you are really thinking or not revealing, and you have little sense of what they are drawing from their speculations. I make this point with conviction but some embarrassment. I have said it to my husband repeatedly over the last forty years and it has had no impact. Not little impact, but no impact at all. He often cries, "I didn't say anything" and my reply is, "yes, but that said it all".

Quiet

So why quiet? To dream, think, hear, storytell, see and interpret. Let us work through these.

▸ *To dream*

Gen Barr is an actress and has a very particular angle on quiet: "I am deaf, so being in a room full of people means I need to read lips that are this small," Gen's finger and thumb almost touch, "and I have no capacity to predict who in the room is going to speak next. My hearing aids have no volume control, so I cannot isolate individual voices, tune them out and focus on the one that I want to listen to.

"So 80% of the time, what I'm looking at is what is quiet. Body language and the rhythm of who likes to speak and when. It can reveal a lot about character – sometimes more than what is being said. I am paying attention to what is not said. Aside from that, picking up a couple of words from here and there and loosely connecting them into a narrative can take me to a completely different place. Wildly off the mark at times, but oftentimes a creative bubble that can be productive. Let's be honest, conversation can be boring and made up of decorum, processes and being seen to say the right thing. In a way, being deaf – working in the absence of sound – means I step out and take a few steps ahead. I can then steer the actual conversation to a positive result."

It is a delicious concept, isn't it? My father would tell me so often to stay quiet just for a moment. He would say, "switch the wireless from transmit to receive." He meant that I should listen for a change. I doubt he was thinking, as Gen suggests, that I should dream of a better conversation. Anna the musician says if you listen, "sometimes you even hear the silence between the notes."

▸ *To think*

Alison says that yoga has taught her this: "When I cannot practice my yoga – and sometimes you just cannot because you are too busy – I really think about it and think about what I am going to do when I do yoga next. In leading, we are human beings, not human doings. We need to sometimes think really carefully about what we are about to say and not just jump in and say it. Thinking about it can be hugely important to our effectiveness. It sets the tone before you then quietly speak.

"You see examples in sport. Think of the football players standing on the field holding back on that kick as they first just think about the kick."

▶ *To hear*

Paula Marra feels passionately about this: "I learned so much about cooperatives through starting Matriarca, in Latin America. The aim was to empower women and it empowered me just as much. It taught me that it is very important to take the time to be quiet and listen. When I first met the women, I was asking questions like crazy because I was curious about their culture. It is a very untapped community in the middle of a region in the middle of nowhere. I asked questions, simple questions, and it took forever for them to reply. They were talking between themselves. I thought it was because I did not make myself clear, so I started to speak louder and faster.

"Then one of the women said, 'I am sorry, if you continue to ask so many questions, it would be very difficult for us to come to an answer.' I realised what they were doing. After each question, they would talk between themselves, develop some ideas, and the person who knew more about what I was asking would then give me the answer. 'You have to give us the time to think ourselves and to get a consensus.' That was the first thing I learned. That there are people that know a lot more about things than me, and it is nice to keep quiet, ask fewer questions and await their thoughts." (Podcast 14)

After I spoke to Paula, I thought again about the expression I hear used a lot: the 'radical listener.' It sounds quite threatening. Maybe just listen and be 'quietly curious' with your questions. That will do. It's not about being radical, but more about being genuine and listening properly and not for show. This is something that upset Harriet Adong deeply when she was asked to speak at a global peace conference: "I was sharing my experience of bringing women who are survivors to peacebuilding. Even as I was talking about empowering women out of conflict, I was speaking for them and not with them. They were

not invited to this peace process. So they were not given a chance to even decide if they wanted to forgive or not to forgive, or if somebody should be held
accountable or not. Everyone at the conference wanted to be seen to be hearing;
they were loud about their listening, but it was for show. They did not really
want to hear the voices of the survivors." (Podcast 6)

▶ *To storytell*

Melissa Berman, who has backed some of the most interesting social entrepreneurs across the world, says, "The best storytellers are always the best listeners.
In the oral tradition, they learn their stories from listening to others because
nothing is written down. They do not see themselves as the creators of the story,
just the vessels of a story that belongs to everybody.

"This helps when you lead. If you listen to and engage with the voices of
the people around you, and if you listen to the fairy tales of their culture, those
fairy tales, folk tales and legends hold truths about that culture – and not just
the old ones, but the new ones too. Be sure to listen to the stories behind the
most popular songs and of the musicians who perform them. Then you find out
why they are so powerful.

"All this gives you a kind of authenticity that becomes extremely powerful.
You can tell the story. You understand the imagined, potential or actual audience, and can tell a story in a way that will resonate with them. It is physical and
it is visceral. It is not just about the head and the heart, but the gut too, the full
body. It is the ability to turn it from 'the' story or 'their' story to 'our' story. In
doing so, you change the narratives.

"This is a critical feature of how women lead. It provides an opportunity to
build successful movements that might bring about change with less fighting. It
is a skill that emerges from being quiet and listening, the ability to describe and
understand the protagonists, what their story is and, crucially, why should the
listener have empathy with the protagonist? How their story connects to my
own life that helps me understand their life." (Podcast 30)

Helena Kennedy, a barrister who has campaigned on behalf of women all
through her life, agrees: "It's all about being able to tell the story if you are go-

ing to make a compelling case for what you are doing and why you are doing it. People are being asked for things all the time. You have to remind people what is involved and why it is important." (Podcast 29)

▶ *To see*

Someone over the length of the Expedition – I cannot, however hard I try, re-member who it was – said something wonderful to me: "If someone says or does something that seems strange to you or that you disagree with, ask yourself: is it because they see less than I see, or is it that they see more than I see?"

Anna's expression, "the silence between the notes" is compelling. Maybe in the silence, we find what others see. The silences often reveal more than the words. For Anna, it is between musical notes, but the idea translates.

Vivi Tellas, as a theatre director, says it does: "When we direct, we tend to look at the figures on the stage, the main characters, but if we have two peo-ple, what I watch for is the space between them, because what is in between them may be invisible and quiet, but it is more interesting and often creates the drama." (Podcast 31)

▶ *To interpret*

Words can reduce a message to a simplicity that is not there. They can confuse, especially in the retelling, and above all they are absolutely not up to the chal-lenge of translation. We have to somehow reduce our over-reliance on words and instead leave time to digest and share understanding.

It was creating podcast episode forty that illustrated this for me, when I asked the members of the First Expedition to translate the definition of leader-ship we had all agreed on into their mother tongues.

The episode ended up with twelve women and twelve languages. Can I please recommend that you listen to it? I cannot capture it for you on paper, but here are some of the things they said:

"I need to find an old Chinese poem or saying to represent the meaning."

"That means something very different in Creole."

"You can have a literal translation, or we can use personification."

"So that is my translation, but it doesn't mean much."

"'Catalysing' in Greek can mean the opposite to what it means in English."

"When you use that word on its own it's fine, but when it is surrounded by other words the meaning changes."

"As a scientist, 'catalyse' means something very different."

"In Polish, 'catalysing' mostly refers to speed."

"Maybe, maybe, we can try. No, that will not work."

"'Momentum' is a very formal and strong word in Arabic."

"In Bangla, that means a blending of the flavours."

"I found it! I found it! In Chinese with this poem, it becomes simple but classic and very very beautiful."

"I have got it in Bahasa. When you listen, it sounds so beautiful. I have been thinking, I do too much in English. I like my native Bahasa more. I don't feel nervous in Bahasa."

Afterwards I asked Uma how she felt about English. "I don't resent it, but there are times when I feel a little disappointed that my native language is not something that I have been able to weave into aspects of my life. At the same time, the English language helps me to connect to millions of others. I owe so much of friendship and wisdom to it. Having said that, if there was more space for two languages to be able to flow into each other, able to weave and be used together, it would be ideal."

Ana Luz agrees: "English brings connection and it is a gift. But it needs to be wielded with awareness and we must be mindful that what we say in English may be perceived very differently by others." (Podcast 40)

Using words with care calls for a lot of quiet to be around them.

Loud

So when does leading require us to slide into loud in the moment and at the right moment? Because a decision has been made and needs briefing, something needs challenging, a question demands an answer, a message needs to be communicated or, quite simply, because leading requires us to be visible.

► *To brief*

Liz: "Sometimes a situation will demand careful listening and extensive consultation, and sometimes it doesn't. It requires decisive action by the person who is leading, and it must be communicated well. There are times when there has to be absolute clarity on the direction and the instructions must remove any doubt. You are not inviting discussion." I asked Liz how she had felt in such circumstances. "I know that in these times – and you have to judge them carefully – people crave relatively loud and one-way messages."

► *To challenge*

Jacqui: "Leading means challenging pretty much all the time. We must be allowed to do it differently from men, but we must actually do it. We have to resist the temptation to seek the calmness of everyone being happy. And we must resist the temptation to agree when it is false and stop nodding and smiling and keeping quiet. It is not really about being loud. We can do it quietly. But even when we do it quietly, it will sound loud. I have always said, on the day I die, I will be in my coffin saying, 'just one more thing before you put the lid down.'" (Podcast 27)

Mai agrees: "There is never going to be the right time to challenge. There will always be some who will fight you. Half of them will do so because they underestimate you, the other half because they are frightened of you.

"You will be told that you simply have to challenge the right way. But there is no right way, and it is never the right time. Sometimes you just have to do it. Prepare yourself, prepare your words, make sure that you are well briefed, anticipate what will trigger you, get yourself under control and strike first if you can. If you wait until the end, they will see you coming and may well cut you off and silence you. Above all, expect pushback from the ones who do not want you to speak too loudly as they benefit from the status quo, and remember that all major change is created by people speaking out."

▶ *To question*

When I met Meera Baindur, a scholar in India, I asked her why she had decided to give up being a guru. "I found that part of the guru's role was to answer questions and solve people's problems, yet I felt that people could solve their own problems. What I needed to do was to ask them the right questions so that they could figure out the answers themselves.

"It was thinking about Gargi in the Hindu writings that persuaded me to become an academic instead. Gargi did not teach wisdom; she just let students shine by asking them the right questions. She offered no solutions, did not write any great treatises or produce lengthy commentaries. She just asked questions.

"I began to realise that, as a guru, I was not following Gargi's approach. I was trying to solve people's problems.

"The trouble is that people do not expect gurus to ask questions. They want answers. I began to fear that the whole point of the guru seemed to be making your disciples dependent on you. I had figured out that everybody is a light unto themselves. So I became a philosophy teacher instead, loudly asking questions all the time. Even when I am on a bus." (Podcast 22)

▶ *To say no*

Think back to Erica's advice on deciding on a promotion: "It is your journey, no one else's. Do not live in somebody else's profile of you. When people say, 'you have been nominated,' or 'you are being put forward for this,' you may feel honoured, but do not bow to the tremendous pressure to say yes.

"Do not worry about what they will say. Just say no loud enough so that they hear." (Podcast 10)

This resonated with me so much. I am clear that sometimes you must loudly and against all advice say no. I remember my first boss saying to me, "I don't pay you to say yes. We know that the people around you will not need to wait for you to say yes. What I do pay you for is occasionally to say no and to say it loudly and infrequently enough so that the people around you will hear and stop."

▶ *To be visible*

Of course, you do not always have to be loud to be visible, but you do sometimes. Never forget that leading means occasionally standing firmly, loudly and clearly so that you are heard. I have done many speeches in my life, but the ones that always terrified me, that stopped me in my tracks with nerves, were the ones to my colleagues, the people I lead.

What a mistake it is when you see chief executives attend the major staff gatherings of their organisations and stay silent. They don't stand up to thank or to encourage, to remind people of the purpose or to paint a picture of the future. They pass on the opportunity to share the vision, to build the commitment, to make people feel inspired. If it's the public speaking skills that hold them back, they can learn them, watch others, practice and keep going until they have acquired them. If it's humility that holds them back, then they need to overcome it.

This must surely be even more important in today's world. Back to Claire: "It is changing at a terrifying speed, and people in power are not giving sufficient explanations, sufficient assurances about what the changes mean for people's livelihoods, security of jobs, families, opportunities." (Podcast 38)

I hear you say, "but we don't know the answers," but remember that silence is the worst option. Silence will lead people to think about the worst possible scenario and assume that you are not speaking to them because it's likely to happen.

'Loud' may indeed not be quite the right word, but it will feel shockingly loud the first time you visibly brief, challenge, question or say no. And it probably always will.

And quiet is the wrong word too. Maybe it is about having the quiet, the space and the humility to genuinely listen to what people are saying and to hold back before quietly speaking. Not to listen for what you want to hear or to find the thing that is going to confirm that you were always right. It is really being quiet so that you understand what the situation is and what people need from you.

So we combine the two: just quiet enough to hear or, as my father would say, "Switch the wireless from transmit to receive." Liz believes that it is this combination of quiet and loud that is the joy of leading: "When you look into someone's eyes and have enough of a relationship with them that you can sense what is needed in that moment."

Vulnerable and Strong

Unlike quiet and loud, there is no flipping these. It has to be both and at the same time; you have to be strong enough to be vulnerable and vulnerable enough to be strong.

Mistakes

Combining the two feels very tied to making mistakes and how to deal with them when you do. Because if you get it right when you do, you can often turn a situation around.

Luseshelo Simwinga, a midwife in Malawi, illustrates: "I was on midwifery night duty. We had a woman who was in labour. Her baby was going into foetal distress. We called the operating theatre team to come, but then we did not have fuel in the hospital car to get them to us. We asked to use the boss's car because it had fuel, but we were told it was only in service of the boss. By the time the operating theatre team arrived, the woman had lost her baby in uterus.

"In the morning I went to the boss and confronted him. He was quick to say, 'I am very sorry that happened. From now onwards, you can use my car whenever you need it.' That gave me a lot of respect for him, that he can say sorry to subordinates."

Looking back, Luseshelo had expected him to hold on to his car at any price and she had certainly not expected him to reveal even an ounce of vulnerability.

"But he showed me vulnerability by apologising and strength by apologising. It disarmed me. For me personally, most bosses bring out aggressiveness and defensiveness in me, but as soon as I realised that he was leading and not bossing, I became a good subordinate. I became defenceless. Because I said to myself, 'I am glad to work under him and to follow what he wants.'" (Podcast 28)

Honest

The combination of vulnerability and strength also ties into honesty. Helena says, "I have spent my life in courtrooms. It has developed an instinct in me. Witnesses are brought to the court, and before I stand up to cross examine them, I watch them very carefully. It is almost as if I can smell it in the courtroom when someone is going to tell the truth or when they will dissemble and deny or reach easily for a lie. I just know it.

"I think this is an important lesson. If you want to lead, you have to really be honest, and that means be vulnerable about your failures and be strong enough to learn from the times when you get things wrong. You have to be truthful when you feel fear or worry or when you have made the wrong call. People prefer that to overconfidence and the denial of any frailty." (Podcast 29)

Rouba agrees, but warns not to go too far: "It is very important to be vulnerable sometimes and to show that you are human, but don't forget that it's not always vulnerability people crave from you, but also strength. They look to you to make them believe in themselves and the future. And you have to remember that one strong word from you has a lot of power." (Podcast 10)

This combining of apparent opposing versions of you can sometimes become worrying to the people around you. Stephanie says it is why you must take the time to explain your apparent dual personality.

Stephanie herself is a good example. She is known as deeply kind and generous but, when she goes into a negotiation meeting, she is the toughest of negotiators and far from vulnerable. People around her seem surprised, even recoil when they see it, maybe even question her authenticity. But there is no inconsistency – she is a tough fighter for the things she cares deeply about.

This is why, if we are leading, we must explain ourselves. But even in this, we need to take care and ask ourselves all the time just how much is really helpful. It can tip into confession or even abdication too early. Hearing too much sometimes risks undermining people's strength to keep going.

Hopeful

Leila picks up on this theme: "More often than not, leading is about being strong and hopeful even when you are not feeling either. Granted, hope can vary in degrees. In situations like being in a refugee camp or tackling immensely challenging problems, your hope may never reach a hundred percent. However, leading involves acknowledging that there is always a kernel of hope. For if you become hopeless, apathetic to the cause and disengaged, those around you will follow suit. Even if hope is as low as two percent, there are moments when you must confront the severity of the situation, acknowledge formidable barriers and not overlook the lack of progress. Somehow you have to acknowledge vulnerability honestly but still strive to find that two percent of hope.

"During challenging times, it becomes vital to purposefully seek out these almost daily moments of hope. We should not solely focus on grand achievements but also find inspiration in the small things as they have the power to evoke awe and wonder. These small moments sustain hope, and they gradually emanate from others within the team too.

"To lead a fight, you cannot be the only person instilling optimism and hope on the long journey. It is important to foster an environment where others in the team also become champions of hope." (Podcast 36)

Harriet Adong reflects on the role of that smile in combining vulnerability and strength. When she gets a smile in return to hers, it tells her one of two things: "Sometimes it is a smile of pain, and sometimes it is a smile of anger. Neither is a real smile. When it is anger, it is, 'Why did this happen to me?' It is a smile of hate, regret, the feeling of not being able to put anything into words.

"And then there is a third a smile, of relief. It says, 'I am happy and happy to talk, because I have reached my moment of healing.'"

I ask Harriet about the original smile, the one that came from her, that elicited this smile in return.

"Mine is a smile that builds a culture of peace. That says, 'you can always connect with me. You should not be scared to reach out to me.' It creates the culture of connection. You have to hold onto that smile whatever you are going through. Most times, we do not want to bring out and speak of our vulnerability, but if we smile, we can connect with our vulnerability without words.

"It creates hope with those that I work with. If I don't give it, the survivors will lose their belief that something new can happen to them. You have to do this even if your heart is breaking inside. Even in your darkest time, as a leader, you have to create that smile, even when you do not feel like smiling.

"It is the smile of vulnerability, but the very fact that you can smile sends a message of strength. When things around seem very dark, you have to hold on and people have to see you holding on. They say, 'If she is not broken, if she is keeping positive, if she is still smiling even in the dark times, then I think we can still also hold on and give her the support she needs.'

"Sometimes, I tell them, I look strong but I am not that strong. Of course, they do not really hear me. Their looks say, 'Do not give up, do not give up.' I do have a sort of innocent belief that somehow we will make it work, that things will come good." (Podcast 18)

As you read Harriet's words, I have no doubt that you can feel her combining and living the two: vulnerability and strength. Olivia thinks it is almost a superhuman combination: "Leaders somehow have to muster this Energy, and when they do it creates a sort of magic. Even if it is just about being happy with their job and enthusiastic about what they are doing. Because the Energy transmits to the people around them if they are positive, optimistic and believe in what they are doing – or at least if they can hide the fears enough so that people have this feeling that it is magic, what we are doing together." (Podcast 42)

Dogged and Agile

The world is moving fast and as leaders we must move fast too. Yesterday might give insights on tomorrow, but only insights. Change is everywhere and its speed is compounding. So we have to be agile, but at the same time dogged enough to see change through. We have to flip in an instant from agile to dogged and then back again. To think again, try something new, stand under a shower as Rachel suggested; if it doesn't work today, it might work tomorrow. Have crazy ideas and test them. If they work, do them more. If they don't, stop, apologise and rethink. Follow our instincts. Say no sometimes. Question the data. Use all our human skills. And then pace ourselves; don't give up, keep going.

Dogged

Women seldom give up. It comes from our Essence. We decide to stop, for sure, to regroup, but keep moving.

Hatoon Alfassi, a scholar from Saudi Arabia who has led some brave campaigns, tells me that women have never been inclined to give up. Her inspiration in this is Hagar in the sacred texts: "Hagar was abandoned with her child in the middle of the desert without food or shelter. She did not sit still, even though she was sure that God was by her side. She did not just stay waiting for a table of food to come down from the sky. She was in Makka, which lay in the middle of nowhere. It was then a barren place, the heat was unbearable. And when the rain came down, which was rare, it flooded. Surviving with her little child in such an environment without breaking down was remarkable and required courage, determination and intelligence.

"She inspires me to keep on going. I try not to concentrate on the past or on what might bring me down. I think this is what she did. She went on building her life step by step. I reach the small dreams ahead of me and each day leads to another. I hope that I have some of her courage and resilience. I keep reflecting on her story. I think that there are always ways; the small lamp that shines from her story brightens my sad times.

"And I remind myself that she eventually became a free woman, head of her household, leader of her own town, a matriarch of a people and of a faith. "(Podcast 23)

Uma's grandmother gave her a poem: "In difficult times, you move forward in small steps. Do what you have to do, but little by little. Do not think about the future, or what may happen tomorrow. Wash the dishes. Remove the dust. Write a letter. Make a soup. You see? You are advancing step by step. Take a step and stop. Rest a little. Praise yourself. Take another step. Then another. You will not notice, but your steps will grow more and more. And the time will come when you can think about the future without crying."

What is the secret to such doggedness, I asked Julienne Lusenge, who fights on behalf of women in the Congo. Because there must be moments when even Julienne is tempted to give up. "To alter the lives for women in the Congo requires stamina. One day I decided, 'now I think that I need to stop because nothing's happened. No result, no success, no change and no change is coming.' I was tired, always tired, so I told my family I was stopping, and they said, 'we will see.'

"Soon after, I was in a car going from Kinshasa to Mombasa and I saw police being aggressive to a woman. I said 'stop' to the driver. I got outside and asked the woman what was happening. She explained that these police had arrested the husband. He had done nothing. Now the police were asking her for money. I asked the commander of the police to explain to me what the law was. I called the prosecutor in Benny and told him the story and he sorted the problem.

"I got back into the car and my husband said, 'you start again?' And I say, 'can you think that I can just leave this situation and go?' So my husband and I and the driver continued to Mombasa.

"In some of the fights I have fought, I get so caught up that I forget to go and spend enough time with the people I am fighting for. And if I don't, I sort of forget and I begin to get tired. When I meet them, it gives me Energy. They tell me their story. Some stories are very painful, but some make me happy." (Podcast 36)

Agile

Melissa Kwee tells me what she sees as the secret to her agility: divergent thinking or, as she puts it, zagging: "Leading is about being a prophet for an alternative future and hopefully a better one; one that is glimpsed but does not yet exist. Often it is very different – if not the opposite – from what we see around us.

"I was once trying to choose the right creative agency for some work. I walked into this one place, and they had a big poster in their entrance. It was of a whole bunch of white sheep walking in one direction and then one black sheep walking in the opposite direction. The caption read, 'when the world zigs

– you zag.' I chose that agency because there is not enough zagging going on. It is not rewarded enough or protected enough.

"You have to lead so that your team never stops zagging. There have to be proponents of the zag. They have to be almost appointed 'Apostles of the Zag' because it is too difficult if it is only one person's job. You need people to cover each other's backs. You almost need a network of zaggers disrupting each other at speed." (Podcast 69)

We know what Alia would recommend they do: play. "Because it allows us to build trust with one another, find fulfilment, develop our brains and deepen our creativity. To become more emotionally attuned to one another's needs and to step back and see problems from a new light, both of which are critical aspects of agile leading. We can shift the Energy in a room using play and even overturn a power differential and flip a hierarchy.

"Of course, one snag is that play is received differently in different cultural contexts. In some cultures, people are hesitant to participate in any activities where they could 'win' when playing with their managers. It takes time and work to cultivate a safe space where the hierarchy and power differential can be dismantled so that people can play freely and be agile without thought of workplace dynamics."

I love to play too, and know the eternal risk you run of being told to 'stop being silly' or 'grow up.' I remember being told off in a lift one day. My colleagues and I worked on the top floor. Other leaders in the building found it strange and perhaps embarrassing that we were always laughing – sometimes giggling – in the lift. This made us seem not serious, or perhaps it made our neighbours seem too serious. Who knows, but the word 'unprofessional' was used. I thought how sad that to appear professional you must be serious, maybe even boring. They asked me to request less laughing from my colleagues; I didn't. I couldn't have.

Alia laughed at this: "I was regularly given advice or reviews about the ways *they* felt I could become more 'effective.' To cut my hair, wear darker colours and boxier clothing, lower my voice, square my shoulders, limit my hand gestures, be less friendly and smile less. More serious and less playful." (Podcast 8)

Vivi suffers in the same way: "As a young theatre director, I soon realised that people think that leading is a serious affair. To lead you must be certain, strong and have a booming voice. I have chosen uncertain, fragile and playful. They all make me more creative and agile. But it is not always easy, especially because I need my backers to trust me.

"Yet how could I possibly be a creative theatre director without being childish? Because I am very childish. I have this personality and I have to work with it. And from it comes my ideas, my creativity, my agility and my ability to relate to others. I have a childish curiosity and if it is not satisfied, I am not interested and I stop doing anything. I still have my very little voice which does not sound like a theatre director's voice. But it is."

I asked Vivi if 'childish' was really the right word. "Maybe it is just being irresponsible. Like a child, I am always playing, and I do not think too much about consequences. For me the work in art is to be open to things we do not know and have the agility to respond to them." (Podcast 31)

Olivia Grobocopatel offers a suggestion from her frustrated next generation: allow rule breaking: "Encourage people to do things that are not in their job descriptions and do not let others block ideas even when they do not fit. Too often we see a job through a job description. The employer uses it to put boundaries up and the employee uses it as a defence mechanism.

"I think my generation will find a way to break down job descriptions, make them more open, even add in that one third of the time should be spent exploring new ideas. Let us build in agility to our systems and our cultures." (Podcast 42)

Roll on Olivia's generation.

Allyson Nicholson, who leads supply chain management at Moderna, says agility lies in curiosity and that it should be allowed to rule: "I like to be busy. It keeps me out of trouble. And I am very busy. I always have more things to accomplish in a day than I could ever do. I like a challenge. In a situation of a panic or chaos, you would want me with you. I realise that the objective of supply chain management is tidiness and the smooth flowing of water. But the stream never flows beautifully; there are rocks, there is chaos, there is dirt and pipes and rubbish in the way. It is not that I love the chaos, but I love sorting it. Constantly finding which way is up and which way is not. Like Alice in Wonderland, we need to decide what path is the right one.

"I think this is why supply chain management benefits from having women involved. We are more open to quickly pivot and find the potential solution that might require more collaboration between groups. And we do things that have not been done before because we are willing to speak up and propose the things that are not obvious at the first sight."

Aparna says that the agility breakthrough comes when you see that "life is cyclical and not linear. It is not just a direct climb up the stairs. You go up and come down and go around and pick yourself or someone else up. That is what agile leading is to me, simply being able and willing to adapt and drop everything for the people around you. You cannot stay fixed. There are times when you have to be more humble or less humble, more strong or less strong, more vulnerable or less vulnerable. I love the combining idea." (Podcast 51)

For me, the breakthrough came when I realised that you could move around and lead from different positions, from the middle, the front, the back and the sides. You move to where you are needed and are most effective. Perhaps most importantly, you can move to the front when it is needed, but only when it is needed and only for as long as it is needed. You have to be ready to do so at all times; whether it is to get things back on track, to move things forward faster, to take the flack, to remind people of the vision, to spot what is ahead, to generate Energy visibly from the front. But when you do go out front, it is with the clear intention of stepping back as soon as possible.

You must also be prepared to lead from the back, when you are hardly needed because things are flowing almost without you. Let us be clear that you are not back there because you are hiding; that is not leading. Nor are you back there because it is a collaboration; they require very active leading and sometimes even from right out in front.

Or you may need to lead from the sides, because you may need to deploy quickly but it is best to keep out of the way just for now.

Then there is leading from the middle, where you can see everyone, sense movement, taste the air, feel the vibrations, love everyone, delight in the triumphs, hold hands, giggle together, watch for shifts, smell the risks and spot the moments.

I think I have revealed my favourite place to be. I know that I will always find Paula Marra there too, in the middle where "you feel that sparkle that you cannot describe. Ideas are everywhere with no idea who from." (Podcast 14)

But, however much I love the middle, I will pivot to the front, the back and the sides with agility and without a moment's hesitation, moving positions doggedly, inching forwards as we go. I think agile and dogged are starting to merge, though I am not sure. Too dogged and you remain suboptimal, too agile and you may run out of steam.

Inclusive and Boundaries

Every one of our seven pieces of Essence, from motherness to education, formed the roots of a common element: inclusive. The word dominates. But even it has another element to combine with, and strangely one which appears quite incongruous: boundaries.

Inclusive

I asked Selvie to start us off by reminding us of what it feels like to be included. Selvie has been on the receiving end of non-inclusive leading, when she felt barely tolerated: "The leader sent a message: 'I care about myself and you are under me, therefore you need to do the things that I ask you to do. If you do not deliver, then you fail. If you fail to deliver something, then I am here to remind you that you did not do what you should for our team.' Most of the time I had no precise idea on what 'the things' even were."

And she has also experienced the opposite, which she encountered when she moved jobs and got a new boss: "I suddenly felt like my leader cared about me as a person. What surprised me the most was realising that my opinion was valued, even though I might not know much. The love and the forgiveness took me unawares too. When I committed a mistake, I was forgiven for committing it and even encouraged to take a look at why it happened. I felt like we were on the same team, in the same boat. There was alignment of interests. It was very nurturing.

"I smile when I think about how different it is now. When I am asked to do work, I want to finish it because I really want my team to do well. In the past I might have said, 'I need to finish this work because if I do not complete it my boss will give me a very bad review.' Now, leading is something that motivates me internally. I am part of it, and it makes me want to stay." (Podcast 7)

There are so many more grim daily accounts of deep prejudice and absence of inclusivity, of cultures in which Selvie would not have even got an interview for either of the roles she describes. Accounts of injustice and bigotry, of missed opportunities and squandered talent, of suboptimal, homogenous teams delivering reliable group think, of people leading who do not put inclusivity as a priority or who make sure that it absolutely isn't. And even if inclusivity is introduced into the systems, diverse talent is so often then met by leaders who are hostile, ignorant, careless or self-centred.

We know that the prize for inclusive leading is people such as Selvie describing her job with such commitment. There is, however, a long way to go to get to the prize. Martyna says it is not easy even with the will to be inclusive because so many people have become accustomed to the opposite: "In many parts of the world, it is not what people have been programmed for. As a conductor you know that to produce a beautiful piece of music you need the intellectual and emotional engagement from all the players, but you cannot find a way to do it. You have to break through this barrier that has been put up in some cultures where people have no experience of inclusivity. The barrier has written on it, 'I am untouched. I will do something with my hands, but you cannot have my head or my heart.' People have switched off; their bodies are still doing the task, but their hearts and minds are not there. They are empty.

"I have seen this in many countries. I call them feudal countries because that is the mentality. People do not involve themselves intellectually or emotionally because freedom has not been given to them. They have just had to obey. If they do not agree with the oppressor, withdrawing their emotions and intellect is their only way of showing this. The rest of it they do with the hands. Their heads and hearts disapprove; they keep them to themselves.

"This mentality is rooted deep. So when you lead, you must overcome it. Break in with a new light, a new stream of hope. Somehow you have to instil that you as the person leading are not the enemy. This is not easy. For centuries, people have not felt equal because the leader has been the oppressor.

"This feudal mentality exists everywhere – not just in orchestras and not just in my part of the world. It is the challenge of leading, not to be the enemy and to persuade people to bring their whole selves to the task." (Podcast 45)

For such a breakthrough on inclusive leading to happen, Catherine and Terri suggest that two myths about inclusivity need busting: the meritocracy myth and the melting pot myth.

First the meritocracy myth, which makes Catherine despair: "In many organisations, many ambitious people have a stake in believing in it. The trouble is that it is not a meritocracy, there is no level playing field and, in fact, it is a very uneven playing field.

"This myth does so much damage. Too many people have fallen for it. The result is that women think that if they don't succeed at something, it is their individual fault. And men see very few women around and conclude that women must not be good enough to get in.

"Challenging the myth gives you a hard time because the people that have made it in the meritocracy obviously believe in it; they think the system works. So if you start challenging it, you are challenging their value and that is not going to get you very far in climbing the ladder.

"I think, in order to really make a difference, you have to not care about climbing the ladder, and it is only with privilege that you can do this. If you don't need the job then you can challenge, but if you really need it, it is really hard to do any challenging. I think this is more true the more you do not fit the mould. In effect, the more you are a marginalized group the harder it is to challenge, and the more you are part of the majority group the easier it is.

"So the myth continues and, in my world, women keep on being told they have to promote themselves to get on in this glorious meritocracy. Basically, 'fit in, play the game and you will rise.' But you won't. It's a myth." (Podcast 33)

The second, the myth of what Terri calls the "quote-unquote melting pot", causes her to despair too: "What it actually does is distil away all that is uniquely 'you.' Women can get caught up in this whole myth.

"When I think of the relationships that I have with women in the United States – White Hispanic, Asian, African-American – we are each from our own places in American society, trying to carve out not only our identities but how we are moving through time and space and how we even connect with one another. We do not want to play games as to whose oppression is the worst or most restrictive. One thing we have in common is that our society has made us feel deficient and devalued because we are not white. It applies to every woman of colour in the US by nature of our skin colour, hair texture, sometimes our accent and what kind of dress we choose to wear, because race and class intersect in the US.

"We just have to start thinking about what really matters, how we value humanity and even how we value differences of opinion. Difference simply cannot be made deficient, because that is at the heart of racism and it is a stain that the US still needs to name, own, understand and work to repair.

"The melting pot mentality does not help. How I even move in the US as a Black woman is very different to my college colleagues. Some of my white female colleagues have an advantage in how they move through the world simply because of the American construct that allows white women to assume a place of supremacy. I have to assimilate, to give up everything that makes me who I am in order to be accepted as American. There is a certain form of almost whiteness that I must clothe myself in. There are certain kinds of music I should listen to so that I am seen as 'cultured.' But I will not 'melt,' whether it is pretending to like opera so as to fit in with people in power or pretending I do not like opera (which I do) to fit in with women of colour.

"If only we could get beyond this notion that somehow women of colour are deficient and 'not your sisters,' only then could we unite and advocate for a healthier society for us all. But for now, the spectre of racism that stains and plagues us continues even to the point where it divides women who should be natural allies."

After speaking to Catherine and Terri, I offer a third myth. I spent a year writing a book on CQ, or cultural intelligence. There is too much emphasis on IQ – helpful but only first base – and on EQ – important but often limited to 'leading people like me' – and I have become convinced that we need more emphasis on CQ – or 'leading people not like me' – if we are ever to reach inclusivity. I spoke to people from different generations, geographies, sectors, specialisms, backgrounds and beliefs as I wrote the book. Almost everyone I spoke to thought that CQ began with 'walking in other people's shoes.' They spoke about seeing difference differently and some talked of 'cracking other cultures.' It had become formulaic. One woman I met had been on a course to understand Chinese culture before taking on a big new role; she had been told all about how to hand over a business card in China, holding it out with both hands and bowing over it. Unfortunately, the first person she met in China had also been on a course to understand Western culture; she had been told that it was crucial to establish eye contact from the start with Westerners. When they met, they almost knocked each other out.

I don't mean to ridicule with this story, and such courses are without doubt helpful, but to really develop CQ you have to overcome this myth that you must focus on other cultures when in fact it is your own culture that needs the focus, so that you see when your own culture helps you to understand others and when it does the very opposite. It gives you blind spots which you have to address if you want to be inclusive as you lead.

Ayesha agrees wholeheartedly, and says it is a very long and tough journey: "I have been steeped in that scholarly work around inclusivity for years, but I repeatedly find myself harsh towards none other than myself and my own culture. In being receptive and curious about the 'other' culture that I am learning from, I lose sight of my own. I fall victim to conscious and unconscious biases in my own self, my own heritage, my cultural nuances and the impact of internalised colonialism and patriarchy on me. I urge every woman who leads to go through a journey of self-reflection and to, as much as possible, courageously confront our own biases about and towards ourselves."

Ayesha then goes a step further: "We have to be inclusive to ourselves before we can hope to be inclusive to others." This resonates with Ana Luz: "I have come to see my multi-cultural identity as rich and full of complementary dimensions. Now I embrace its contradictions, but it was not always this way and it is not always easy. I embrace my multi-dimensional identity now. I acknowledge it, own it and make it explicit."

In acknowledging, we also recognise that it will come with blind spots too. Even if we perceive ourselves as inclusive, there will be people whom we come across less and people who confuse us more, and we will not always meet our aspiration to be inclusive. There will be people whom we openly or subtly benchmark against ourselves, judging them as quicker or slower, more or less fun, more or less intelligent, more or less fair-skinned, even more or less inclusive than me, with 'Me' too easily becoming the benchmark.

Inclusivity requires us to break away from this way of thinking. Having firmly decided that we are not the benchmark against which to judge others as lesser or more. It was one of my proudest days when Terri, whom I admire so very much as a Black woman in the US taking vast challenges head-on, adopted as hers the expression, "I am not the benchmark."

But why, then, does inclusivity need combining, and how could boundaries possibly be the element it needs to be combined with?

Boundaries

Sometimes inclusive is seen as holding an open space with no boundaries – everyone feels included and able to fill the space as they wish. It makes sense in some ways, and it is truly important that the space is open but not that it has no boundaries.

Sometimes, in leading, we beautifully include all, and then in the name of inclusivity let all do anything. We justify a lack of boundaries in the name of inclusivity. I hand over to Uthara and Alia to explain.

Uthara: "I did finally realise that I was expecting everybody to be just like me. So how I lead had become almost as if I was leading myself.

"I believed in complete freedom being given because I was committed to 'leading inclusively and democratically.' I would sit everybody down and decisions would never be made because we would keep going round and round.

"I finally got it. A blank sheet of paper to draw whatever you want is not what everybody likes. Many want structure, to be led. It was a like slap in the face." (Podcast 64)

Alia picks up from this point: "Providing limitless space to teams can actually be problematic and far from empowering or inclusive. It can even be harmful. Leading is about offering people a space where they feel safe, which means providing clarity on the parameters. Only then do people feel empowered and able to do great work. I've found that unlimited space for creativity can be paralysing."

I asked Alia if she had always seen it this way. "A hundred percent I did not. I used to think that the fewer the boundaries, the more liberating it would be. Now I see a container as deeply liberating. For me to thrive, I need to know boundaries for my own sense of safety, structure, direction. It's helpful to know the mission, what's in scope and out of scope. This can actually be generative and give me space to run with clarity. For me, this is deeply liberating. It allows us to have much more productive conversations, and at times to push back. If the boundary is set in the wrong place that is fine, we can review it, but having boundaries allows us to have a much more fruitful conversation and collectively go further together.

"The truth is that it took me a while to learn this. Not till my mid-thirties. I think my twenties was probably spent in thinking that the emptier the space, the better it was. I deliberately set out to destroy boundaries. Now I have this concept of leading being about creating a vessel, and the vessel to me now helps create freedom and liberation.

"I look for boundaries in the leaders who lead me now. Yes, I want a say in setting those boundaries, but I want to know where we are going and what our constraints are. The boundaries have to be wide enough, and I must be allowed to question them. But they must be there."

Thoughtful and Risky

These two are switchers. You move from one to the other when you know the moment is right. As you go, you need to watch out for the strong forces that push you away from both of them: from risky, because the price women pay for risks and mistakes is very high, and from thoughtful, because the speed of change all around us pushes us to think that thoughtfulness is not an option. Yet both are crucial – both feed each other, and avoiding either of them does not work. Nor, of course, does getting stuck in one or the other. If you do, people either get tired of waiting for your thoughtful decisions or fearful of what risk you are going to drag them into next.

Thoughtful

Folawe is clear: "At times, you have to resist the sense of urgency and the instinct of fight or flight. The prevailing systems and culture will always push you to rush, to deliver, to action and to keep going. Make sure you push back." (Podcast 10)

I remember being sent away in the early days at Common Purpose, by the chair of the board, spitting with anger, to produce a growth plan. He had over 10,000 staff in his organisation, so a vast fleet of people to delegate to. I had ten at the time, and a vast list of actions to be done by the end of the week. I was outraged by his blindness. But it didn't take me long to realise what a fool I was. I was ignoring data, missing trends, blissfully ignorant of dependencies and living on a diet of risk. Years on, I still get embarrassed when people remark on my foresight in investing very early on in IT and remote working. It was all because of that chair. He forced me to take a step back, to get thoughtful as well as risky.

Latanya says she sees it over and over again: "People just go from challenge to challenge, from fight to fight, neither recognising success nor being strategic." (Podcast 29)

Melissa Berman says thoughtful moments sometimes lead you to call stop, "because you see that you will not get the success you sought. Or because this is the moment to step out so that a new person can take over leading. Or because the game has changed, and it needs even more of a rethink. Or because the vision has shifted, and it is no longer you.

"Or even because your own life has changed, and you cannot give it what it needs. This final one is too often recognised at the last moment when you realise that nobody can go on forever. Burnout is real. You stay too long and then you start to feel shut out. Of course you must lead for the long game, but you have to be astute about when to either step back or eventually step out." (Podcast 30)

Risky

As thoughtful as we may want to be, risks are required, moments need to be seized, decisions need making even when we don't have the complete data or full picture. Our Essence tells us to take those risks as our ancestors did, as nature does, as mothers do, as our education demands of us, and despite the trauma we may feel. And we know that in some situations the riskiest thing we could possibly do would be to do nothing and avoid taking a risk at all.

Nichole and Hila say there is no alternative as we look to the future.

Nichole Bradford, a professor at Stamford who anticipates huge shifts ahead, is clear: "Leading will require us to keep going when everything around us is spinning and changing so fast. However fast you think things have changed, they are about to speed up dramatically and the impact will be compounding. It will be in five major areas: data, materials, energy, food and transportation. And Artificial Intelligence is coming to all five to take the change curves and put grease on them.

"An example of this is that until about five years ago, when AI was first getting applied to material science, all of mankind had come up with maybe six to seven new materials each year. This has now gone to 36,000 per year. This is happening in all different areas, and they are triggering each other so that the speed of change is compounded." (Podcast 39)

Hila is of a generation that can see what is coming and knows the risk-taking and bravery it is going to require. There is an urgency for leaders to act, bravely act. Her generation is almost unique in human history because the problems it faces have a limited deadline to fix. As she says, "this will definitely define how we lead. I think my generation has witnessed a lot of avoidance and faffing about and I am not sure how this will play out when people my age get to those positions of power. We will not have the time to avoid the issues and we also know that avoidance does not work. I think that as a generation, we are very good at seeing through the smoke and mirrors and getting to the root of the problem and realising that what we need right now is action. We do not need talk. We need brave action." (Podcast 16)

If this level of risk is demanded of us ahead, we will need to face head-on the problem that the price of mistakes for women is very high. If our actions immediately yield results, we are judged effective at leading. If results are not immediately forthcoming, we are judged for being a woman. There is little safety net, if there is one at all. And when a woman anticipates the challenges, she is often portrayed as emotional or even unprofessional.

The danger is that we become less inclined to take risks and give the impression that we need protecting. Lailamah Khan, a young student in Pakistan, resents this: "There is this stigma here that girls are unsafe, weak and vulnerable. We cannot be left alone. We cannot take care of ourselves. That may be true for some girls, but there are a lot of women out there who are perfectly strong and perfectly capable of taking care of themselves. I know some of them. And I like to think I am one of them." (Podcast 21)

The unequal risk barometer makes many of us angry, but when we express this, we are usually dismissed on the basis that anger is one of those emotions to be avoided when leading. We are told that it is the first step towards losing the argument.

As an aside, I want Hila, Helena, Latanya, Hinemoa and Folawe to explain the disdain they feel these comments deserve.

First Hila: "I think that anger is extremely important. It has always been a very important tool for successful movements, even the driving force." (Podcast 16)

Then Helena: "Of course you get angry and feel let down. My own government did nothing to help the women jurists we got out of Afghanistan last year. In fact, they got in the way. I used to stop myself from displaying anger. I would hold myself back. I still occasionally do. But now I have learned to be much more directional about how I place my anger. At the right time it can prompt a useful response. I do know that I express it in a way that people find it hard to hear, but I think that they have to hear it." (Podcast 29)

Over to Latanya: "Anger is an emotion that can drive a lot of change, generate a lot of Energy. I think if you are not angry, then you are probably in the wrong game. If it does not make you angry, it probably will not make you do anything much. Anger fuels people. It's curious watching women lead. They often become hard as nails with people who get in their way, and then they are deeply loving and soft when they care for their colleagues." (Podcast 29)

And then Hinemoa: "We need to express our anger about some of the stuff that is going on. Frankly we have all been conditioned to a greater or lesser degree to be 'nice' about things. To always look for some kind of middle ground. That is a skill, but that is not the only skill." (Podcast 1)

So anger is not to be dismissed, but we must not let it drive the risks we take. We are too thoughtful to let that happen.

And the same can be said for fear. Latanya has read many of the writings of modern-day women who have been murdered for their actions or beliefs: "I don't believe that they were fearless. I think that is not the word. Many of them knew that they were being followed and they were being openly threatened, but that fear did not immobilise them. They kept going. It did not stop them. To be fearless is one thing, but they were with fear." (Podcast 29)

Camila Pontual, who works on the protection of the Amazon in Brasil, described her friends in the same way: "They decided to combine their inauguration events as government ministers. To do it alongside each other, to showcase union. It was the day after the terror attack on the Brasilian parliament. They were in the same building, the same rooms. The cleaners had cleared them up and repaired overnight.

"Both of them avoided the usual boring speeches. Instead they spoke from their hearts. They were orators. People listened to every word. Some were sobbing because it was such a beautiful moment. And they ended up with music. It was an indigenous traditional ceremony there in the middle of that palace. The beautiful lyrics were based on the fight of many Black women who have been silenced for centuries in Brasil."

I asked Camila if she thought that her friends were terrified inside, as they did what leaders must sometimes do: hide their fears and use symbolism to persuade people to lift above their own fears. Camila answered, "courage is not ignoring the fear, but it is doing it regardless. Of saying 'look where we are. We feel imposter syndrome but we are in a good place, a place that generations of women have never been allowed into. We are here together.'" (Podcast 44)

There are just so many amazing women who risk it all and lead. Their stories are endlessly inspiring and, if you are like me, they are also daunting. I think of Stella's words: "I am a vulnerable Black woman." I hope Stella will forgive me for editing them so that I can use them too: "I am a vulnerable woman."

We all have our doubts as we take our risks. Even the author of the *Rebel Girl* books does. Francesca: "When I started *Rebel Girls*, what kept me going was this idea that I could not fail. People were looking up at me as the first Italian female founder that was accepted in an incubator in Silicon Valley. On one side, this was a positive feeling that gave me the fuel to keep going not just for myself but also for other people. But on the other side, it made me convince myself that if I failed it would be because I was bad at leading and that I did not deserve any of the opportunities that I had got.

"As female leaders we want to be perfect. We want everybody to like us. We want everybody to say that we are great at leading. But in reality, leading is establishing priorities, getting people out of their comfort zones, then enabling them to do the work that they would not do if you were not there. It is often uncomfortable and sometimes we do not know exactly how uncomfortable it can get before it becomes really toxic. We make all sorts of mistakes, have to be incredibly vigilant, accept that we know more or less what we know. Take time out to rethink and know more. We try to have a sense of what we are doing and what its impact will be. We have to take risks and allow ourselves to make mistakes all the time."

Last word to Susan Whitehead, for many years a leader at MIT. She reflected on how long it had taken her to get to this point in her career: "I silenced myself and I kept on silencing myself. I wasn't fearless. I wonder whether many of us are the same. Are we silencing ourselves or are other people silencing us? What has become very clear to me is that you can't do anything of meaning in this world unless you are conscious of what you are fearful of. You have to 'go to the mouth of the dragon' with your fears if you want to live a full-bodied life. Name your fears, whatever they are – small or large – even if they seem foolish or embarrassing, and live with them. Otherwise those things that you're afraid of will rule you, and you will not take the risks you know you should take."

Risk-taking is required, combined with thoughtfulness. And let's not pretend; they are often propelled by anger, and they carry fear.

You now have our eight combines. Some are switchers, some are overlappers. I am sure that all seven must resonate with you to some degree, but you are sure to have some of your own to add. In my Elements for combining, I would add serious and fun. Mona tells me she would add into hers risk and fear.

Journal

Solo

Go back to your map and keep filling in the Elements circle. As you add the combines, maybe think about which of the two you tend to revert to. The size of the combine circles can indicate this.

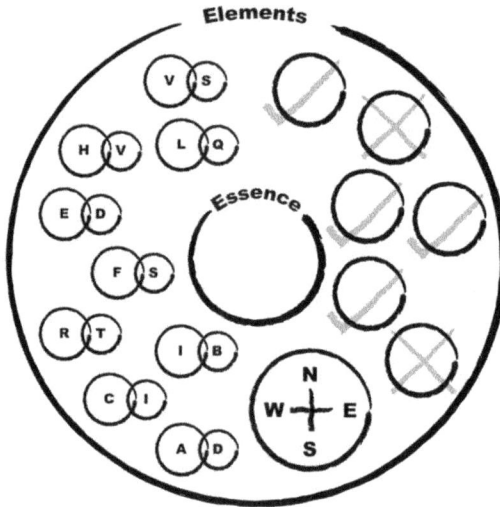

Figure 9: The combines

Now go a step further. Draw a horizontal line across a page in your journal. Add one line for each of the combines. At each end, put one of the two Elements that need combining. Treat each line as a sliding scale. Now put a green dot where you are on the sliding scale now. Find another coloured dot and place it where you think you want to be on the sliding scale in six months' time. And then choose another colour and do the same for where you think it might have been in the past.

Talk to one of the leaders on your list about the combines you find most challenging. How do they get the combining right?

In a group

It's about time for the group to do some play. Here are two suggestions:

Write some group poems:

Every group member completes the following sentence at the top of a page. It starts with:

"She used to think leading was about..."

Once done, each member folds the page over so that what she has written is not visible and hands it on to another member of the group.

Each member will now have received a folded piece of paper from another member. Now, without reading the sentence above, complete the following next sentence at the top of the folded page that you have been given. It starts with:

"Then she started to lead by..."

Once done, each member folds it over so that what she has written is not visible either (so there are now two folds) and hands it on to another member of the group.

Each member will now have received a piece of paper from another member with two invisible sentences on it. Now each member completes the final sentence:

"And as a result..."

Last step now. Hand it on again. Each member unfolds the page they have been handed and reads it out to the whole group.

Create a mask:

Each member creates a mask. The front of the mask should illustrate the kind of leader you want to be. On the reverse, illustrate what is holding you back from being the kind of leader you want to be. You can create a beautiful, elegant mask or you can use a paper plate and draw on it quickly.

Explain your mask to others in the group and ask them about their mask.

Expression

We move now to the outer circle and to how Essence and Elements play out in how you lead. Much of your Expedition up to now has taken you inwards; now look more outwards and get practical. Talk to women you admire, whom you have observed chairing meetings, or doing talks, or driving negotiations, or surviving upheavals, all doing the hard work involved in leading and doing it in a way that reflects their Essence. Talk to them and ask the 'who, what, when, where, how' questions. The feet on the ground questions. Capture all the tips you know will work for you or that you want to try out for yourself.

I have met countless women on the First Expedition and through the weekly podcast episodes. This section captures the highlights from some of those conversations. I offer them as illustrations of the discussions you might have and of the practical tips you are after so that you can build up your Expression circle.

Keep to precise questions. It's those tips you are after. For example, I have always struggled when chairing a meeting to find a way to close people down when they are banging on. My Essence has in it, amongst other things, mother-ness. And this shows up in my Elements in many ways; one of them is kindness. So how do I express this in meetings when I know we have to move on? How do you do it without crushing people but equally without implying that you agree with them? I saw someone do this well, and I have stolen their technique. They interject, "that is very helpful" just at the right moment when the person is about to draw breath again. It works, and now I use it a lot. I shall be very nervous about using it on the podcast now! This is an example of the granularity of tips you are after. This one works for me and it connects back to my Essence.

Here are eight extracts from interviews rich in tips:

Leading Performance

Monica Medina has led schools in multiple countries across her career and knows a great deal about leading those difficult conversations about performance, the ones we all have a tendency to put off. I asked Monica how to make them go as well as possible. She made a list of what not to do.

Babble

"I grew up in a home where English was not the only language. I consider Portuguese to be my first language. I find it is helpful for me, as a second language learner, to plan what I am going to say. Sometimes it takes just a couple of minutes to capture some key points. Other times I actually have notes in front of me. If it is a really tricky meeting, I go to one of the assistant principals and he always asks me, 'are you in the zone?' If my answer is no, we rehearse carefully. The more prepared I am, the more succinct and clear I am. I am also always ready to give examples of what the expectation is, how to move forward, how I am going to help the person to get to a better place.

"I am a talker, you know. I can talk and talk. So I really have to be sure that I go into the meetings ready to focus on what is important. So absolutely no babbling."

Confess

"No confessing. I mean, honestly. People do not come to my office to hear my problems. So no expressions such as 'this is really hard, but it is even harder for me.' Leave all your own issues at the door.

"You just want to stick to very simple messages. Like, 'I hear you' or 'I am sorry that you feel that way, but this is how it needs to be.' Sometimes, 'let us take a break. Let us talk again tomorrow'. This gives you and the other person the opportunity to start a conversation fresh. I think it is a really healthy approach. Especially at those times when you have not slept the night before or you are dealing with personal issues or other professional issues at the school, and you are not at your best. Just say, 'I hear you. You hear me. Let us meet again tomorrow and see if we can move forward.'"

Fast forward

"This is pretty heavy stuff you are discussing. You are talking about someone's performance. If you rush, you are saying, 'this really is not important. You as a person are not very important to me.' I think that is a bad message. You have to send a message that you are supporting them in whatever shift they need to make."

Collapse

"Prepare yourself mentally so that as soon as the meeting gets tough, as soon there is an ounce of resistance, you don't change or, worse, collapse your position.

"I remember being in an open faculty meeting when a couple of teachers told the principal, with me seated there, that they did not like me, they did not want me there as the assistant principal and they were not going to do what I said, whatever I told them to.

"I knew moving forward that I was perceived as unimportant, ineffective, ignorant, was no added value to the school. As a result, initially I found myself backing down on just about everything, but I quickly learned that what I then said was deemed even more unimportant. I was seen as uncommitted because even I did not believe what I was saying. Everything they thought about me was just illustrated by my behaviour.

"If, in your meeting, you can feel yourself starting to give in, then take a break. Because if you do cave, let me tell you that person will tell everybody who will listen the moment they leave the meeting, 'I told her, she pushed me hard, but I told her, she tried to get me to do x, y and z, but I told her.' And that message will travel through your school like wildfire."

Wing it

"You have to prepare. To ask yourself if the issue is skills or will. If it's skills, then the solution is straightforward because it is a matter of filling the skills gap, of providing opportunities to practice in a safe environment, of giving them short term wins and giving regular feedback.

"If it is about will, it will need unpacking. There are times, not often, when the person raises a good point. You listen to their thinking, and you say, 'I really want to think about what you just said. Can we talk again tomorrow?' Because maybe they are right.

"And there are other times when the person says, 'I have been successful as a teacher. My parents really love me. My kids love me. I am popular. Now you want me to risk all this to do as you want?' There are times when you have to face the fact that this teacher is not going to change. They are either unwilling or unable to shift their practice. And that is the hardest conversation of all. You will support, but you need to be firm that this is what you expect, in this timeline. And there are no more questions. If it goes this way, you have to be one hundred percent certain that this is what you need to do; there is no turning back.

"Using this process has helped me to not lose a lot of sleep, because by the time I have got to the crunch point, I have felt that I had done everything I could to support.

"So no babbling, confessing, fast forwarding or collapsing. And be prepared. But all this does not make it easy. It doesn't mean that I didn't feel bad after each meeting, that I did not have a lot of empathy for the teacher. However, my bottom line is: 'I have two sons. Is that a classroom I would put my own child in?' If the answer is no, then I was really doing a disservice to the school and to the students by not being firm and clear. Let's face it, that is the job when you are leading. You are the one who is responsible, in the end, for the performance of your school and students." (Podcast 34)

Monica's advice covers pages and pages in my journal, mostly with lists of my mistakes alongside it. Sometimes because I did everything I could to avoid having these conversations because I did not want to upset people, or because I had convinced myself that it was all my fault and that I was being unreasonable, but most of the time it was me not having the courage of my convictions. And sometimes it was because I did the opposite; I jumped in too quickly to a conversation because it had been weighing heavily on me and I wanted to get through it. Inevitably, I started ill prepared and ended in a mess.

I keep that old saying 'mortgaging the future' firmly in my mind, knowing that if I ignore difficult conversations, things just get worse and worse and then boil over. Because problems don't go away, and if I don't deal with them I also risk losing a great performer in the team because they get fed up with carrying the extra weight.

Leading Teams

Kelly McCallum's experience comes from leading a major sports team, something I have never done. This made Kelly the person for me to talk to about teams. She gave me one thing to recognise, two things to do and two things never to do. She began with the 10,000 hours concept, a new one for me.

10,000 hours

"As women, we were born into relationship building. It is how we are socially constructed. There is a saying in sport that 10,000 hours of practice makes a person an expert in a skill. As women, I guess we have reached those 10,000 hours of relationship skills by the time we are eight years old. So we have that edge because for whatever reason we have had lots of practice at relationships. We have done our 10,000 hours.

"If relationships are ingrained in women, they are also ingrained in leading. Women have this by just being women, and it is about time we recognised our edge. I don't think we often put our hand up going into interviews or boardrooms and say, 'I have 10,000 hours of skills in relationship practice.' We don't give ourselves enough credit for this."

People, people, people

"There is a saying: 'it's about people, it's about people, and it's about people.' Team sports give us relationship practice over and over again. My priority as the captain every time is to form connections with every single player on that field in some way that shows them that I care.

"For example, I remember playing the Singapore National Team. One of my team made that game hers; she must have scored about eight tries. She was absolutely awesome and she knew it. When later, we went to play for Canada. We had a general call out and I just looked at her and just said, 'Singapore.' She gave me the nod and a smile. It was a special connection that me and her shared and it was really important."

Communicating

"Team sports are an experience of uncertainty over and over again. We can prepare as much as we want, but we cannot predict the outcome because there are just so many complex things that can happen in a game. Either side can be winning at any time.

"So communication in the moment, which is clear and heard by the team, is paramount. What I mean by heard is that there is recognition by everyone that we are still on the same page and moving forward to our vision. That nod or that eye contact is really important to understand that we are all in this together. When you communicate well, you bring down the uncertainty. You control those negative emotions. It feels good. There is connection and synergy within the team. You know that uncertainty will fail to break those connections.

"I remember a game when we only had four minutes to try to win. A little bit of synergy was feeling broken, the negative emotions were coming in, the uncertainty was flooding in about winning or losing. I was full on with mini bits of communication, getting to every single person on that field very, very quickly. A word, an eye contact, a small gesture individual to each player. It's quick, sometimes it's just a little wave.

"One of my teammates used to say that when she saw me flick my ponytail at her, she knew that I was okay and that we were still connected. People say there is no time for this, but there is always time, always a moment. And that is what I love about leading. There is always a moment that you can connect. Flick your ponytail.

"And when you do, remember it is also about keeping your head up. Especially when a mistake has happened. Head up, chest up, look forward whenever those negative emotions start to come on."

No overthinking

"Never, ever overthink. It is the number one of the most important things I have learnt in leading sport teams. If you overthink, they will score while you are thinking. Of course, before the game you think a lot, but during the game you need to think in the moment. Leaders must react quickly to turn a negative into a positive. Doing so will define your leading. Think before and think after but not in the middle of the game.

"Often, it is about reframing very quickly. I remember when we were playing the USA and the referee was penalising us all the time. After the third penalty, I brought the team in. I said, 'we are going to create a situation where we take the referee out,' It was my decision."

I jumped in here with Kelly. So far, the sports examples had made a lot of sense, but 'take the referee out' was a new one. Kelly explained: "The referee was controlling our emotions, so I had to bring the control back to me. We changed our game; we stopped going in to contest the referee's decisions and that took the referee's controlling factor out of it. Players don't like doing this, so it was hard, but it worked.

"Leading does involve some very hard decisions. We mustn't avoid them. The decision I took that day was not easy or at all popular, because it was not how the team wanted to play. But as much as I believe in collective leadership, this decision was mine."

Humiliating

"Don't humiliate anyone in your team. If someone has made a mistake, do not humiliate them by amplifying it to the whole team. You can crush a person in a second if you do, and that is not what you need. It destroys the connections, the synergy, right across the whole team and there is no easy coming back from it.

"If you do ever get in that situation, because we do sometimes, it will just be a long process of lots of conversations to build the trust again. You have to restart from the beginning. So the best way is to not get into that situation." (Podcast 19)

The sense of Energy and pace talking to Kelly was inspiring and empowering, too. When we had finished speaking, I immediately regretted not asking her for advice on how to put a team together. Martyna's orchestra is so carefully chosen. I suspect Kelly's team is too. What does she look for? How does she balance the skills? What characters, temperaments, cultures, attitudes does she look for? How does she cover the blind spots? I will ask Kelly next time and I promise a podcast episode with her replies.

In the meantime, I have adopted many of Kelly's tips, especially the small rituals you need to establish with each individual member of your team. It's a powerful concept. I think that I have often done it subconsciously but not deliberately and consistently and with every single member of a team. Now I will.

Leading Trust

You will have probably picked up my obsession with midwives by now. I have become fascinated by how lightly they choose to lead in a labour room and how hard it is for them to lead outside the labour room. So I turn to Harriet Nayiga in Uganda about the first and then Sylvia Hamata in Namibia about the second.

Trust others

Harriet: "It is very tempting to be the health professional in the room, the one with all the knowledge, to assume things before they happen, to know better than the women who are giving birth, to quickly forget that everybody is unique. But you can't go this way. When you walk into the labour room, you have to make sure that every assumption, any knowledge you think you have, you drop it. You need to remove yourself from that high position of power that you think you have.

"The real meaning of midwife is 'to be with a woman.' We forget this and yet most of the time women do not need us because the body is designed to deliver babies. The midwife is just there to jump in if there are complications, to make good decisions only because the woman will be vulnerable and cannot do things on her own.

"I try to ensure to drop every form of power that I think I have. To strip myself of power and ensure that I am working with the woman. To listen to her, to trust her instincts about her own body, to be empathetic with her. And when I do this, and she sees me doing this, I find that the woman responds by trusting me back. She tells me things and does not keep things from me. She trusts me more because she sees me listening and then acting on her words as a result. She knows that even if I am not able to do something, I will explain to her why.

"I can think of many times when the woman has been right and by building the trust between us, we have prevented something disastrous happening. She would say, 'I am not comfortable' and I would reply, 'what do you mean you are not comfortable?' And then she would tell me the problem, and I would check and say, 'Are you sure? I have checked and I do not see anything' and she would ask me to check again, and I would go back and realise that 'oh no, we need to do something about it now.'" (Podcast 28)

To me, this was a beautiful story of leading. These are learning points that go way beyond midwifery. You take on a role, you are given training, you get a job title and with it, power, and then if you are Harriet you choose to give it all away. Because then the person you are leading will trust you and work with you. Then, because most of the time you are not needed and it's best for you to be out of the way, you step back until you are really needed, and then you take action decisively and quickly and colleagues will allow you to do so because you have built up trust. If the word midwife means 'to be with a woman,' maybe our new definition of the word 'leading' should be 'to be with people.'

Trust yourself

Sylvia: "It is suffocating the moment you walk out of the labour room. You have no voice. There is so much that you see and so much that needs to be said but it continues to go on without your voice. You may want to say something, but nobody would listen to you. It is like you open your mouth and nothing comes out. There isn't anybody to listen to you.

"Soon you start to doubt yourself, to no longer trust yourself. You think that the real reason why nobody is listening to you is that what you say doesn't mean anything. You think maybe you are not smart enough, simply not good enough. Or maybe you are just wrong. And so you stay away, you pull back into that little corner where you feel it's safer. You think that if you do not say anything, you won't get criticised. And you become scared of what people would say if you did speak out.

"You remain this person who doubts herself, wondering if you belong. Then one day you just boil over. Everything comes out at once. That is the day when everybody says you are emotional and irrational because you do not make much sense as you try to put everything together. Someone suggests it is 'just that time of the month.' I think that is the most demeaning statement ever. And it is even worse if it is that time of the month. You become a perpetually frustrated person and even when something good is happening, you miss it because you only see what is wrong.

"I have been in there. I left practising midwifery because of it. I moved to family planning and immunisation for women and children. But it was the same there. Eventually, if nobody wants to listen to you, you start taking action. What finished me off was running a clinic every Wednesday in the morning and our uptake was very poor. The only source of local employment was picking grapes, and no woman was going to lose out on income on a Wednesday morning. So I started offering immunisations at night. When I was found out, I was in trouble.

"It was then that I thought that I had to get out of midwifery completely and when I did, people started talking to me, listening to me and telling me that I mattered. I met successful women doing great things and discovered that I was not the only one with self-doubt. I stopped being scared of highly achieved people. I realised that they know what they know, and I know what I know. And I started talking." (Podcast 28)

In some cases, during the First Expedition, I learnt tips from the women that I met, like Harriet; at other times I made promises to myself. Sylvia prompted a promise. I have her words pinned up above my desk. They tell me to take time to listen and never ever (I hope) fail to. Because to make someone like Sylvia feel small, and that she cannot trust herself, that is not right, never mind not clever.

Leading Creativity

Jennifer Stein and Vivi are theatre directors, one in a Canada and the other in Argentina. I think about leading creativity and innovation often, and of how to get beyond group think, but I don't think I have ever spoken about this to a theatre director. So this was a priority.

Jennifer: "At the start, you have to believe in yourself and absolutely believe that you are going to get to somewhere great. It is an act of faith, and you have to believe in the people around you, to know that when you enter the room with your accumulated life experience, so does everyone else. Harnessing all this is where the magic will come from.

"When I began my career as a young theatre director, I watched extremely charismatic – and also extremely forceful – directors come into the room and tell everyone how it was going to be. One particular director, throughout the rehearsal process, used these little cardboard cut-outs of people on a cardboard model of the stage. He would move them around to tell people how each scene was going to go. It was probably one of the first rehearsal processes I was involved in, and I was amazed how it worked. But looking black, it didn't work.

"Slowly, I found my own way and it did not involve standing still. I moved around because I wanted to see what was going on, to see each performer's face and get really physically engaged."

Distance

"I am deeply curious about personalities, but I also keep a bit of a distance at the same time because you need to leave a rehearsal unencumbered by everyone else's emotion. You do not want to take it all in. You learn to do this as a creative person, particularly through the audition process. At the end of a day of auditions, you leave exhausted and completely drained if you absorb everybody's desires and anxiety. You can be sensitive to what people are feeling, you can respect feelings carefully but not take them in. If you do, you lose your vision and objectivity."

Momentum

"But you do use your curiosity to understand different people so that you are able to amplify the voices that are carrying the creativity along. You must be wary of the voices that are bringing the process to a standstill. Sometimes it is about timing, and you will have to say to them, 'wow, you brought up something really interesting, let's schedule some time for you and me to work through it,' and meet the person separately. It's about orchestrating the flow for the whole group. And it's also important to remember that some people are quieter than others and they often have a lot to say when they do speak.

"The other thing to watch for is splinter groups or dissatisfaction and what direction it's pointing in. Yes, you have to let a collaborative creation process run its course. You must let the process breathe. You must give it oxygen, but you must also keep a close eye so that things do not burst into flames.

"Certain things just have to happen, and you have to work through them, and you have to embrace that. I learned early on that you cannot come into the process with everything mapped out. The whole point is that it is a process of discovery. By adapting, you get to a place where the artists own the piece."

Egos

"Crucially, for all this to happen, you have to leave your ego out of the process. Artists will ask probing questions and offer insights – that's why they are there. If you know, deep in your bones, that a particular choice is critical to the whole of a project, then you are going to have to resolve it together and you will need to say so. But if it is a small variation to what you had originally envisioned, and it is not going to disrupt the larger fabric, then you go with it. You have to take a moment to step back and decide.

Pivot

"Maybe you will feel like you are stepping into the abyss because there is no set plan, but go with it. It is live, and it is wonderful. Why do you feel like you're stepping into the abyss? Because you forget you can always change your mind! It's impermanent.

"I call it the goalpost theory of creating. We all have to get the ball within these two goal posts, but there are a million different ways to do this. This is why you are in the room with them anyway, leading. You go through the planning phase and it is really fun envisioning the piece, how the costumes will look, how the set will function, etc. But then you might go into rehearsal, and someone does something amazing, something you would never ever have imagined, and you know that it is brilliant. This can even start as early as in the casting process. You have envisioned who you think would be an ideal person to play a part and then someone walks into the room who is 180 degrees from what you imagined, and you go, 'oh, yes. Wow.' That is your job when you are leading, to pivot and go, 'oh yes. Wow.'

"Leaders, of course, also have to say, 'oh wow, no' sometimes too. Saying no does not have to be so fraught with fear and concern, almost anticipating a negative response. I remember seeing a director say to an actress, 'you know that point when you...' She replied, 'yes,' and he just then said, 'don't do that.' It was said easily and lightly, and everyone laughed and then went on to discuss what they would all do instead. You can lower the stakes. It's not a personal criticism. It's a course correction. It's serving the larger project.

"Stay light in your touch. The best three words you can ever utter in the creative process are: 'let's try it.' Nothing is lost, let's just try it. You are validating other people's participation. You are working together. You might already know how you feel about it. It doesn't matter. 'Let's try it.'"

Resolute

"Go back to that first director I learned from. He had a huge personality. He filled the room. To be clear, I want to fill the room too, but in a different way. There is quiet leading, and there is slow and steady leading, and both are sometimes called for. Often there is no need for a big splash at the beginning, particularly if you are working with new people when it is best to begin quietly, to let your presence and your leading grow. Sometimes you simply have to let people learn who you are, through your actions and decisions. You build trust that way.

And for me, it's critical that there is joy in the process. If there is a lightness in the room, everyone feels it's safe to participate.

"Sometimes we all struggle with wanting to be liked. You want to feel their affection. But this cannot be the arbiter of your decisions. For a while I was making decisions based on wanting people to like me. I learnt that lesson pretty quickly: it does not work. You start letting people run roughshod all over you and soon you have a train wreck on your hands. Sometimes you have to be very decisive and resolute, and it does not matter whether they like you. I had to learn this as a young woman, and I had to relearn it as a director.

"The director's nightmare I used to have was that I would be facing a room full of artists asking questions and I'd say, 'I don't know' and they would say, 'but you have to know!' It was paralysing. I don't have that nightmare any more because I have realised that there is nothing wrong with saying, 'I do not know.' In fact, now I say, 'I do not know and that is why we are here.'" (Podcast 31)

Surprise

Over to Vivi. She goes even further than Jennifer; she deliberately sets out to lose control.

"At the very least put the control in other hands so that you do not have it but share it and then watch carefully where it goes. I see things that are not right, or that I do not like, but I just let it be. I say to myself, 'let's see what happens.' I am not going to rush into correction and say what is right or wrong, because I really want to surprise myself. Sometimes the other person brings something really surprising.

"If you control everything, you won't get surprises. And by controlling, you may miss the new ideas that the apparent 'wrong way' sometimes leads you to. And after all, the right way is so boring most of the time. I think there is nothing new coming up if you take that path of being right or certain. The other side is more unknown. I like the unknown; it is more dangerous.

"It is very peaceful when you get leading right, when all the parts come to place, and you build a whole. It lasts for a little while, then everything moves on again. It is happiness. Simple happiness with a lot of work." (Podcast 31)

The sheer volume of tips I got from talking to Jennifer and Vivi was extraordinary. It's the culture they both work so hard to build that shines through. The expressions, 'let's try it,' 'don't do that,' (said lightly), 'I don't know,' and 'oh yes, wow' stand out. They speak of inquisitiveness and a willingness to go with the flow, combined with crystal-clear boundaries established with joy. They seem to have perfected the art of combining apparently irreconcilable Elements as they lead. They speak of humility and a delight in the ideas, often the better ideas, of others. It is no wonder that actors and audiences chose to follow them.

Leading Chaos

My first boss used to say, "leaders are like tea bags. You don't know how good they are until they are in hot water." Both Elsa Donoghue in Jakarta, Indonesia, and Erin Robinson in Atlanta, USA, were plunged deep and rapidly into scalding water. They survived and learned, and I met both and learned a great deal too.

Elsa

Elsa was the head of a large school when accusations were made of impropriety. I never asked Elsa for details because it was learning about leading that I was seeking. But the scale of the horror was very clear when I spoke to Elsa and she told me that some of her colleagues ended up doing seven years in prison, unjustly so, before the issue was sorted. It was a big injustice that happened.

Elsa started by recalling the moment it started: "I do not know if the word is 'exploded' but in a very rapid amount of time, events progressed to a point at which things were getting out of control. There may have been little mini explosions along the way. But in the end, it was rapid."

Imploding

"I think back about how complex it was and how, at the beginning, we were so naïve. We were certain that we had our procedures in place and that the allegations being made, which were proven in the end to be false, would sort themselves out. They did eventually, but with incredibly horrific outcomes for some of my colleagues.

"'Exploding' may be the wrong word for the school, but 'imploding' would be the right word for me leading. I went through all of the emotions that you can imagine, from concern to guilt and then anger and on to outright fear. And it was not just for me but all the people I was leading.

"As the head, I experienced a tremendous amount of self-doubt. I questioned a lot of things internally and I held back quite a bit about some of the emotions I was feeling. To start with, I felt conflicted because obviously we did not want anything to happen to any of our students and when allegations like that are made your first inclination is to listen to the child. Then as time went by, I started to realise that there was no way this happened. It is then that my attention shifted to the adults with whom I worked, who were being rapidly embroiled in this fantasy-like situation."

Trust

"Somehow, we began to make our way through the maze in a way that not only sustained us, but actually ensured that our students were still learning and our teachers were still teaching. We did it as a leadership team through teamwork. And I learnt a lot.

"I learned not to delegate the in-person communication to faculty or parents. I learned that when it comes to crisis situations, the communication is something that cannot be delegated and that I had to maintain a pretty stable outlook. A lot of it was simply by being there, by my stance, my humility, my ability to listen, not to rebut, not to contradict and not to dismiss feelings or concerns. A lot of this was done nonverbally.

"I had been at the school for over three years when this happened, and we had an incredibly high level of trust with the community. That helped greatly. A message that I have always carried with me is that building relationships and trust is paramount. I had worked on it diligently. When the crisis hit, parents were angry and wondering what was going on, but overwhelmingly, from the very beginning, we had a gigantic team of supporters. They knew me as a professional and quickly realised that there was no way this could have happened."

Open and closed

"I did not always get leading right. On one occasion, I overshared with a couple who then spun the details I gave them to their advantage. Before you knew it, there were more families making allegations. I regretted it immediately, though I did it because I wanted to be human and I thought I could trust them.

"Then sometimes I got it all wrong for the opposite reason. I was too much of a stone wall. I felt at the start that I had to be strong. I thought that as the head I could not fold or show that I was scared and, as things spun out of control, I got more stoic.

"There was a seminal moment when the deputy head told me that they were probably going to prison and that I probably would too. I remember bawling, just having one of those moments when the cry just came from the gut. I had been holding it in for so long. This happened while we were doing orientation at the start of the new year. I remember saying that there was no way I could do it. They looked at me and said, 'yes, you can. You have it in you, you are not alone. Yes, you can.' I cannot say that I believed them, but it was a seminal moment. We opened up school and, as hard as it was, we did it. Soon after, a member of the leadership team said to me, 'stop pretending you are okay.' And I said to myself, 'I am not okay and people are noticing.' I realised that leading can't be done alone. You cannot either hold the power on your own, and nor can you hold the pain on your own.

"There is something else I learnt about consistency and why it is so important for leading. It engenders a sense of safety, security and trust. I was consistently visible, out and about. I was not hiding. I was walking about, being present, being available, ensuring that no matter what, there was something people could count on.

"We created routines, almost rituals. We all – teachers, students, parents, community members – congregated every Friday for seven years, at this iconic part of the campus called the Dragon Fountain. The dragon is the mascot of the school, and that location is beautiful. It was a place of peace for us. If you could not make it every week, it was understood that you were there in spirit." (Podcast 32)

I learnt a great deal from Elsa about visibility, consistency, what not to delegate, oversharing, rituals and holding your nerve. It is worth listening to podcast episode thirty-two, because her voice feels important to hear.

Of the many points Elsa made, this is the one that stood out a mile for me: "Leading can't be done alone." It brings back frightening moments in my career when I thought that leading was about sharing only the good stuff, and that the bad stuff was all for me to shoulder. I carried a lot of the weight and did so gladly and proudly on a number of occasions but, looking back, it was not sensible for me. And nor did it work for the team, who had an exhausted and myopic person leading them for months, and opportunities were probably missed as a result.

Erin

Erin led through a different kind of trauma in her school when a student committed suicide. As we talked, we drew up a list of her learnings.

Individual

"You have to take care of all the technical issues, processes, legalities and systems, but don't let them distract you from the inordinate amount of time you need to spend with each individual. Remembering that not everybody needs the same thing at the same time. You simply cannot broadcast generic messages to cover everybody, because people are going through things in different ways and are on different timelines."

Organic

"You have to avoid getting too formulaic. Of course you need a disaster plan, but use it; do not fall back on it. Be more organic, pay attention, see where you are needed, keep a particular eye on the people who need it, know the networks and understand them, know the informal places to pay attention to as well as the formal places. There is something about a crisis; people default back to more hierarchical structures, but don't forget what you know about the community you lead.

"There is the usual danger of being dismissed as relying too much on instincts and focusing on the emotional, but I would often reply, 'I know that it's not logical, but that doesn't mean that it is not right.' You need to hold the linear and the messy alongside each other. Don't get all messy, because there are linear things that you have to attend to, and don't get all linear because then you will miss the mood."

Compassion

"Leading requires compassion. Not empathy but compassion. To me, compassion is sitting alongside somebody rather than stepping fully into whatever it is that they are going through. If you step in, you are going to lose yourself."

This ties in with so much that Harriet Nayiga and Ayesha have said. Words mean such different things to different people – empathy, sympathy and compassion, used in different contexts but always with a combination of warmth and distance. Yet another apparently contradictory combination.

Looking ahead

"You have to figure out when the community needs to start moving on, because you must always be thinking about what comes next. But be mindful that when something really terrible happens, people need to come back together over time. In a school, things are cyclical, so this is even more pronounced. People will remember the traumatic event the next year, and there will be markers. It does not go away. It resides somewhere and becomes part of the DNA of the place. You have to pay attention to that. There is no 'we took care of this, and then it is done.' It is always there."

Calibrating

"People use the word 'authentic' all the time. When leading chaos, I think it is about being authentic – but only just authentic enough, because in crisis you cannot go too far into the true message, because that message is not for everybody.

"People don't want to feel like you are hiding things, but they also recognise that you cannot tell them everything. For me, it is about watching people, listening – really listening – so that you can figure out what you can give people that they need to hear without divulging too much. If you give too little, you trigger anger and frustration and you lose trust. If you give too much, then people feel overloaded and they cry out 'too much.'"

Help

"I think it helps if you do not lead with ego and realise that you cannot be everywhere and be everything to everyone. What I have to figure out is who are the people that I am going to build up and rely on for support, and I have to be quite clear with them that I need them. Never underestimate people's willingness to step up." (Podcast 32)

Erin's list is in my journal. To me, her advice on authenticity brought back the words of my first boss, who used to say, "give people enough so that they can say 'I note.' Do not try to give people so much insight that they will agree with you because that is probably not going to happen. In most situations, 'I note' is enough and all you will probably get."

I also love how Erin has very firmly reframed instincts and emotions as Elements she values highly.

Leading Together

I was spending too much time with people who lead organisations, and wanted more with women who are leading families and communities. And leading friends too; this felt especially important given that so many younger women are recognising just how crucial friendships are.

I spoke to three young women in different parts of the world. It was a joy. Temi, Meena and Marga in Nigeria, India and Argentina would put female friendships as central, stand-alone pieces of their Essences. Each one has determinedly cultivated their women friends and they see this as one of the central distinguishing features between theirs and their mothers' generation. They say female friendships take time, attention and some basic rules. And that they are crucial for women who lead.

Female friendships

Temilade Salami is an environmental activist in Nigeria: "I have amazing friends who have helped me up and cheered me on at different times. I can be vulnerable with them and share my life with them, the wins and the losses. This is something lots of people do not talk about; we absolutely need to shine a light on the positive side of our amazing female friendships. It needs shining because we are still taught that fellow women are our enemy in Nigeria. We are not expected to have or need any female friends once we marry."

Meena says that it is the same in India: "A girl is someone else's from the minute she is born, so she no longer has a sense of individual existence, which means there is really no need for her to actually have any friendships. And yet they are so essential to women who lead. We need a lot of care, love, kindness, forgiveness and a space to really unwind from what is a high stress activity, which comes with high stakes for women. Who else do we turn to?

"It is not just about creating a network to get forwards; it is about recharging. Leading seems to be a bit like being a sponge; you listen to people and give them the time and space to figure things out, to express themselves and to make mistakes and learn. It is exhausting and it also means you are probably going to bear the brunt of mistakes that happen.

"Then there are the microaggressions in the workplace. They are something that most men don't understand. They cause you to question your self-worth and judgment; they start eating you up from the inside. I think the only times that I have been able to feel better about all this is when I speak to my women friends, because they make me realise that what I am feeling is real.

"To me, it's sad that women in India almost never have female friendships. If they do, it's under extreme pressure, involving lots of lying and saying that I am going here when I am actually going there. There is a really beautiful word in Hindi called 'saheli' or 'saheliyaan' – translated, it sort of means a woman who walks with you. There is just something magical about the word that makes me very happy." (Podcast 48)

Glue

Marga Grobocopatel Marra is a doctor from Argentina; one doctor in a tight group of doctors: "We met in our first year in an anatomy class. We are all thirteen of us now doctors, so it has been seven years. We all shared the same table in class, so we met studying dead bodies. We are very intimate for every exam, we graduated on the same day. We were also footballers together; we won the championship twice.

"I have made a list for you about the secrets of our friendship:

- It is not a competition
- Most trouble comes from misunderstandings
- Each person shines
- Be there, but no dependency
- Do not judge
- Just love and trust
- Eat strawberries with chocolate
- Put in the hard work, starting with understanding yourself

"The most important is the first. I feel like for previous generations, female relationships were like a competition, and this has changed a lot. We feel no need to compete. Every time one of us gets the better grade, it is no surprise because it is always Kata. When she gets the best grade, we all feel like we did it together. When we won the football championship, all of us celebrated together. Our self-esteem is not about competing with friends. Part of this is that we are so different. We each have something in which we are strong and good and for each of us it is a very different thing. We shine with our own thing so there is no place for competition.

"We talk about things in a very honest way. One time we got into a fight because the group split to study for a pathology exam, and we had a very bad communication. A part of the group felt like the other part of the group left them apart. When we talked about it, it got clear very quickly. We joke a lot about our boyfriends, we say 'he has to conquer us all.'

"We always say, 'Live and Let Live.' You have a friend who is there for you and who you can share your time, feelings and thoughts with, but you also know that the person will not absorb all your Energy and become dependent on you. It's a balance.

"It is really important to not judge your friends. I know we all do that all the time. I always say, 'I will judge you, but I will not tell you.' My friends tell me the truth only when I ask them to.

"In some groups of friends, they have lists of things you have to do to be part of the group, like you have to be a feminist and you have to vote a certain way, and you have to dress this way. I think this happens a lot nowadays and it is not good. We love each other and we trust each other, and we like to be with each other. It is not about the way we dress or our political opinions and not where we go to dance or how we use our Instagram accounts.

"We do have rituals. Every night before a big exam, we always have the same dessert that we really love. It is strawberries with chocolate. It makes us feel like everything would be fine.

"All of us feel like this friendship we have is the proudest thing we have done in our life. So when we graduated, we talked a lot that day and all of us agreed that we were very proud to be doctors but we were prouder to have built this group of friends that is so strong and so healthy. It takes a lot of work; I know it sounds easy, but it is not.

"I have come to realise that, at the heart of things, it is often about knowing yourself. If you do not know yourself so much, you start thinking that your friends did something that bothers you when, in reality, it is not something your friends did, it is something that is going on inside you." (Podcast 48)

I suspect that Temi, Meena and Marga are right. Female friendships will be a dominant piece of the Essence of many women of their generation, and Marga's list of how they translate from Essence through to Expression is both delicious and intensely practical.

Leading Against the Odds

I became fascinated by midwives, and then there came another fascination: Botswana, a country where women lead in significant numbers and yet still have to do 'the dance.' I spoke to two very senior women, Joyce Wema Isa-Molwane, a businesswoman and lawyer, and to Pelonomi again about how they dance in very different ways. I sought them out because their experience of dancing is so very different from mine and from each other's.

Boiling frogs

Joyce Wema: "When I speak in boardrooms, the mere fact that I am a woman means I must be tactful as to how I get my message across. My male counterpart could say something today and it is okay, but if I say it tomorrow the reaction could be totally different. You need to read the room, not just in terms of words, but in terms of body language, and ask yourself, 'Should I raise this here and now?'

"If I realise that there are sticky things that need to be discussed, I am better off speaking to my chief executive on the side. I convince him and he will then present the ideas as though they are his own. I do not look for the glory that I made the decision or that I advised him, I just want to reach my objective. I have decided it is good to lead from behind.

"You need to understand the battle that you are in before you can prepare for the war that is going to come. Sometimes the best way to succeed is to take the Trojan horse approach. Fight from within the system, get close to those who are the real decision makers and influence their thinking without them realising it. In this way, you are able to put things in place for those who are coming behind you. As a woman, if you understand the paradigm in which you operate and how best you can make the system work for you, you can make effective change.

"It is an elegant dance. You need to be aware of issues, of the people around the table, of the nuances, and you need to be ahead of the pack. Never get tired of reading and understanding and researching. A woman undertaking the elegant dance, for you to be the best performer on that dance floor, you better have your facts straight, you better know what you are talking about. There is no point in opening your mouth and not having something solid to say. You need to be confident, you need to be assertive, you need to be knowledgeable, robust in your Expression and hold your ground. Be firm but be polite, be respectful. Do not forget about your culture. So the dance is all those Elements put together."

Joyce Wema's dance is designed to ensure that men never recognise that they are no longer in charge. She feeds them her best ideas, knowing that they will claim them as theirs. I asked Joyce Wema if that was enough for her, just to know that she had a part to play in them.

"Yes. You do the dance because recognition speaks for itself. I do not believe in doing something and then saying, 'I did this.' What you have a hand in will show and it will come out. And especially remember: if an idea is not yours, you cannot implement it. So who will the implementation be given to? You, the originator of the idea. When you implement it is when your glory is going to come, but your idea would have gotten the approval at the table, because you did the dance to get it to the table.

"I think all of us need to start doing the same dance and open a dance troupe so that those who come after us do not have to continue dancing. We have to teach each other the steps. The problem is that if you do the dance for too long and by yourself, you will end up perpetuating the dance.

"The females coming up should not have to do the dance, they should not have to fight to be around the table, they should not have to continue being gagged. But for me, this is the start of putting all the dances and the efforts together into one fluid movement that we all understand as women in leadership roles, so that we do not have to have this battle going on forever.

"Keep the example of cooking frogs in mind. First keep it in the temperature that it is used to. If you are getting it from a pond, you put it at pond temperature, you do not start blasting at 100 degrees because it will jump out of the pan. So you slowly turn up the temperature. By its nature, it will adjust its temperature to its surroundings and before the frog knows it, it is cooked.'

"There is a role that we play as we pass through our generations. What we do today will impact generations to come. I do not think many women would openly say that they are doing the dance or cooking the frog, because that is giving away the strategy, but it is okay to plan ahead and be strategic together. This is what we do as Botswanan women. We are stitched to be like this." (Podcast 25)

Head on

With my mind going round in circles, I spoke next to Pelonomi, who performs a very different dance. No boiling of frogs for her. She takes on the fight head on. I asked her how she prepares herself for it.

"You never can prepare yourself absolutely. You will be misunderstood. You will be called names. You will be labelled. There will be backlash. People will retaliate. I was attacked even by fellow women – in fact, mostly by fellow women, the harshest attack came from them. I do not think they are attacking me to defend the men. I think some of them are attacking me because they would have liked to do what I am doing. Because I moved quicker than they wanted to, or because I have done something that they wanted to do but were too scared to do.

"Anyway, my preparation was to decide early on that as an individual I have a mandate to perform. I am very clear about what I am supposed to do, and I believe in my capabilities on the mandate assigned to me. I decide that I am going to do it for as long as I know that I am doing the right thing. And I decide that I am not going to be deterred by criticism based on things that have got nothing to do with the work that I do.

"I do not think that there are people who have been investigated at work as many times as I have been, but those investigations just fell apart. Some of them just died before they started, because they were all based on things that did not match up to the truth. I have never gone outside of the rules of what I do. That is how I survived. Truth: truth and pure brawn.

"I think what we need to learn as women is that leading can bring you the power you need if you do it properly, and that power grows with what you do, because people see what you do consistently and constantly.

"If you allow your history, your decisions, the things that you do to be overshadowed by some male person, you will never be visible and therefore your power will always be under the shadow of somebody. So go out there, do your thing, even your mistakes. Let them come out there, allow yourself to fall and get up again. Once people see you dust yourself down, clean yourself up and come out again, that is when they will let you build your power. That is how they will know who you are and respect you. And the others will get scared because they see you. They know how powerful you are becoming." (Podcast 25)

Joyce Wema and Pelonomi are good friends (the kinds of friends Temi, Meena and Marga are determined to be and for just as long). Both have common pieces in their Essences, and yet the pieces play out in very different ways in their Elements and Expression. It is a beautiful illustration of just how personal leading is. One has a trojan horse, the other goes straight in. Both have been hugely successful.

I wonder sometimes, looking back, if I might have had more of an impact if I had been better at flattering people. I am very much like Pelonomi. It's a fair question to ask myself, but I fear an irrelevant one because I would never have been able to do it. Too much in my Essence would have got in the way.

Leading Pace

Talking to Uma helped me with this. Let me explain.

Pace and speed deeply emanate from my Essence. The piece of my Essence that is education (huge classes and not much learning) made me impatient. The piece of my Essence that is trauma (I have little recollection of my life between the ages of 10 and 15; it was miserable) made me unrelenting. The piece that is motherness (there was never any question in my mind that I would have five children) made me driven.

So with education, trauma and motherness in my Essence, pace and speed was always going to feature in my Elements. But I also knew that how I Expressed it when leading would have to be done with care, and that a lot of leading is about exactly this: judging pace right. Looking back, getting pace wrong has consistently been my weakness. Don't misunderstand me; I know that getting it right has also been my strength because it draws people in. But when I have got things wrong, it has often been about charging into things.

So I wanted to speak to Uma, who has led and is leading glorious movements which require an intricate understanding of pace. I thought she might help me get better at it.

Sprint or marathon

"Leading is like running a sprint or a marathon. It is all about how well your body can distribute its Energy throughout. You must preserve enough Energy for your entire run. You have to judge when to slow the pace and when to speed it up. Whatever happens, there always has to be a flow of Energy. If not, negativity seeps in and a split, a break, a tear emerges. And you can feel it. When something has ruptured, you must attend to the rupture because otherwise the stakes are very high. The movement can be destroyed if you judge the pace wrong.

"Your job is to create an enabling environment in any movement and when you do, then you can sprint. Because you can feel the courage, a shared courage to challenge the status quo. It is palpable. And it comes with an openness to learning, an ability and an agility to act. There is a lightness of play, of imagination, curiosity and fun. When this happens, there is no question about slowing down. It is magic. Sprinting becomes just so easy. You start breathing in sync, you start singing in synergy, you start playing and everything falls in line.

Fogged out

"Fear sometimes emerges about maintaining, sustaining and surviving. This feeling has sometimes frozen me, and that is when I get vulnerable. I feel fogged out. It is then I ask myself: what is the most important thing here? What do I want to happen? What is the price of doing something like this or not going for it? My instinct is to withdraw, but that is when I say to myself, 'this is not the time to withdraw or disengage,' and I now listen to others. I know that I cannot risk seeing the situation only through my eyes, and I stop thinking about winning or losing and start to listen to others. They draw me out and release me from my freeze.

"Of course, movements are usually built on things that we want to dismantle so that we can shift the power around. But when things get tough or stuck or we feel like we are on our last legs, we need to be laser-focused about what we all love and we are trying to create together rather than attempt to dismantle. At the heart of it all, there has to be purpose. Without it, there is nothing. If it becomes unclear or there is a drift or distraction, then we plateau and people start to question everything. That is a red flag, and it is time to regroup.

"This arousal from evocation, rather than arousal from provocation, is what keeps me going. There is a surge of Energy in both positive and negative ways. When this happens, you suddenly realise that you are not the person in control anymore, it has been taken over by a few others. With this comes a real sense of joy as the Energy surges and I know I have been shifted to the backseat. I cannot even tell you how overjoyed I have felt that it just happened.

"Of course, I have also experienced a sense of being played and manipulated, of being hijacked and sabotaged, when control is taken from me. A drama has been created, I have been pushed into the middle of all of it and then been dumped. But with experience, I have learned to identify the signs of when it is starting to happen, though I still feel destabilised and exposed, even disempowered and helpless when it happens.

"But when I do get the pace right, that is magic, magic rooted in care, in accountability, in non-hierarchical, empowered ways of working. It is a flow of Energy and animation. It all lines up. I have felt it, I have experienced it. When our desires, our beliefs and convictions and our actions have lined up together. I have been in that room. I get goosebumps every time I speak about this. It is magical." (Podcast 62)

I hope that as you read this chapter about Expression and pick up tips on everything from tough conversations to rocking boats and from nurturing friendships to boiling frogs, your own list of women to speak to has got longer. And with it, the questions you want to ask them.

You will want to listen greedily to their answers, push them when they don't get practical enough. Make sure that while you do that, you are neither dismissing their ideas nor adopting them too quickly or too slowly. You are looking out hard for the smallest of tips that make sense and will work for you.

As your Expression circle grows, keep a watching eye on its connection to Essence.

And watch out that the infinity symbol does not seize up. It should be flowing outwards from Essence to Elements to Expression. And flowing back too, because as Expression meets the outside world it will discover new things all the time. Essence will adjust.

Don't forget that every one of my conversations in this section is captured in more detail and infinitely more beauty in the podcast episodes. If you listen to them, you will hear the voices, the emotions, the delights. Enjoy.

Journal

Solo

Get out there exploring big time. Go back to your list of people to speak to. Update it. Fill in the gaps now that you are well into your Expedition.

Take time out to have those conversations. Find out how people lead in practice in different situations. Get granular. How do they actually lead a meeting? What do they do that they know they shouldn't do? What really works for them? How do they connect it with their Essence?

Go to the back of your journal and start a list of tips. Nothing in great detail or with too much thought, just tips.

In a group

Find a way to share insights as you go. You might want to create an online MIRO board (or whatever app works for you) so that you can capture and share what you are discovering for the benefit of each other. And regroup whenever you can, so that you can discuss the issues and ideas and even tensions you come across.

Energy

Right at the start of the First Expedition, when we defined the word 'leading' and set out to test our hunch that it was not the word itself that was gendered, but simply that women go about leading differently. Even then I think we knew that we should think of leading as Energy; about managing our own Energy, about sparking the Energy inside the people we lead and about generating a microclimate of Energy in which things happen around us.

Lifeblood

Every woman we met – knowingly or unknowingly – led me to believe more and more that Energy is the lifeblood of leading. Maybe it's not what being a 'leader' – the title – is, and it's not what 'leadership' – the state – is, but it is what the verb 'leading' is all about.

Energy that emanates from Essence. An Essence which guides and grounds that Energy. Energy that shows up in our Elements. It causes us to jettison some of them because they get in the way. It pushes us to reframe others because, reframed, they can turbo-charge Energy. It demands that we land our purpose and keep it under constant review because Energy thrives on purpose. It requires us to combine what may appear to be incompatible Elements because the sparks will fly when they do combine. Finally, it finds its way to Expression as we discover ways to bring Energy into the meetings, problems, opportunities and relationships involved in daily leading.

This is why the infinity symbol lies right across the three circles of Essence, Elements and Expression. The three circles gently build on each other, each one feeding the next, relentlessly building, and then the infinity symbol just strikes across them all. It reflects the flow across them, the constant, dynamic and eternal flow from Essence to Expression. And it's not a one-way flow, it is two-way. Expression flows back into Elements to make sure they adapt to the outside world. In this way, the inner world flows to the outer to hold it accountable, and the outer flows back to the inner to ensure it evolves. This way, we don't get carried away in our leading by the influences of the outside world, and we constantly shine a light on ourselves and don't retreat inwards, failing to adjust in a fast-changing world.

Some people might use the word 'power,' but it's not the right one here. 'Energy' is a very different word. Ana Luz, Liz and Aparna will explain.

Ana Luz: "Too often, power just seems to be something to accumulate, hoard or wield."

Liz: "Even if we stick to the expression 'power with' rather than 'power over,' it's still something you associate with abuse of power, something to steal from another person, to force people to do something that they may or may not want to do, or simply to have more of." (Podcast 59)

Aparna: "Power feels like a force that sits and accumulates in one place. Energy is something that flows." (Podcast 26)

Liz: "It's just much more interesting to create Energy which people feel and want to be part of because it is so infectious." (Podcast 59)

There is another reason why there is an infinity sign stretching across the three concentric circles. It symbolises the Energy that flows upwards from this dynamic exchange. An Energy that generates ever more Energy and enthusiasm that becomes contagious as it spirals upwards.

Liz: "Energy attracts like Energy. Energy is mutually reinforcing and increases exponentially once you create the space for it to reverberate so that it starts to spiral upwards. If we want to get to a place where our leading generates Energy, we have to be aware of the Energy that we are bringing to a situation. It is an exhausting responsibility, but I think it is what leading is all about.

"Of course, the same is true in the other direction, and Energy can spiral downwards. If we show up in a very low Energy state, feeling lethargic or like a victim and not operating at a particularly high frequency, then the likelihood is that others will pick up on that and they will mirror it. They may show up only to do the bare minimum. Low Energy leads to lower Energy and reinforces into ever lower Energy. People feel drained, and it turns to apathy and then maybe even anger and a narrowing down to winning or losing or being right."

As it spirals, it remains rooted or anchored firmly back in Essence. Because Energy must be handled with great care whichever way it spirals, but especially as it spirals upwards, faster and faster. Because with Energy comes huge responsibility.

Rouba: "We are working in a warzone. Some of the decisions I make will impact people's lives, people's futures, people's families; just sometimes, we change the course of history. I am not saying one decision from me would change how things happen in Syria, but it is the addition of all of these small decisions by people like me who will definitely impact our future.

"I think when you realise this, it becomes very frightening, because it increases the responsibility. You realise that people are looking to you for answers when sometimes you do not have them. I think these are the moments when you feel scared about leading." (Podcast 10)

I asked Martyna about being in a different kind of limelight, when as the conductor you walk out on the stage: "It is not easy to lead right up from the front, but I tell myself that I have undertaken the task of leading so I have a responsibility and, ethically, I must do it. I enter the room; everyone notices me, and everything goes silent. It is very intimidating and has been like that for as long as I can remember. I repeat to myself, 'there is a duty behind leading, I should learn how to use the power well.' Many leaders have this challenge. You accept the responsibility of being the leader, and that makes you incredibly visible and vulnerable to your mistakes. The only way to deal with it is to remember that people actually came here because they wanted to listen to something beautiful. That people have come to work with you because they chose to. This adds pressure, of course, but somehow it helps too." (Podcast 45)

This is why the Energy has to be rooted back to, and anchored in, Essence. To both cope with the responsibility and to avoid spiralling in the wrong direction. Because Energy generates power (perhaps not in physics, but in leading it does, at least it does to me) and maybe you need the right Essence to both generate and also to deal with that power.

Spiralling off

Sarah and I made a list of some of the routes the infinity symbol can take if it spirals off in the wrong direction. Sometimes it does without you even noticing. Then it becomes a gargantuan task to put things right.

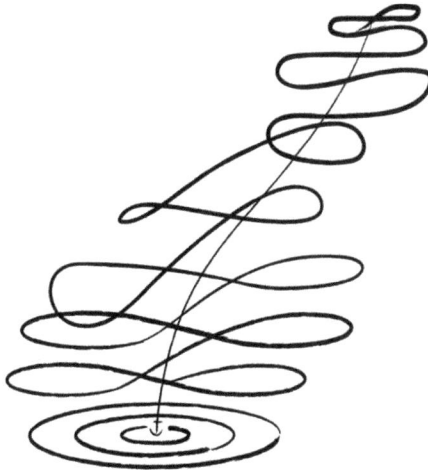

Figure 10: Spiralling off

We thought of four such routes. They are all connected to the power that your Energy brings you. You deny that you now have power, you come to think that you deserve it, you start to assume it or you become consumed with maintaining it.

Deny

"If you don't acknowledge that you have any power, or even deny that you have it, you can't calibrate how you use it, so it will go unchecked."

Sarah experienced this first hand and early on: "I moved into a new position where I had a lot more of both positional and network power. A great deal more clout. I was still the same person who met people for lunch to talk about family, so I really did not explore for myself what it meant to have this power. I realised quickly that people around me showed up differently because, all of a sudden, I had this positional power over them. If I was the first one to speak with an idea that I genuinely thought was merely interesting, I changed the trajectory of meetings with my team. People would try to go with my idea even if it was terrible. I had to understand positional power, the Energy that I created in the room and how best to show up in it."

I asked Sarah if power had really crept up on her or had it – as it is for many – been more about a modesty that caused her to deny her newfound power. "It can be both, but remember too that often it is a false modesty. You say, 'this is all because of everyone else's work and the work that everyone has done.' I think that to be authentic, you have to take credit for the things that you have accomplished. We have been conditioned and coded as women to make ourselves small even when it is at the detriment of actually moving something forward."

Deserve

"If you believe that you deserve power, that you earned it, you stop being curious. You surround yourself with people who want to be close to power, people who will never tell you under any circumstances that your idea was no good. Then you start believing your own spin. You tell yourself that you 'pulled yourself up with your own bootstraps.' You become blind to your unearned privilege, and you find that you are no longer creating Energy.

"I suspect that this is the dominant model. After all, power does corrupt. You become incredibly vulnerable to flattery. People who lead are all to some extent vulnerable in this way, but you are particularly vulnerable because you seek it out. Because everything needs to validate your deservedness. It is a very dangerous place to be.

"What you don't see is that it's really a trap, a plateau, a dead end, and it stunts your growth. How could it be otherwise given that you think you have come to the culmination of your game?" (Podcast 61)

While Sarah is talking, I am thinking that my birthday is next month, and I will be 65. It is sad that too many of us at 65 are in this category, but then again, I have seen 25-year-olds in this category. Even 18-year-olds.

Maintain

If you get to the stage when your sole focus becomes maintenance, all your Energy becomes consumed in maintaining your position and power and everything becomes solely about 'me,' 'my' and 'mine.' You have forgotten any compass that you might have set and even why you set it in the first place. You have almost started hoarding your Energy so as to build your own fiefdom because your scarcity mentality has convinced you that there is not enough Energy to go around.

Sarah has seen founders who suffer from this, and the organisations that they founded suffer as a result because, "the organisation becomes about the person and not the purpose. The structures, incentives and culture get built around a person, their Energy and their apparent 'magic.' It is like Gollum from *Lord of the Rings* in the cave with that precious ring. You have to keep feeding it because it's insatiable. The founder will have tasted power, and now loves their own Energy and the position and successes that emanate from it.

"In some ways, maintenance becomes about survival. You know what you are up against and how much of a fight it will be. You know that the system will begin to gaslight you soon, it will tell you that you are wrong when you are right, and it will pit you against even your greatest of friends. All this means that you feel the need to hold on ever tighter to the power that you have. After all, 'there are limited places at the table.' You will not have jettisoned this Element. So you maintain, build up and hoard because you need power at your fingertips."

So there you have Sarah's four dead ends – but as she says: "These don't have to be permanent states. They are only a mental state, so you can catch yourself and adjust your route. The key to this is remaining curious, knowing that leading is a practice and that you can always grow." (Podcast 61)

This is why the infinity symbol is so important: it flows in both directions. When you connect with your Essence you can realise that you have to rethink the Energy you create. And when you engage with the world around you and see how people respond to your Energy, you can go back and think again about your Essence. Your Essence evolves continually, as does your Energy, and this way you can avoid spiralling off in the wrong direction.

Sarah's list surely prompts the question: how do you get Energy back on track? How do you reverse the spiral once it has gone off course, or when it has started on a downwards spiral and you can feel it draining away towards an Energy you don't like? What then?

I asked Alia: "I first check my own Energy and to what extent I am contributing to the spiralling. Do I need to eat or go for a walk, spend time with friends, do something that is going to spark joy in me? My aim is to ground myself and stay steady.

"Then I have to bring the team back to where we should be. Sometimes there is somebody who is really rocking the boat in a way that is unhealthy for our team's Energy and I need a direct conversation with them to help shift their Energy. It is not an easy thing to do. It is hard, it is uncomfortable. It is not something I enjoy, but it is part of our collective Energy, which is sacred. After all, our time and Energy are our most precious resource.

"Sometimes we all need to go away together as a team to change the dynamics. At other times, there is a need to bring in somebody new into the team because one person moving can change things dramatically.

"Above all, my favourite way to shift the Energy is through play. As adults, we often leave play behind in childhood. Yet play is a wonderful tool to tap into our creativity, shift power dynamics and spark joy and innovation. It appeals to a different part of our brains and injects a new Energy. "

I am with Alia on this. I would never go anywhere without my bag of props – coloured pens, scissors, glue, post-it notes, mouth organs, stickers of animals and smiley faces, play doh, Lego bricks, rolls of paper, packs of cards – so that people can create sculptures, draw pictures, build models, cut out designs, play music, sing, laugh, giggle, challenge, redraw, recreate together. One of my favourites is a file of photos printed out. They are of mountains and waves, of people making all kinds of different faces, of famous and hidden places, of familiar objects and strange unidentifiable shapes. I have collected them over the years and never know quite how they will be used. People just pick them up to illustrate a point, or to express a feeling, or to play a game they have newly invented.

Back to Alia: "You don't always have time to go take a nap or give yourself space or design a session of play but, even then, you can pause in the moments when you are overwhelmed, take a breath and be thoughtful about how you are showing up in the storm.

"In times when you are surrounded by negative Energy, you have to almost create a little bubble around your team. Though you may find that when there is opposition all around you, it actually makes the Energy in your own team even stronger. It can generate an intense sense of purpose and determination to have each other's backs and not allow differences to drag the team into the negativity. Everyone is stronger when holding each other tighter."

Alia and I spoke about this bubble you have to deliberately create to protect your positive Energy from the surrounding negativity. For me, it is not always negative Energy you have to protect against the most. It is a total absence of Energy that I find the hardest. With negative Energy, at least there is Energy to work with. There is the possibility that you can turn it around into a positive. The killer for me is no Energy at all: there is nothing to turn, and everything is an uphill battle.

Alia: "I want to add just one thing. Energy can feel very different in different cultures. People show up in different ways from you. This can be a gift, but sometimes it is difficult to understand or recognise. If you do not take time outside of your daily tasks to know people as humans, you are unlikely to understand the Energy around you.

"In Sri Lanka, for example, tea is an important ritual for many. You often have tea before you start a meeting, and discuss people's families. You are able to understand each other and where everyone comes from before you start talking business. Over time, this helps you understand each other's Energy. And it is not just me understanding people, but also them understanding me. This relationship building is an important part of leading and shaping the narratives you build about others, and others build about you." (Podcast 60)

Spiralling Up

Moving on from the deathly spiral or the directionless spiral, back to when Energy is spiralling upwards in a beautiful direction.

Liz: "It's a mutually reinforcing Energy that enables more to be done, a flow state with a real focus on the most important task. The distractions are tuned out, creativity is flowing everywhere, momentum is building, things are happening and nobody has even noticed how much effort is being put in. People have moved out of a low Energy state and stopped thinking about who is winning or how, and have got to the place where everyone is winning. It's then that the Energy skyrockets. The expression 'high Energy' is often used to describe when Energy is really flowing well, and yet when you get there it actually feels peaceful and calm, full of synergy." (Podcast 59)

I made a list with Liz of what causes a spiralling upwards to what she describes unexpectedly as this peaceful and calm state.

Calibrating

"There is a time and a place for different Energy levels. Really effective leading involves identifying in the moment what the situation needs. You may need lower Energy and a slower pace when really intense listening is required. This will be very different from the kind of Energy you need to generate an action phase. Then a different Energy might be needed if say people need to vent and express frustrations or anger. It is not always about being in this super high Energy phase that can be exhausting.

"We make choices about how long we stay in each Energy state. When we choose to remain in a certain state, we need to be aware that we are doing so and of its impact on the people around us.

"This judging of the Energy level is what makes leading so critical. You have to use your intuition and learn to trust it. You have to be in a good place yourself to do this, not so exhausted or upset that you can't see clearly. This is so much easier said than done. It relates to so many different human dynamics, but it speaks to leading requiring the ability to pick up on different Energy levels and judge them right. You have to make calls all the time, like whether it is worth spending time forcing through an issue or whether to regroup and reconsider, knowing that either way there has to be closure and some kind of shift in the Energy." (Podcast 59)

Judgement

"We are often drawn towards external factors like logistics, systems and processes because it is less uncomfortable looking at them. Somehow they feel easier to fix. Leading does attract inherent problem solvers who tend to stick to the external factors like changing a policy or moving an office, things that are not necessarily related to people. Actually, the real blocks are inner blocks. It's about the person or the people, the mindset, emotions and the limiting beliefs. Often there is less desire to go there because it feels like it might be a little bit messy and might result in people's feelings being hurt.

"Sometimes you are in situations where somebody is completely stuck in a low Energy state. They are dragging a team down and despite lots of different attempts, the person is just not shifting. Then you have to have one of the difficult conversations that Monica has talked about. You can't afford to put a plaster over the problem and see the Energy drain. Make sure you have that conversation today, because the team will be tired and looking to you to raise those Energy levels for everyone else.

"At other times, you will find that the problem is the combination of the people in a team, that they just do not really gel. There are conflicting personalities, none of whom are wrong, but they struggle to work together. You cannot duck this one either. Sometimes it's as simple as just getting out of the office, especially if you see the impact of your work by getting out and reconnecting to the purpose."

"Sometimes it's not systems, logistics, processes, people or teams, it's you. There will always be people you struggle to work with. There will be times when you run yourself down and struggle to inspire yourself, never mind others. There will inevitably be triggers that go off in you, no doubt emerging unanticipated from your Essence. There will very rarely be moments when you get anything resembling a round of applause; mostly you will feel flattened by the regular insights into your failures that everyone around you provides.

"You have to tune into how your Energy is transferring to others and also how theirs is transferring to you. There will be people who make you feel drained and tired and a bit overwhelmed, and there will be others who have the opposite effect on you. Pay attention to that Energy transfer and how you want to adjust it, then start experimenting in how to bring in your Energy in different situations when you pick up different vibes. When to stop and listen.

"When you do, you may find that the Energy level is sliding downwards because people are feeling vulnerable or angry or afraid or all of these and more. And you are feeling these things too. Don't just become some sort of cheer-leader who brushes concerns aside. Or you may find that it's sliding because people have lost sight of what it was all about. Then it's not cheerleading they need from you, but rather a beautifully expressed reminder of what the purpose is, why it is important and how it will be achieved. Because you need to scoop people up, lift their sights, throw your own Energy in and ask them to rally." (Podcast 59)

This elegant judgement must be the magic Olivia spoke of when she described leading done beautifully. It's the invitation that Martyna made with an elegant hand gesture that had no need for words. It's the ponytail flick that Kelly gave when she called for more from her star player.

Shedding

Melissa Kwee is adding to our list now. Just as Sarah has warned us about being hoarders of Energy, worried that there isn't enough to go round, Melissa says you have to do the opposite and just give it away.

"Energy is ultimately something to give away, responsibly, so that people feel trusted, responsible and empowered. You share energy with care: the intent is that it moves in a direction that is broadly established and agreed upon, that it rests not on a single party but within and across a group of individuals who have chosen a common destiny. After all, it takes a network to fight a network.

"So it's not occasionally, but really as often as is appropriate, and I hope it is often and that there is a great joy in giving Energy away."

Harriet Nayiga smiled when I met her soon after and I told her about Melissa's words. She then brought a note of caution in: "Don't forget that it is easier to give it away when you have masses of it. Take care not to be too generous. If you strip yourself of power in order to create the Energy for change in a traditional space, it will not always work. You may have to hold onto your Energy and use it yourself. Otherwise you get thrown to the back. Be careful about restricting yourself or showing that you are vulnerable, because they will use your vulnerability against you." (Podcast 28)

Olivia came in rapidly behind Harriet and then went in a different direction. She sees change coming and predicts that it will be very different for her generation: "Before, I think we could find Energy and power was measured on how much information you had that other people did not have. Now, with my generation, it is more about how we can combine our knowledge and Energy together. So it is all about sharing, everything is about sharing: how can my idea be improved or implemented, how can my Energy be exponential if I do not share it with someone else?" (Podcast 42)

Positioning

Olivia then asked me about whether it was best to generate Energy for change from outside a system or from inside. I took this one to Lissa and Uma. Lissa chose the inside, Uma the outside. They both recognise the need for both to combine.

Lissa "It's best to combine the internal and external energies. It takes both. Because once you get labelled a radical, you will struggle internally and you will no longer be heard. So as an insider seeking to produce the Energy for change, you carefully cultivate relationships with 'radicals' from the outside, to learn their perspective and translate it into one that can be heard internally."

Lissa saw this happen in the US military "On the issue of allowing gays and lesbians to serve. You had all of these perceived radicals on the outside demanding change, and it was very easy for the United States Congress and the US military to say, 'we cannot hear you; you do not understand our world' and 'the walls will crumble if we allow gay people in.' But over time, gay people in the military became more visible, and because they were such a deep part of the culture, it was impossible for the military to not hear them. Particularly because so many gay people were great soldiers. It took a long time, but it was those gay soldiers who were carefully aligned and in relationship with the external 'radicals' who pulled it off.

"It's these coalitions across the institutional membrane that maintain the Energy to drive change because, from the outside, you risk being ignored and from the inside you risk being rejected. But even from the inside, sometimes, very rarely, you have to toss a hand grenade in the room and blow some things up to get the attention and to focus the Energy change. The hand grenade in the context of the US military was some of us coming out of the closet and saying, 'I'm gay.' That just completely blew things up. All of a sudden, there was this cognitive dissonance. They had a respected and esteemed colleague in one part of their brain and in the other part they thought gay people were bad generally and really bad for the army. 'Gay person, great soldier' was confusing. That is what prompted real change from the inside. In the end, it was all about timing.

"For sure there are some change agents who believe in just blowing stuff up so that it has to be recreated, but I love the military too much for that and I think I can create Energy to change it in easier ways." (Podcast 5)

Uma opts for the outside. She has spent years creating Energy from there and recommends it because, for her, it 'connects to my Essence and soul' (Podcast 62) and for five other reasons:

- You get the benefit of more solitude, during which you can connect better with your Essence.

- You have more freedom to listen to the voice of intuition within yourself. You can also sense more from the outside.
- Being on the outside means that you know what it feels like to be excluded, which makes you much more inclusive in your leading.
- You can see the bigger picture and you don't get lost in the details of the systems you are supposed to be maintaining.
- You are unconstrained by rules, beliefs and loyalties that you are expected to accept inside. It gives you more room to grow in whichever way you like.

Then Uma reflected some more on the effect that being an outsider has on you: "You are less easily frightened by the prospect of being on the outside. You know what it feels like and have survived it, so it is no great terror. This gives you an edge because, for many, losing their power is the greatest of terrors."

Of course, there are shadowy sides to being an outsider, as Uma says: "There is a real danger that you begin to believe that you will only ever belong when you are on the outside. You get entrenched in the margins and can slip into destroying and disrupting things around you without a purpose. You start feeling like you are a stranger to yourself, someone who does not fit in anywhere, who is only ever an observer on the outside looking in. Sometimes you then start to read all the things that happen to you as people trying to keep you out. You can become quite paranoid. You believe that the world is unsafe, that nobody wants you and you cannot connect with anybody because they are all there to harm you or keep you out." (Podcast 62)

With this daunting warning in mind, I reflect that as someone who invariably chooses the outside (it's in my Essence). I will at least always be with Uma. And that's good.

I have a feeling we might find Ayesha there too, though she has a condition as she joins us: "Outside is good, but let's not waste too much Energy creating new spaces for change. Let's find the ones that are already there and use them".

So outside and inside will need to be added to our ever increasing list of Elements that we must combine as we lead. Creating Energy from the inside or the outside, both feel right at the right time, and for the right person. And this brings me back to something Alia said at the start of her advice on how to reverse a spiral. She said, "First I Check my own Energy".

It's You

When you are leading, whether you choose to lead from the front, back, middle or sides, your own Energy level is key. As the person leading, the Energy level is your responsibility, and quite a personal one. There is no getting away from this.

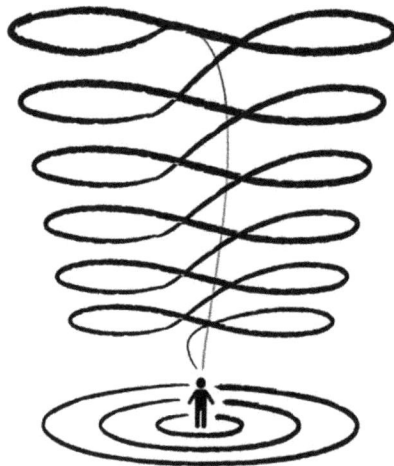

Figure 11: Energy from you

Helena: "It's your own personal enthusiasm that generates the Energy. People who seem to be flat in their engagement often have difficulty generating it. Your enthusiasm, passion and persona often create – if not stimulate – the Energy. It is an Energy that people feel externally from you, but which is really a manifestation of the Energy inside you." (Podcast 29)

Helena is well known for her straight talking. And so is Uma; she says she calls for "women to claim their Energy and their resulting power in its purest sense."

Uma: "I don't mean this in the usual way, in the context of position, structures, titles, budgets and institutions. There have been moments when I have experienced immense power and there are moments when I have felt extremely powerless, and neither had anything to do with the positional power that I have enjoyed.

"I see Energy rather as being in your own space, where your voice matters and your opinion is valued, and you are authentic and true, whether that is a playground or a parliament. It is a very calming space, and also extremely excitable because you are so full of Energy. Not an Energy that is driving you to do something, but an Energy of simply being."

I asked Uma for an example of when she last felt so powerful, and the example she gave me was drawn from motherness. As she spoke, her eyes shined. I am not sure whether it was with pride or with tears or a combination of both.

"The last time I felt very powerful was with my 17-year-old daughter. She was going through an internal critical crisis; she was very sad and very vulnerable. She called me. I was about an hour away from her by car. I said, 'let's just talk.' We cried together, we laughed together, it was an extremely vulnerable and intimate time for both of us. She influenced me. I influenced her. It was an hour and fifteen minutes before I reached home.

"I call those seventy-five minutes powerful because for me they came from a deep space of self-efficacy and compassion. We connected very deeply and intimately as two women sharing things about our lives.

"When I reached home, we just hugged each other and then I went to do chores and she went to study. In those seventy-five minutes, I was connected with myself and the purpose of my life, the meaning of being born a woman, of having the privilege to mother a daughter."

Uma's story is of her daughter. But it is not just about daughters. What Uma describes is certainly how I have occasionally felt with people I have led. When I get it right – which doesn't always happen – it feels right. It's why leading is wonderful.

"It is when your spirit, your will and your intellect come together. It brings vitality and gives you an Energy. As women, we have been outsiders to power for such a long time. Maybe we need to recognise just how much that has framed what we think about power. There is a danger that we concentrate on the powers we do not have. Maybe we must take care not to dismiss all the infinite Energy that we possess." (Podcast 62)

Temi, the young, passionate Nigerian environmental activist, feels it as she grasps the Energy her generation of women know they possess: "We give ourselves permission to create Energy. The tides are changing. And it is really beautiful to see." (Podcast 42)

Journal

Solo

Focus on Energy. Talk to people who create it. Ask if you can shadow them. Watch what they do and how people respond.

Look at how they manage their own Energy, how they stimulate Energy in others and how they build a microclimate of Energy around them.

Really quiz them on avoiding the dead ends, whether they have always managed to or how they have learned the hard way.

Make sure that you are still talking to people from different cultures, generations, beliefs and geographies. People who do things in a very different way from you. How does someone half or double your age generate Energy? How do you avoid the Energy dead ends if you are in the global north or the global south? What causes Energy to spiral upwards when you are leading in one setting and yet has the opposite effect in another?

Distil what you think will work for you. Some will, some won't. Take snippets from every conversation and build up how you will create Energy in the different settings you lead in.

In a group

You will have got to know each other by now. Give each other feedback.

And invite me to come and join you on your Expedition for an hour or so. I would be honoured.

Finale

So that's it. We are done. Over to you. Don't ask me to summarise; that's not how Expeditions work. In any case, it really is up to you now. Your journal must now be very full. Your map is no doubt creased and scribbled on (if not physically, at least metaphorically). Don't stop now. Just take a breath, then keep on exploring.

My Expedition

As I draw breath myself, I think about how the First Expedition has caused my Essence to evolve. I have discovered pieces that I had not recognised before, like 'the body'. I have put names to other pieces, like 'motherness'. It has prompted me to think again about pieces that I would once have considered small – 'ancestors,' for example – and now recognise as much bigger. It has challenged me to rethink the relative sizes of the pieces: for me, 'education' is now bigger, relative to 'trauma'. It has uncovered pieces that are individual to me, such as 'outsider'.

I have jettisoned and reframed Elements and added a few of my own to these lists. I have tested my purpose in leading – but I am not sharing the outcome of this one (it's private). I have gloried in the newly discovered 'combined' concept. I just wish I had found it earlier. I have always described myself as a 'strategic opportunist,' and have always been told that it doesn't make sense. Now I know that it does.

I have gladly taken many new tips from every single woman I have met over the last year. And I intend to continue my hunt (or rather my podcast hunt) for Expressing my leading.

Finally, I have realised that leading really is a verb. And I now know its secret ingredient: Energy.

How do I know all this? Because my Essence has breathed the fresh air of the First Expedition. I have been put to the test, leading such a glorious group of determined women: Alia, Ana Luz, Andini, Anna, Aparna, Ayesha, Camila, Erica, Fatima, Folawe, Hinemoa, Isata, Katrina, Katya, Laura, Liz, Melissa, Mona, Rouba, Sarah, Selvie, Uma, Vidya, Yvette, Lissa, Stephanie and Maria. It feels like my infinity symbol has been set to fast forward over the last year, flowing in both directions. I lead differently today because of it.

Your Expedition

So now it's your turn. And all I can say is: go. Go and lead, because we all have to. There is so much that needs leading – and so much that needs a fresh eye. We cannot let leadership get stuck in titles and definitions. We have to bring our Energy to leading – starting now.

And keep exploring as you go. Don't stop your Expedition now – it has only just begun.

There are only 101 women's voices in this book. There are more things to read, people to talk to, podcast episodes to listen to, questions to ask, answers to be dug out. There are more pieces to uncover in your Essence and more Elements to draw from them. And there are so many different ways to express them. Learn all the time, and let the infinity symbol flow.

Build your Energy, because it's a force that spirals upwards when you get your leading right. There are so many ways to make sure that the Energy you generate is effective, inspires people and has purpose. Try them all.

There is a golden moment when Essence becomes clear: the three circles align; the Elements get jettisoned, reframed, found and combined; the infinity symbol flows gently across the three circles, connecting them as the inside questions the outside (and vice versa). It is a sweet and dynamic spot, and from it the infinity symbol takes off and spirals dynamically upwards, generating Energy as it goes.

So keep exploring. Find your own approach to leading that works for you. There is no single universal way: because that central circle – our Essence – is so very different and personal to each of us.

And yet, is it entirely different? As women, we share so much. For all our individual differences, there are many common pieces – and that is what makes us full of Energy when we are together.

Beyond the goal of all of us finding our own individual way to lead, just think, for a moment, of the bigger prizes to be won.

When enough women choose to lead in a way that works for them, we might just begin to redefine leadership so that even more people choose to do it.

Women will no longer feel that they have to be something that they are not, and our sons will discover that this approach to leading resonates with them too.

And finally, women will take their rightful central role in leading a world that is facing huge challenges.

More than ever, it needs us leading the way.

Go go go

As you set off, I shall delight in watching your triumphs, quietly hoping that your Expedition played a small role in them.

I have two more hopes: that my map – and what is now your map – serves you well, and that, as you explore, you will tell me what you discover along the way.

I will be there for as long as I can – with luck, every week with another podcast episode, and every three weeks for a live session. I'll be doing my best to address your questions, learn from your answers and add them to my journal, which is already bursting with ideas and images from the explorations that led to this book.

'"Popping colours." "The body is a barometer." "The infinite game." "10,000 hours." "Strawberries with chocolate and chocolate with tea." "Let's try it." "The three seeds." "Justajoo." "The Vā." "The silence between the notes." These are just some of the words that are now etched into me, along with these images: a Polish conductor's inviting hands, a rugby player rucking or flicking a ponytail, a frog boiling, a Wonder Woman suit, a tiny theatre director with a tiny voice in Argentina, a 'nosey' supply chain director in the US, and the smiles of both a survivor of war in Uganda and a nun in Nepal. Leading, every single one of them.

Now it's your turn. Go, go, go. This is leading – and you're in.

Love Julia

Last Word

It was helping Julia to curate the Expedition, waking up at the crack of dawn to strategise with her and Vidya, and then becoming a member of the First Expedition, that led me back to leading. For a few years, I had refused all offers, preferring my portfolio life. But discussions around leading made me think about myself and realise that, as someone with influence, how could I encourage other women to be authentic leaders if I did not show up myself?

My journey of leading has followed a circular path, often tumultuous and non-traditional.

I started as an investment banker: a very male dominated world. It rewarded leading that was aggressive and intent on power-grabbing. Our compensation, rather than being judged on performance, was judged on who stood up for you in the room when evaluations were discussed.

Now I am Global Executive Director of Equality Now, an organization that promises to shake up a system that was not created by or for women.

In this new role, I have used many of the lessons highlighted in this book: understanding my Essence (deep commitment to gender equality), leaning into Elements (intuition, listening, purpose) and then being bold in Expression (an inclusive and abundant mindset, working hard but smart) so that I generate Energy.

I feel like I am in the sweet spot of my life, and being in the company of the most soul nourishing women during the First Expedition gave me the fuel I never knew I needed. We talk often, but most of all know we have each other's backs, not just in leading change but in our lives as well. I am available at any time of night or day to every member of the group and feel a deeply affirming sense of solidarity.

After all, together we unlocked a way of leading that is true, fundamental and life-affirming. And the most beautiful part was realising that leading is individual and unique. This book will have helped you to find your way and, after all, for it to stick, it must surely be self-defined.

Only then will we become streams of light, feeding into this beautiful prism of leading change.

I hope that you are enjoying your Expedition. It is a journey worth stepping into.

Mona Sinha
Global Executive Director, Equality Now
Curator and Member of the First Expedition.

Appendix 1: The 101 women

Alex Moore, Director, J&J Medtech Education UKI

Alia Whitney Johnson, Founder, Emerge Lanka Foundation

Alison Coburn, Founder, Sky Blue

Allyson Nicholson, Vice President, Supply Chain Strategy & Design, Moderna

Ana Luz Porzecanski, Conservation Scientist, American Museum of Natural History

Andini Makosinski, Inventor, Filmmaker & Writer

Ani Choying Drolma, Buddhist Nun & Singer

Anila Dehart, Global Talent Managing Director, Deloitte

Anna Afeyan Gunnarson, Co-Founder Afeyan Family Foundation

Anna Kuk, Director, Son Organique & Artistic Director, ReVerb Ensemble

Anne Rugg Onwusiri, Client Account Manager in Sports, Stonewall

Antonia Belcher, Chartered Surveyor & Businesswoman

Aparna Uppaluri, COO, Tata Trusts

Asifa Hassan, Founder & CEO, She Matters Project

Ayesha Mian, Founder & CEO, Synapse & The Pakistan Neuroscience Institute

Bin Wolfe, Global Deputy Talent Leader, EY

Camila Pontual, Rio Climate Program Manager, Columbia Global Center

Camilla Sievers, Co-Founder & CEO, Qi Health

Chulu Chansa, Founder, Africana Woman

Catherine Ruggles, Director, Software Engineering, Google

Claire Yorke (Dr), Fellow, Center for War Studies, University of Southern Denmark

Elsa Donohue, Head of School, Vientiane International School

Enaya Noor Mian, Student, Karachi Grammar School

Erica Su, Head of Strategy and Transactions, EY Greater China

Erin Robinson, Associate Head of School, Atlanta International School

Erum Khalid Sattar, Sustainable Water Management Program, Tufts University

Fatima Zibouh, Co-Chargée de Mission, Brussels2030

Fiona Campbell, Associate Partner, Aberkyn at McKinsey & Company

Folawe Omikunle, CEO, Teach For Nigeria

Francesca Cavallo, Founder & CEO, Undercats, Inc

Genevieve Barr, Writer & Actor

Harriet Adong, Executive Director, Northern Uganda Foundation for Integrated Rural Development

Harriet Nayiga, Founding Director, Uganda, Midwife-led Community Transformation

Hatoon Alfassi, Honorary Fellow of Arabic and Middle Eastern Studies, The University of Manchester

Helena Kennedy, Director, International Bar Association Institute of Human Rights

Hila Davies, Environmental Community Strategist

Hinemoa Elder, Māori Child & Adolescent Psychiatrist & Author «Te Aupōuri, Ngāti Kurī, Te Rarawa, Ngāpuhi nui tonu"

Isata Kabia, Founding Director, Voice of Women Africa

Jacqui James Gavin, CEO, 5 Senses of Inclusion

Jennifer Stein, Theatre Producer & Director

Joyce Wema Isa-Molwane, Director Legal, Compliance, BOCRA

Jude Kelly, Founder & CEO, The WOW Foundation

Baroness Julia Neuberger, Rabbi

Julienne Lusenge, Director, Congolese Women's Fund.

Katja Weisheit, Corporate & Private Donations, Turtle Foundation

Kate Middleton, CEO & Founder, The Wren Project

Katrina Webb, Founder & Director, Newday Leadership & Paralympic Gold Medallist

Katya Guryeva, Officer, C40 Cities

Kelly McCallum, Lecturer, AUT Sport Leadership & Management

Lailamah Giselle Khan, Student, Nixor College

Latanya Mapp Frett, President & CEO, Global Fund for Women

Laura Fleming, CEO, Hitachi Energy UK & Ireland

Lee Sue Ann, Coordinator, Regional Strategic and Political Studies Programme, ISEAS, Yusof Ishak Institute

Leila Toplic, Chief Communications & Trust Officer, Carbonfuture

Lissa Young, (Dr), Associate Professor, United States Military Academy, West Point,

Liz Bloomfield, Executive Director, Ripple Effect Images

Lulu Raghavan, Vice President APAC, Landor & Fitch

Luseshelo Fanny Simwinga, Nurse-Midwife Mentor, GAIN-GAIA

Mai Chen, Barrister, Public Law Toolbox Chambers & President New Zealand Asian Lawyers

Margarita Grobocopatel Marra, MD Hospital de Clínicas José de San Martín, in Buenos Aires!

Martyna Pastuszka, Artistic Director, Concertmaster, {oh!} Orkiestra

Meenakshi (Meena) Arundhati, Actor, Writer & Researcher

Meera Baindur (Dr), Associate Professor, School of Liberal Arts and Sciences, RV University

Melissa Berman, Founding President & CEO, Rockefeller Philanthropy Advisors

Melissa Kwee, Co – Creator, General Worker, National Volunteer and Philanthropy Centre Singapore - City of Good

Mona Sinha, Global Executive Director, Equality Now

Monica Medina (Dr), Literacy Consultant, International & US schools

Myrna Atalla, Executive Director, Alfanar

Nandita Das, Actor, Filmmaker & Social Advocate

Nichole Bradford, Executive Director & Co-Founder, The Transformative Technology LAB

Nosipho Siwisa Damasane, Chair of Board, Richards Bay Coal Terminal Ltd

Olivia Grobocopatel, Consultant, IDOYA

Paula Langton, Partner & Head of Sustainability, Campbell Lutyens

Paula Marra, Founder & CEO, Matriarca

Paula Alvarez Vaccaro, Founder, Pinball London

Pelonomi Venson Moitoi, Former Minister, Botswana Government

Princess Ashilokun, Poet, Strategist & Founder, Atinuda Productions

Priyanka Handa Ram, Founder & Chief Energy Officer, Learn to Play

Rachel Middleton, Consultant, Odgers Berndtson

Rouba Mhaissen (Dr), Founder & Director, Sawa Foundation

Saba Al Mubaslat, Regional Director MENA, Ford Foundation

Samia Latif (Dr), Consultant in Health Protection and Global Health

Sarah Henry, CEO, Tandem

Selvie Jusman, Investment Banker

Sheila Paylan, International Human Rights Lawyer

Sina Wendt, Board Member, NZ Opera Foundation Trust

Stellah Wairimu Bosire (Dr), Founding Director, Africa Center for Health Systems and Gender Justice

Stephanie Khurana, Chief Executive Officer, Axim Collaborative

Susan Whitehead, Founding Lifetime Trustee, Whitehead Institute, MIT Corporation

Sylvia Penelao Hamata, Midwife & Legal practitioner, High Court of Namibia

Tebogo Matenge, Entrepreneur

Temilade Salami, Founder, EcoChampions

Rev. Terri Hord Owens, General Minister & President, Christian Church of the Disciples of Christ

Twila Moon (Dr), Deputy Lead Scientist, National Snow & Ice Data Center

Uma Chatterjee, Founder & Director, Sanjog India

Uthara Narayanan, Chief Changemaker, Buzz Women & Director, Avantika Foundation

Victoria Cordoba, Director, CliniQ

Vidya Shah, Executive Chairperson, EdelGive Foundation

Vivi Tellas, Theater Director & Curator

Yvette Hopkins, Director, The LeadHershipXchange

Zenna Hopson Atkins, Board Member, SaxaVord

Appendix 2: Women Emerging Podcast Episodes

The voices of many of the 101 women are captured in these podcast episodes. We have released an episode every week since the start of the First Expedition. Go to our website to access them all Womenemerging.org .

1. **Why a Women Leadership Expedition?**
    Hinemoa Elder, Vidya Shah

2. **How Will the Expedition Work?**
    Mona Sinha, Ana Luz Porzecanski

3. **Who is Going in the Expedition?**
    Yvette Hopkins, Anna Kuk

4. **Is it Really a Better World for Women Now?**
    Isata Kabia, Ayesha Mian

5. **Disruptive Leadership**
    Katya Guryeva, Lissa Young, Camila Pontual

6. **What does Women's Leadership in Different Countries Look Like?**
    Harriet Adong, Saba Al Mubaslat, Sina Wendt, Katja Weisheit, Chulu Chansa, Erum Khalid Sattar, Victoria Cordoba

7. **How Important Is Listening within Leadership?**
    Selvie Jusman, Uma Chatterjee, Liz Bloomfield

8. Discovering the Ugly Reality of Systems Thinking
   Sarah Henry, Alia Whitney Johnson, Melissa Kwee

9. TheFuture of Leadership: Beyond Binary Choices
   Fatima Zibouh, Andini Makosinski

10. AHA Moments of Women Leaders Across the Globe
    Rouba Mhaissen, Erica Su, Folawe Omikunle

11. Avoiding the Feminist Trap & Prioritising Your Well-being
    Laura Fleming, Katrina Webb, Aparna Uppaluri

12. Expedition Launch Episode
    Jude Kelly, Deepali Khanna

13. Interview with Julia Middleton
    Amy Stillman, Julia Middleton

14. A Human Approach to Leadership
    Bin Wolfe, Paula Marra

15. Zeitgeist Part 1: Illiberal Democracy – Secretly Impacting Your Leadership
    Nicole Anne Boyer, Lee Sue Ann

16. Zeitgeist Part 2: Angry Young Women – On Politics, Refugee Camps & Climate Change
    Megha Harish, Asifa Hassan, Hila Davies

17. Zeitgeist Part 3: The Hunger Games – Stop the Manipulation
    Sarah Henry, Paula Alvarez Vaccaro

18. Happiness in Leadership
    Ani Choying Drolma, Harriet Adong

19. Leadership Outside of Work
    Kelly McCallum, Alison Coburn

20. Answering the Unsettling Questions About Leadership
   Mona Sinha, Laura Fleming, Isata Kabia, Yvette Hopkins, Katya Gurye-va, Ana Luz Porzecanski, Vidya Shah, Alia Whitney Johnson, Anna Kuk

21. Teenagers & Leadership
   Rania Mumtaz, Wayna Ahmed, Aymen Tamur, Rija Ali Khan, Eshal Fatima Haque, Lailamah Giselle Khan, Marya Zulfiqar

22. Leadership Within Faith Part 1
   Dr. Meera Baindur, Terri Hord Owens

23. Leadership Within Faith Part 2
   Hatoon Alfassi, Amany Lubis, Ani Choying Drolma, Julia Neuberger

24. Leadership Lessons from Botswana part 1
   Priyanka Handa Ram, Tebogo Matenge, Rosalind Kwinje, Kelly Ramputswa, Sharifa Noor, Rebecca Binns

25. Leadership Lessons from Botswana part 2
   Joyce Wema Isa Molwane, Pelonomi Venson Moitoi

26. On Privilege and Power, Spirituality and Womanhood
   Aparna Uppaluri, Katya Guryeva, Ana Luz Porzecanski

27. Leadership Insights from Successful Transgender Women Leaders
   Antonia Belcher, Jacqui James Gavin

28. Midwife Leadership
   Olajumoke Adebayo, Harriet Nayiga, Luseshelo Fanny Simwinga, Neha Mankani, Sylvia Penelao Hamata

29. Women Who Lead Movements Part 1
   Latanya Mapp Frett, Baroness Helena Kennedy

30. Women Who Lead Movements Part 2
   Melissa Berman, Uma Chatterjee

31. Creativity & Leadership
    Jennifer Stein, Vivi Tellas

32. Leading Through Trauma
    Elsa Donohue, Erin Robinson

33. The Myth of Meritocracy
    Catherine Ruggles, Nosipho Damasane

34. How to Have Difficult Conversations as a Leader
    Monica Medina, Karen Lord

35. Different Cultures and Countries Affecting Women's Position in Society
    Anna Afeyan, Alfonsina Penaloza, Anila Dehart, Selvie Jusman

36. How Do You Lead a Fight?
    Leila Toplic, Julienne Lusenge

37. How Privilege Affects Leadership
    Deepali Khanna, Theo Sowa, Marianne Schnall, Stephanie Khurana

38. The Context in Which We Lead Part 1
    Francesca Cavallo, Twila Moon, Dr. Claire Yorke

39. The Context in Which We Lead Part 2
    Nichole Bradford, Leila Toplic, Paula Langton

40. The Role of Language in Leading
    Selvie Jusman, Uma Chatterjee, Isata Kabia, Hinemoa Elder, Katya Guryeva, Ana Luz Porzecanski, Fatima Zibouh, Rouba Mhaissen, Anna Kuk, Director, Erica Su, Maria Karageorgou

41. Groundbreaking Learnings Mid-Expedition
    Julia Middleton

42. How Young Women Think About Leadership Part 1
    Olivia Grobocopatel, Temilade Salami, Karimot Odebode, Meenakshi Arundhati Banerjee, Enaya Noor Mian

43. **How Young Women Think About Leadership Part 2**
   Dimple Barwani, Esther B.R Fornah, Ines Palacios

44. **Leading Miraculously Through a Building Explosion**
   Camila Pontual

45. **Leading an Orchestra**
   Martyna Pastuszka, Anna Kuk

46. **Mothering & Leadership Part 1**
   Rachel Middleton, Myrna Atalla

47. **Mothering & Leadership Part 2**
   Saba Al Mubaslat, Samia Latif

48. **Women Leaders Need Female Friendships**
   Temilade Salami, Meenakshi Arundhati Banerjee, Marga Grobocopatel

49. **Exclusive Heartfelt Sharings as Expedition Culminates**
   Sarah Henry, Anna Kuk

50. **Accidental Leadership**
   Folawe Omikunle

51. **Essence 1: The Sacred**
   Aparna Uppaluri

52. **Essence 2: The Body**
   Katrina Webb

53. **Essence 3: Nature**
   Ana Luz Porzecanski

54. **Essence 4: Motherness**
   Melissa Kwee

55. **Essence 5: Ancestors**
   Hinemoa Elder

56. **Essence 6: Trauma**
    Dr. Ayesha Mian

57. **Essence 7: Education**
    Isata Kabia

58. **Essence**
    Mona Sinha

59. **Energy 1: Leading Is Energy**
    Liz Bloomfield

60. **Energy 2: Managing Energy**
    Alia Whitney Johnson

61. **Energy 3: Avoiding Traps**
    Sarah Henry

62. **Energy 4: The Outside Edge**
    Uma Chatterjee

63. **'If That's Leading, I'm In'**
    Julia Middleton

64. **Five Objects 1: Leading Beyond Perfectionism and People Pleasing**
    Uthara Narayanan

65. **Five Objects 2: Leading as a Rebel**
    Paula Alvarez Vaccaro

66. **Five Objects 3: Leading with Vulnerability**
    Dr. Stellah Wairimu Bosire

67. **Five Objects 4: Tackling Team Challenges**
    Lulu Raghavan

68. **Five Objects 5: Learning Leading Through Rugby**
    Anne Rugg Onwusiri

69. **Five objects 6: Importance of Divergent Thinking**
    Melissa Kwee

70. **Five Objects 7: Dreams in Leadership**
    Juliana Algañaraz

Julia Middleton is host of the "Women Emerging" podcast and a best-selling author of two previous books: "Leading beyond Authority" and "Cultural Intelligence". She is deeply committed to helping people from all backgrounds to develop as leaders, and speaks regularly on leadership to audiences around the world.

In 2020, Julia launched Women Emerging and went on to lead an Expedition of 24 women to find 'an approach to leadership that resonates with women'.

Prior to that, she was founder and, for over thirty years, Chief Executive of Common Purpose, which grew to become one of the biggest leadership development organizations in the world.

Born in London and brought up in New York, Julia was educated at French Lycées and graduated from the London School of Economics. She is married, with five children and lots of grandchildren.

Milton Keynes UK
Ingram Content Group UK Ltd.
UKHW011324091223
434087UK00001B/131

9 781739 222918